POP
GOES the
LIBRARY

Using Pop Culture to Connect
With Your Whole Community

Sophie Brookover
and
Elizabeth Burns

Information Today, Inc.
Medford, New Jersey

First Printing, 2008

Pop Goes the Library: Using Pop Culture to Connect With Your Whole Community

Library of Congress Cataloging-in-Publication Data

Brookover, Sophie, 1975-
   Pop goes the library : using pop culture to connect with your whole community / Sophie Brookover and Elizabeth Burns.
      p. cm.
   Includes bibliographical references and index.
   ISBN 978-1-57387-336-9
   1. Libraries--Special collections--Popular culture. 2. Libraries and community. I. Burns, Elizabeth, 1966- II.Title.
   Z688.P64B76 2008
   021.2--dc22

                                                                    2008019509

Printed and bound in the United States of America

President and CEO: Thomas H. Hogan, Sr.
Editor-in-Chief and Publisher: John B. Bryans
Managing Editor: Amy M. Reeve
Project Editor: Rachel Singer Gordon
VP Graphics and Production: M. Heide Dengler
Book Designer: Kara Mia Jalkowski
Cover Designer: Shelley Szajner
Copyeditor: Beverly Michaels
Proofreader: Pat Hadley-Miller
Indexer: Sharon Hughes

For our families

Contents

Acknowledgments xi

Foreword by Erin V. Helmrich xiii

Introduction xv

About the Web Page xix

Chapter 1: Defining and Using Pop Culture
            to Connect 1
   An Interview with Judy Macaluso 4
   Sidebar: Making Sure That Worlds Collide by
       Debra Kay Logan 8
   Voices from the Field 14

Chapter 2: Creating a Pop Niche for Yourself
            and Your Library 21
   Surveys: Real Time and Online 23
   Focus Groups 26
   Statistics 28
   Voices from the Field 30

Chapter 3: Building a Collection That Really Pops 39
   Collection Development Strategy 40
   Pop Culture Materials Selection: Print Tools 41
   Pop Culture Materials Selection: Online Tools 42
   Pop Culture Resources: The Human Factor 43
   Beyond Books: Pop Culture in All Its Many Formatted Glory ... 45
   Sidebar: Alternative Formats: A Director's View by
       C. Allen Nichols 45
   Methodology: Hand Selection and Standing Order Plans 48

Sidebar: A Brief Word About Centralized Selection 50
The C-Words 53
It's a Process 54
Voices from the Field 55

Chapter 4: Advocacy, Marketing, Public Relations, and Outreach 61

Think Big, Start Small 64
Sidebar: An Interview with Ilise Benun 67
External Constituents 69
Internal Marketing and Advocacy 70
The Value of Cross-Training 71
Continuous Training 73
Not Like a Needle in a Haystack: Connecting People
    and Materials 74
Sidebar: Marketing Tips That Pop by Jill S. Stover 76
Avoiding Flubs: Practice, Practice, Practice 78
Maintaining Your Pop Collections 82
Pop Reach (Pop Culture Outreach) 83
Taking the Pop Approach 84
One Word, Multiple Possibilities 86
Voices from the Field 88

Chapter 5: Trendspotting 97

Identifying Resources, Extrapolating Ideas 100
Developing Tie-Ins and Establishing Trust 101
Sidebar: An Interview with Christine Matteo 102
Voices from the Field 105

Chapter 6: Information Technology Is Everyone's Job 111

Technology: Fun and Easy 112
Voices from the Field 140

Chapter 7: Programming That Pops 151
Finding Inspiration, Valuing Preparation 152
Sidebar: Get Their Attention! by Debra Kay Logan 156
But at My Library 160
Sidebar: An Interview with Carlie Webber 163
Voices from the Field 166

Chapter 8: Pop Programming Year-Round: Pop Goes the Year 173

Appendix A: Core Pop Culture Resources for Library Professionals 227

Appendix B: Pop Programming Year-Round Calendar 245

Appendix C: Survey Questions 251

Appendix D: Websites 255

Resources and Recommended Reading 269

About the Authors 281

Index 283

Acknowledgments

We are deeply grateful to the members of Team Pop, without whose assistance and support we could never have completed this project. Melissa Rabey, John Klima, Sue Quinn, Carlie Webber, Karen Corday, and Eli Neiburger: Y'all rock.

Many thanks to the wonderful interviewees and sidebar writers whose invaluable insights are essential to making this book shine: Karen Avenick, Ilise Benun, Nancy Dowd, Jill Faherty, Chris Herz, Debra Kay Logan, Judy Macaluso, Christine Matteo, C. Allen Nichols, Jill Stover, Carlie Webber, and Katy White.

We are indebted to the fabulous team at ITI, especially Rachel Singer Gordon and Amy Reeve, who held our hands throughout the process.

Foreword

Welcome to the real world—the world where libraries aren't foremost in most people's minds, and where even avid readers don't necessarily use our services. As institutions we often do a poor job of advertising our basic services, let alone those with which we're trying to attract new users. This often occurs because we're all too "inside" it to notice that we have fallen off the radar—or that we never even made the radar in the first place. Sometimes, though, this happens because we take a stand, making a conscious effort *not* to join the "fray." You know the type: those who would rather lock themselves up with the reference books and close the library doors, principles intact, than roll with the times and embrace the changes that have besieged our profession.

However it has played out, the fact is that the real world has passed some libraries by. It's time to stop arguing about these aforementioned principles and call for triage. At the top of your triage list? Relevance.

Embracing what is popular in your community is about embracing relevance. You already own books and offer programs that are relevant to your users, they just don't know it—yet! Never stop advertising your *free*-ness. "Oh, but people already know that!" Do they? Do they know a library card is free? Do they know that you rent DVDs for free—or at least cheaper than Netflix? Do they know that they can send their teen to the library for a free program that may also feed them? Do they know that they can place holds from home and pick things up at their own convenience?

Ask your front line staff: "What are the top 10 questions you get on a daily basis?" Eliminate where's the bathroom, and you have nine really good questions showing how you're not getting the word out about basic services. Delve a little deeper, and you have the basis for a good marketing plan; use the tactics in this book to help you take it a step further.

Some of you holding this book are sighing with relief: "Finally, a book that supports what I have been saying for years!" Others may be skeptics—do you really need to watch TMZ to be a good librarian? Absolutely not! As Sophie Brookover and Elizabeth Burns show, you need only to be willing to reframe. Reframe the way you advertise the things you are already doing. Reframe the way you plan future events and how you market them to the community. Reframe the way you talk about your services, depending on who you are talking to. Reframe the way you think about the library. Pretend you hate to read (yes, it will be hard), and you have no idea why *anyone* would ever go to the library. This book will teach you how to make your library relevant to your best user, your worst user, and the person who never wants to use you!

Consider yourself a library user Nanny McPhee: "When you need me, but do not want me, then I must stay. When you want me, but no longer need me, then I have to go." Unlike Nanny, if we do our jobs right, our users will always need us—once they know how relevant we are to their lives. This book will make that happen.

—Erin V. Helmrich

Erin is currently a Teen Services Librarian at the Ann Arbor District Library in Michigan and has been writing the thrice-yearly Teen Pop-Culture Quizzes for *VOYA* since 1999. She is currently a member of the YALSA Board of Directors and a YALSA Serving the Underserved Trainer. Active in the Michigan Library Association, she was the 2008 recipient of the Frances H. Pletz Award for excellence in teen services, and is a frequent writer and speaker on pop-culture, teen services, and advocacy. Write her at erinhelmrich@gmail.com.

Introduction

Welcome to *Pop Goes the Library*, the book!

"Pop Goes the Library," the blog, is the brainchild of Sophie Brookover. She launched it as a solo project in April 2004; Elizabeth Burns joined the blog almost exactly a year later—and, at the time of this writing, Team Pop now includes eight pop-savvy bloggers from public, school, and academic libraries.

You may be thinking, "Oh, another blog-turned-book." Well, not exactly. When Sophie started writing the blog, its manifesto was *"We're public librarians. We believe libraries can learn from and use Pop Culture to improve their collections, services, and public image. We love TV, music, the movies, comic books, anime, magazines, all things Net ... you get the picture."* Since then, as the number of contributors has increased and we've all followed different career paths, this manifesto has changed, broadened, and deepened. So, too, has our appreciation for how pop culture can contribute to *any* library, library system, or library setting.

Also, the blog is, well, a blog. Its content reflects what is going on in the world at a given moment in time; it is filled with short snippets of ideas and programs and commentary. The book, however, provides us the luxury of exploring in detail what pop culture is and what it is not, what it means to create a pop culture collection, and how to use pop culture to generate staff support and public support for your library.

Great ideas result from brainstorming, and some of our best ideas (if we may be permitted a moment of bragging) are the result of our back-and-forth discussions, usually via Google Talk. Writing this book taught us never to work in isolation, and this is probably the biggest lesson we'd like to impart to our readers, too. (Oops, we gave it away! Please read the whole thing, anyway!) Involve your staff, from the pages to your director, and, above all, involve your community, from school visits to focus groups and surveys to frontline conversations. We cannot emphasize this point enough: This book is about identifying and harnessing the power of your community's pop culture. It's about your library, your community, and how to build better and stronger relationships between the two by using pop culture.

We turned to the real experts for advice and information: you. Throughout the book, you'll find "Voices from the Field" sections, where we highlight what librarians and library staff have to say about pop culture, collections, and programming. We also share some of our own experiences.

Between completing this manuscript and seeing it to publication, Sophie changed jobs, from working as a teen librarian at the Camden County Library in Voorhees, NJ, to a position as a school librarian at Eastern Regional Senior High School (also in Voorhees). When you see references to Sophie's library, its collections, and programs, they reflect her experiences at the public library.

Some things we'd like to say, straight up:

Pop culture comes in all sizes. Yes, there are big, showy programs and collections, but you can also easily add a dash of pop culture to a traditional "get to know your library" scavenger hunt by giving it a reality TV show name such as *Library Amazing Race* or *Library Survivor.*

Pop culture varies by community. Your library's pop culture might involve engaging students in support of the school curriculum and academic goals—with author visits, workshops, etc.; or it might involve buying more needlework books—because that is what your customers want. Pop culture can also be anime, manga, and gaming in the library, or any of the many other ways libraries engage with their communities' interests.

Finally, a lot of libraries are doing things with pop culture, but just not calling it pop culture. Yes, we do consider your mega-*Harry Potter* program that coincided with the release of *Harry Potter and the Deathly Hallows* to be pop culture.

We hope you find what follows to be useful, thought-provoking, and fun. We always welcome your ideas and comments at the blog (www.popgoesthelibrary.com) or via email (sophie.brookover @gmail.com and lizzy.burns@gmail.com).

Read on and—we hope—enjoy.

About the Web Page

www.popgoesthelibrary.com/popbook

This book references dozens of online resources and sites about pop culture, programming, and Web 2.0 technologies (see Appendix D for a list of URLs by chapter). Websites come and go, and pop culture changes rapidly and in surprising ways: This year's Sweet Little Miss is next year's Unwed Mama, last year's Bad Boy of Hollywood is this year's Oscar-nominated Do-Gooder, and tap dancing could be the Next Retro-Cool Thing. Technology is another area where we'd love to have a Magic 8 Ball to predict what the next big thing will be (and if you discover a reliable one, please let us know!). In order to make *Pop Goes the Library* more useful and enduring to readers, the resources listed will be maintained and updated on one handy blog.

Please visit www.popgoesthelibrary.com/popbook, where you'll find a clickable link to each site mentioned in this book so long as the site is current. We will also be updating the blog regularly with new sites that are pertinent, useful, and popalicious, as we become aware of them.

Feel free to email any changes, comments, and suggestions to us at popgoesthebook@gmail.com. Thanks for reading, and we'll see you online!

Disclaimer

Neither the publisher nor the author makes any claim as to the results that may be obtained through the use of this website or of any of the Internet resources it references or links to. Neither publisher nor author will be held liable for any results, or lack thereof, obtained by the use of this page or any of its links; for any third-party changes; or for any hardware, software, or other problems that may occur as the result of using it. This website is subject to change or discontinuation without notice at the discretion of the publisher and author.

DEFINING AND USING
POP CULTURE TO CONNECT

You're reading this book because you've decided that pop culture belongs in the library. Or, you're curious about how pop culture could fit in with your library's mission. Or, maybe you're looking to shake up your existing materials, collections, programs, and outreach. You're itching to try something beyond the same old, same old. Why not pop culture? And what exactly does "pop culture in the library" mean? Having *Entertainment Weekly* in the magazine section? Showing a movie in the library?

In this chapter, we'll talk about what pop culture is, and explain why we believe that embracing pop culture is so crucial to vital library services, programs, and collections. In short, we'll evangelize for the value and usefulness of pop culture. We hope you'll be engaged, whether you agree with us wholeheartedly, are incensed by our intention to shake up library collections and services, or fall somewhere in between.

So, what is pop culture? The simplest definition we've found posits that pop culture is no more than "commercial culture based on popular taste."[1] Put another way, pop culture comprises "those trends in art and entertainment that society [finds] most appealing."[2] A *Dictionary of Sociology* offers a more nuanced definition, setting popular culture into a framework of culture in general, and comparing it with high, or elite, culture:

> Culture denotes all the knowledge, technologies, values, beliefs, customs, and behaviors common to people. While simple societies may have only a single integrated culture that is shared by everyone, complex societies can accommodate many layers and levels of cultures and subcultures.
>
> One important distinction is between popular culture and what is usually called high culture. The latter includes things like classical music, serious novels, poetry, dance, high art, and other cultural products which are usually appreciated by only a relatively small number of educated people. Popular culture, sometimes also called mass culture, is far more widespread and accessible to everyone. The main business of popular culture is entertainment and, in Europe and the United States (for example), it is dominated by sports, television, films, and recorded popular music. The distinction between minority and majority cultures may often involve a value judgment in favor of high culture.[3]

Finally, we found much to reflect on in this definition of popular culture, drawn from a retrospective study, *With Amusement for All: A History of American Popular Culture Since 1830*:

> Popular culture must enjoy at least fairly broad support from ordinary people and be accessible to them. But what separates it from noncommercial neighborhood and family games, for instance, is that its creators and/or

disseminators seek to profit from it; they are in the business of merchandising entertainment.[4]

It's important to consider the commercial aspect of popular culture, because the consumption aspect makes such a difference.

Now, how can we synthesize all of these explanations of pop culture into a definition that you can put into practical use on a daily basis at your library?

We define popular culture very broadly: To us, pop culture is whatever people in your community are talking, thinking, and reading about. The breadth of this definition can be intimidating—after all, it includes *everything!*—but we think it will give you the flexibility to identify and meet the pop culture interests and needs of your particular community. This definition also addresses the commercialism issue, which we think is key: It is increasingly difficult to discern a bold line marking the boundaries of high and popular cultures. To be sure, it is easy to find examples at the extremes—opera (which was itself once pop culture) on one side; the continuing saga of Britney Spears (which we think is really sad—almost operatically sad) on the other. But what about a topic like faith? At first, this seems like a no-brainer. Religious faith, in all its forms, is clearly high culture. What, then, do we do about a book like Rick Warren's runaway bestseller *The Purpose-Driven Life: What on Earth Am I Here For?* What about *Dangerous Surrender: What Happens When You Say Yes to God*, by Mr. Warren's wife, Kay? What about magazines that explore faith, from the amusing and thoughtful (but borderline blasphemous) *Heeb* to the serious Roman Catholic journal of opinion *Commonweal?* Each of these publications addresses high culture topics, but by appealing to the interests of a broad public through a commercial mechanism, they enter the realm of popular culture.

We also insist on this potentially challenging definition because we want to encourage you to see popular culture everywhere around you. By viewing the world through this lens, you open yourself and your library to an overwhelming abundance of possibilities.

Of course, some popular culture trends are fleeting or faddish. Every year seems to bring new hot topics to the fore, so it is essential to update your collections and programming regularly, guided by complementary sets of information such as circulation statistics, patron survey data, and articles in national and local newspapers, as well as popular periodicals and review periodicals. (See Appendix A for an annotated list of pop culture resources we've found useful, reliable, and entertaining.)

When we present workshops on using pop culture in libraries, we like to emphasize that although pop culture is often associated with youth culture, it is not limited to the interests of any particular slice of the demographic pie. Although it's natural to conflate pop culture with celebrity news, music, and movies, because pop culture magazines from *InStyle* to *Entertainment Weekly* to *In Touch* report on these areas regularly, this definition is too narrow. It ignores the great wealth of pop culture topics that lie outside of those areas regularly canvassed by *Entertainment Tonight*.

Please don't feel overwhelmed! And don't feel that you have to become someone you're not—a pop culture junkie—in order to deliver quality pop culture services to your customers.

BRITNEY WHO? ANI-WHAT? WHEN YOU DON'T KNOW (AND DON'T CARE) ABOUT POP CULTURE

Judy Macaluso, teen librarian extraordinaire and Teen Services Coordinator for Ocean County Library, Toms River, New Jersey, shared some wisdom about pop culture with us. In a nutshell: It's not about you. It's about your customers and your library.

What are some of the pop culture collections and programs you've worked on as a teen librarian?

Anime, manga, *Lord of the Rings* and anything fantasy, comics/graphic novels, MySpace (www.myspace.com).

Did you begin as an enthusiast for each of these pop culture areas?

Not for all of them. In fact, I consider myself pop-culture ignorant. I don't watch TV or listen to Billboard music. If it was not for needing to know this for my job, I might not even have manga or Facebook (www.facebook.com) on my radar. It is totally irrelevant if *I* have an interest in or value something— what matters is what today's teens care about now. That is the hook that teen librarians are continually looking for. This is why using teens as advisors, with a Teen Advisory Board, is so vital. Teens help us do our job. For example, Ocean County Library now has an outstanding manga and anime collection, and believe me, I didn't read it or watch it, but nine or 10 years ago I paid attention, found teens passionately absorbed by it, utilized their expertise to learn, and knew our library needed to add these collections and resources.

What is your trick for finding, embracing, and promoting a pop culture interest that is not yours?

I pay attention—very close attention—to teens. What they are talking about, seeking on the Internet, listening to, and watching (TV and movies). I engage them in conversations and activities to learn what the latest buzz is. I also subscribe to YPulse (www.ypulse.com), Trends & Tudes (www.harrisinteractive. com/news/newsletters_k12.asp), and other trend-forecasting websites. And I have to say that I believe *not* being a fan of or being into the latest pop culture thingy is an advantage. I just surrender to the knowledge and expertise of the teens themselves and let them teach me (and the library) what it's all about. In this way teens are much more in the driver's seat with library projects. Good old youth participation rules!

To encourage you to think more broadly about popular culture and its place in your library's collections and services, here's a generation-by-generation breakdown of just a few common pop culture enthusiasms and concerns of the major demographic groups (arranged by age) alive today:

Tiny Tots and Grade Schoolers

- PBS Kids
- American Girl
- Disney Princesses
- Magazines
- Crafts and cooking
- The Wiggles
- *Dora the Explorer*
- *High School Musical* and its many spin-offs

Tweens and Teens

- Social networking technology
- Anime and manga
- College and career choices
- Faith and spirituality
- The environment
- Sex, drugs, and rock n' roll

Generation X and Generation Y

- Career development
- Family and work balance
- Aging parents
- Home ownership
- Retirement planning

- Gadgets
- Politics

Baby Boomers

- Retirement
- Aging parents
- Refilled nest syndrome
- Educating young children
- Health care costs
- Leisure pursuits

The Greatest Generation

- Vintage films and TV shows on DVD
- Using technology to keep in touch
- Active senior citizens
- End-of-life planning

Because people are passionate about the aspects of pop culture that interest them most, these topics can be a powerful lure into the library, not only for your supportive veteran users, but also for those elusive and tantalizing nonlibrary-users. Although many people have positive feelings about libraries in general—the 2005 OCLC report on perceptions of libraries noted that the English-speaking world views its libraries as trustworthy, and values the collections and computers found in libraries[5]—many of those same people don't see the library as indispensable to their daily lives. Enhancing your library's popular culture collections and pop-related programs is one way to change that perception and make your library indispensable to its community.

You may have noticed that we haven't mentioned "coolness" yet. We value indispensability over coolness for two major reasons. First, coolness implies detachment, and libraries are anything but

MAKING SURE THAT WORLDS COLLIDE BY DEBRA KAY LOGAN

When it comes to infusing your library's services with pop culture, nothing is more important than authenticity. We've said it before, and we'll say it again: You don't have to be an expert to give pop culture a place in your library. But you don't have to take our word for it—veteran school media specialist Debra Kay Logan of Mount Gilead (OH) High School gives us a glimpse of how she melds information literacy with well-placed pop culture savvy.

Their World

Concerts, video games, MP3 files, zany morning radio shows, MySpace, the latest TV craze, podcasts, the hot new advertising slogans, anime, iPhones, You Tube, alternative music, blogs, and diverse fashion trends are all forms of information. Students do not wait to be bombarded by this kind of information; they go out and find it. Students are immersed in and soaking up popular culture.

My World ... A World Not So Far Apart

As the school media specialist, I am the Information Guru, and my job is to teach students to deal with information. I am all about teaching them how to negotiate questions like: What do I need? Where do I find it? How do I negotiate and navigate resources? How does this work? Is it accurate? Is this what I need? How do I use it ethically? What do I do with it once I find it? Are there shortcuts?

I may be the Information Guru and have the tools and knowledge that students need, but let's face it, I am a member of the teaching staff. Kids look at me and think ... old. Really old. One of the first things I teach them is to look beneath the surface ... my surface and that of the information they crave or need. That means I need to be current. While I work to engage students, my real goal is for my students to see what I offer as more than just up-to-date; it is cutting edge and relevant. I want to be the person they come to when they get a new technology or information source and are not sure how to use it.

The Collision

Who says that the "information" in information literacy has to be dry? By making an effort to monitor and integrate current media stories, trends, forms, and formats, I work at making a "mash-up" between the teen world and the world of information literacy. Integrating popular culture helps to make what I teach accessible. By making applicable connections to information, media, technology, and reading literacies, I work toward the goal of helping students to become successful users of all kinds of information in ancient, new, and yet unimagined formats.

Walk into our library and evidence of this collision between popular culture and library goals for students is immediately apparent. Displays are never repeated; they are nearly always based on a hot media topic. *CSI* inspires a display case about evaluating information. *Who Wants to Be a Millionaire?* leads to a bulletin board promoting print sources. A pirate-themed display is timed to the release of the most recent *Pirates of the Caribbean* movie and is used to reveal a relevant treasure. Current information about average annual salaries is given step by step for different levels of education, from no high school degree through postgraduate education.

Whenever appropriate and if the fit is natural, popular culture is also part of face-to-face teaching and learning. Listening to the morning news and the crazy, number one, big city radio show on the way to work provides a treasure chest of current news stories, commercials, celebrity gossip, and other resources that can frequently be infused into class discussions about using information. Did you hear WNCI this morning? Did you see a particular product placed in the number one movie last weekend? Nostalgic movies and music can be effective, too. In *Grease*, Sandy and Danny both sing about the same summer nights. They are both primary sources. Why are Sandy and Danny telling completely different stories? What is bias?

Some lessons are designed to engage students by giving them opportunities to bring what they know and find interesting to the learning process. Students brainstorm about subjects like music, while learning about keywords and skills like broadening, narrowing, and restating topics. This is always a quick update for me on what performers, groups, and types of music are hot or not. Pop culture can be used to build excitement into a project as well. Instead of having students make a poster, have them use Microsoft Publisher to make a faux MySpace page for a mythological being.

Truth in Advertising

Integrating popular culture has to be honest, authentic, and appropriate. Using popular culture just for the sake of using it would be like namedropping: phony and ineffective. Students are astute and will lose trust if the use of "their" culture is abused or ingenious. For example, I keep current on pop music because I enjoy pop music and love going to concerts, but no, I have never listened to performers like Marilyn Manson or Insane Clown Posse. I would destroy my credibility if I said otherwise. However, when there is a natural fit and if popular culture examples selected are relevant and appropriate, pop culture helps to build excitement, interest, credibility, and learning.

detached from their communities. We are deeply invested in the concerns of our communities, and closely woven into the fabric of our communities. We care earnestly about our patrons and exist to help them find the materials and information that they need. These are wonderful values—but they're just not cool. That doesn't detract from their importance, though, because often things that aren't cool are valuable in other ways. Secondly, coolness implies a value judgment that our notion of pop culture does not make. Coolness is both elusive and subjective. Pop culture is obvious (once you know where to look), largely objective (Does it sell well or get high ratings? Then it's popular!), and well covered by media outlets large and small. Additionally, you'll have your work cut out for you just keeping track of pop culture; keeping tabs on what's cool or not cool is an even more difficult (and thankless) task, because it's so subjective and changes even more quickly than pop culture trends.

The following table gives you an idea of cool vs. not cool things, trends, and people. To be honest, we're having a little fun here, but we're being a little bit serious, too. We're not saying the Not Cool things are bad—we're quite fond of shimmying to KC & the Sunshine Band and have been known to wear khakis ourselves—but by our lights, at least, they're just ... not cool.

COOL	NOT COOL
Johnny Cash	Kenny Chesney
David Bowie	KC & the Sunshine Band
Jay-Z	Russell Simmons
Post-incarceration Martha Stewart	Pre-incarceration Martha Stewart
Jeans	Khakis
Black T-shirts	Button-down shirts
Martinis	Cosmopolitans
iPods	Zunes

In short, we need to leave the determination of coolness up to our customers. We provide them with the right mix of materials, and let them sort out what is cool or not cool by their own mysterious and individual processes. Even circulation statistics may not give you what you're looking for in a hunt for what's cool, because all they tell you is what your users think is worth checking out of the library, not how much or how little they liked it. Happily, providing materials your users will think worthy of taking home for further investigation is exactly what embracing pop culture in your library is all about.

To illustrate the differences between an established trend and a more ephemeral one, let's look at the subject of cooking. As of this writing, cooking is an extremely hot topic, thanks in part to the success of cable TV celebrity cooks like Rachael Ray, Dave Lieberman, Jamie Oliver, and Nigella Lawson, whose shows are popular on networks such as HGTV and the Food Network. In addition to hosting cooking programs, these chefs are also building small media empires. Rachael Ray hosts several television programs, including a talk show, writes cookbooks, and in 2006 launched an eponymous lifestyle magazine. This trend has been going strong for at least the past five years and doesn't appear to have peaked yet, so now is an ideal time to jump on the cookery bandwagon and leverage this trend to your library's advantage. Thanks to the hotness of cooking and celebrity chefs, there are a number of enticing opportunities:

- Contact a local cooking school and invite some of its students and instructors to offer a live demonstration of how to prepare seasonally appropriate foods (make sure you let attendees sample the goods, too).

- Take a hard look at your cookbook collection. Is it up-to-date? Are some of your classics worn out? Purchase replacement copies where necessary, and select new titles to reflect changes in local tastes and cooking interests.

- Display your cookbook collection prominently, highlighting staff picks. Take a page from the big-box retailers' playbooks and include staff commentary on the books—this could be just one or two enthusiastic sentences handwritten on an index card and paper-clipped to the cover.

Of course, not all trends are as durable as cooking. Right now we're in the middle of a perfect storm for the enthusiastic home cook: interest in celebrity chefs, combined with a resurgence of value placed on domesticity in a post-9/11 world, mixed with the increasing popularity and availability of organic products, and multiplied by hundreds of cooking shows on a variety of network and cable channels—a foodalicious bonanza. Other trends, however—

Crocs brand shoes, hit TV shows that flame out after two or three seasons, teen versions of popular women's magazines—are more mutable, largely because they're not interconnected with other trends and so aren't in a position to leverage those trends' popularity. This mutability doesn't make these trends less important, exactly, but it does mean that libraries and library staff need to become comfortable with the ephemeral nature of certain trends. Once-hot magazines will go out of print, former ratings-catchers will be cancelled (along with their tie-in novelizations), and beloved fiction series will come to an end.

To continue working with our broad definition of popular culture, we'd like to introduce a corollary: You don't have to like pop culture to embrace its importance to your library. You read that right: You can be uninterested in pop culture, or even harbor a bit of antipathy toward at least some aspects of it, and still put it to use in your library's collections, services, and programming. So take a deep breath—if you don't watch *American Idol*, have no interest in anime, or think most Top 40 music is unlistenable—it's okay. Obviously, we encourage you to enjoy a varied media diet and to experiment with your listening, viewing, and reading habits—after all, having access to all of your library's holdings is one of the small luxuries of working there, right? But we recognize that not every pop culture trend is going to float everyone's boat. That's reality, and it's perfectly fine. What's not fine is dismissing pop culture as something that's of interest only to teens (or any other demographic group) to rationalize its perceived unimportance.

Reports in national magazines and major newspapers look at pop culture from a broad perspective, so they naturally tend to concentrate on big, almost inescapable facets of popular culture, such as celebrities or youth culture. But pop culture in libraries is about popular culture as it is embraced by *your* community, both by current patrons and potential patrons. And while sometimes this community pop culture will overlap with national pop culture, at other times it will be uniquely your own. That's why it's essential to look not only at what is popular across the country, or what is popular in the next town over, or what is popular with teens according to MTV, but to look at what is popular in your area, your neighborhood, and your schools. This is the heart of what we'll address in Chapter 2, Creating a Pop Niche for Yourself and Your Library.

Voices from the Field

At the end of each chapter we will feature "Voices from the Field," selected responses to questions in the online survey we conducted in July 2007. The survey was posted on SurveyMonkey.com, and, in the three weeks it was available online, it received more than 700 responses. (We were amazed, thrilled—and a tiny bit overwhelmed!) Each "Voices from the Field" section provides a representative sample of the best responses to our questions. What do we mean by "best?" The best responses are the most thought-provoking, or insightful, or infuriating, or witty ones we received.

In this chapter, we share selected responses to our survey question, "How do you define pop culture? What do you include or exclude in your definition? How does your definition (and inclusions and exclusions) of pop culture change when you apply it to your work in libraries?"

"Pop culture is ephemeral, simple or simplistic, predictable, repetitive, formulaic, and generally different in those ways and others from the arts that survive the test of time, break barriers, are original, creative and thought-provoking." —Anonymous Public Librarian

"I think about this a lot. When I say 'pop culture' or call something 'pop,' I mean quite simply that it is something that is in the public's consciousness, something that has, at the very least, a great deal of name recognition. I hate when people use 'pop culture' in a pejorative or dismissive way and the general attitude that if something appeals to the masses it must, by necessity, be less than worthy in some way. Pop culture is always intersecting with what is considered more highbrow, literary, and classic with the most interesting results. *East of Eden*, for example, was rotting its huge self away in the literary canon until Oprah decided to make it a book club pick, and it suddenly hit bestseller lists and became, as far as I'm concerned, part of pop culture. You look at a show like *Spring Awakening*, undeniably pop-y, certainly in its music, but it is based on an obscure 19th century German play. It has the kind of subtlety associated with literary drama, but it also completely rocks. At this point, I think it's hard to use the term 'pop culture' as a synonym for 'bad' without sounding ignorant (and, yes, I mean you, Harold Bloom)." —Adrienne Furness, Children's and Family Services Librarian, Webster (NY) Public Library

"Pop culture feels like those things that you picture your 5, 10, 15, or 20 year-old self in 10 to 45 years from now saying, 'I remember *that*!' It's the ephemeral, trendy, oh-so-important stuff without which you'd feel out of step with your peers. With regard to libraries, I tend to think 'inter-library loan' rather than 'what a good addition to my collection!'" —Anonymous School Librarian

"Pop culture, to me, is what is happening at the grass-roots level with regard to entertainment and social interactions, including fashion and ways of communicating. Even though I am no longer a young adult, I feel that as a teen librarian I can do my job best when in tune with what teens feel is important." —Anonymous Public Librarian

"I think pop culture is any entertainment or style that the majority of people have a passing familiarity with. This is not necessarily what is trendy, but it is also not obscure. A critical mass of people needs to have an awareness of something for it to be pop culture. For example, in libraries, *Harry Potter* is pop culture while *Twilight* is a niche." —Gretchen Ipock, Young Adult Librarian, Sellers Library, Upper Darby, PA

"I define pop culture as whatever our patrons are talking about and interested in." —Michele Lipson, Computer Services Librarian, Bryant Library, Roslyn, NY

"Whatever captures the imagination of my student population in the micro and macro senses of their lives; whatever they think is popular in their world, is then available in my library." —Stephanie Rosalia, School Media Specialist, Eileen E. Zaglin School PS225K, Brooklyn, NY

"I define pop culture as whatever is going on in the mainstream consciousness (Top 40, popular magazines, *Entertainment Tonight*, *Inside Edition*, nightly news, etc.) as well as what is popular amongst sub-cultures (hipster aesthetic, gay/lesbian/bi/trans, knitters, romance readers, etc.)." —Daniel Barden, Technical Services Administrator, Alachua County Library District, Gainesville, FL

"I think pop culture is a slippery beast. It's constantly changing (as far as specific content goes) but it's made up of movies, music, television, books, current events, etc. that are happening right now. Anything going on is pop culture. But today's pop culture is not necessarily tomorrow's pop culture." —John Klima, Access Services Librarian, Palmer College of Chiropractic, Davenport, IA

"Pop culture is about the new, new thing, about being connected to the pulse of the now. It defines mores and shapes lifestyles, activities, and goals. Pop culture has a youth connotation, but can be more broad based and can be influenced and molded by all ages. Advertising and sales promotion seem to dominate modern pop culture. Maybe the decentralization of the media through the Internet will change that, but the 'sellers' will just find a way to buy the sites and make them advertising vehicles—the kids will be one step ahead—someplace else." —Anonymous School Librarian

"To me, pop culture is anything—and everything—people talk about to entertain themselves or to provide information on things that are important to them. This includes computers, media, music, TV, radio, reading (all forms, including reading online or listening to spoken audio), sports, politics, religion, arts, and theatre." —Jay Wise, Youth Services Coordinator, Chillicothe and Ross County Public Library, Chillicothe, OH

"I think a couple things that make up pop culture include ready availability, marketing, pervasiveness, and visibility. Because pop culture is what people are generally interested in, people come to the libraries to find these things (knowing, perhaps, that pop culture items are faddish and maybe aren't worth the trouble to own or maybe to try them out before owning). Pop culture changes in the library a little because we're dealing with discussions of pop-cultural artifacts or discussions or representations of how pop-culture manifests itself. Maybe we don't have a Wii in our library, but maybe we buy a book on Wii culture." —Anonymous Academic Librarian

"I think pop culture covers a wide variety of topics. It's not just who's famous right now, or what's in the news; it's not just the fads and fashions. It's so many little things that we don't even think about, like advertising, games, Internet sites, slogans, and slang. In my particular job I try to apply what's popular and eye-catching, and what's up-and-coming, in such a way that it attracts people visually to our programming, and turns their standard ideas of what a library is and ought to be on their heads." —Anonymous Public Library Associate

"Something that is in fashion now, wasn't six months ago, and probably will not be in 12 months." —Anonymous School Librarian

"I think of it as all the stuff I have to know in order to not be a crazy lady trying, unsuccessfully, to relate to teenagers." —Anonymous Public Librarian

"Pop culture is the collection of materials and knowledge about materials that make up the collective imagination of the general public, creating a shared realm of knowledge from which social relationships can form." —Anonymous Public Librarian

"Pop culture is the stuff that people talk about, read about, listen to, and watch—the public conversation we're all having. I could have a conversation with my friends on the West Coast and then go to the East Coast and pick up the same conversation with a group of strangers and not miss a beat. It's so pervasive in our society (even the news can't get away from it—see CNN's ticker) that it's hard to say what is excluded or how I use it in my work in libraries—it's everywhere. I suppose I use it most when booktalking, to relate books and their plots to something relevant in the lives of the audience." —Anonymous Public Librarian

"It is anything that has an effect on our culture as a whole. It can help define who we are as a people as well as be an example of the things we find entertaining." —Anonymous Public Librarian

"Pop culture is all of the celebrity crazes, slang, and entertainment information that works itself into our lives every day. Television, movies, books, celebrities, magazines, and anything that sticks in people's consciousness are part of pop culture. The library is truly all about pop culture: Most of what people want information about or are interested in are in essence passing fads of pop culture." —Anonymous Public Librarian

"Even what we consider classics today was pop culture once—just look at Dickens." —Anonymous Public Librarian

"I would exclude the term 'pop.' It implies that it is not something to be taken seriously. I remember being a teen in the 60s, and I still take the popular culture of that time seriously. All librarians need to remember that the current 'pop' culture is no less serious to these young adults than was theirs. I get furious when I hear another librarian my age making fun of teens' styles—after bell-bottoms, micro-minis and those stupid-looking hats? Get real!" —Anonymous Public Librarian

"I don't know that I explicitly include pop culture in my work in libraries but the fact that I am pop culture literate (in fact, more so than most of my teens) helps me build relationships with them much more than the other librarians I work with." —Anonymous Public Librarian

"Pop culture would be those areas and things that change with the whims of the masses. Popular materials requested by patrons without regard to literary value." —Anonymous Public Librarian

"Pop culture is everything that goes on in the world today, from current events in politics to entertainment. I think it's important to cover all aspects in the library because everything in the modern world is somehow related." —Anonymous School Librarian

"In my library, it means timely displays connected to what's happening in the world, it means having the books/movies/music that people are talking about, and it means having librarians knowledgeable enough about all this stuff that they know how to spell the name of an anime series or a rap artist when someone asks for it!" —Anonymous Public Librarian

Endnotes

1. "pop culture *n.*" *The Oxford American Dictionary of Current English*, Oxford University Press, 1999, Oxford Reference Online, www.oxfordreference.com/

views/ENTRY.html?subview=Main&entry=t21.e23613 (accessed June 11, 2007).

2. Sarah Brenner, "popular culture, post-World War II," in Allan M. Winkler, Susan V. Spellman, and Gary B. Nash, eds., *Encyclopedia of American History: Postwar United States, 1946 to 1968*, vol. 9, New York: Facts On File, Inc., 2003, American History Online. Facts On File, Inc., www.fofweb. com/activelink2.asp?ItemID=WE52&iPin=EAHIX198&SingleRecord=True (accessed June 11, 2007).

3. John Scott and Gordon Marshall, "popular culture," *A Dictionary of Sociology*, Oxford University Press, 2005, Oxford Reference Online, www.oxfordreference.com/views/ENTRY.html?subview=Main&entry=t88.e1 753 (accessed June 11, 2007).

4. LeRoy Ashby, *With Amusement for All: A History of American Popular Culture Since 1830*, Lexington: The University Press of Kentucky, 2006.

5. Cathy DeRosa, et al., *Perceptions of Libraries and Information Resources*, Dublin, OH: OCLC Online Computer Library Center, Inc., 2005, www.oclc. org/reports/pdfs/Percept_all.pdf

CREATING A POP NICHE FOR YOURSELF AND YOUR LIBRARY

In Chapter 1, we discussed defining and using pop culture to connect with your community—and touched on the difference between "pop culture" and "cool." In this chapter, we'll delve more deeply into what it takes to create a pop culture niche for yourself and for your library.

We cannot emphasize enough that your pop culture collection, materials, and programs must reflect *your community's* wants and needs, not your own. Every now and then a question comes up on a library email list such as, "I have some extra money to spend on teen magazines/games/manga. What should I buy?" Librarians on the list chime in with excellent suggestions. However, the just-right answer to this kind of question cannot be found on a list—the question has not been posed to the just-right audience. That questioning librarian is really trying to find out what *her* teens want, not what other, perfectly lovely teens in Ohio, or Oregon, or on Ogontz Avenue want. (Unless, of course, you happen to live in Ohio, or Oregon, or on Ogontz Avenue, and serve the same teens!)

Please don't misunderstand us—these lists of suggested titles generated by colleagues are a great resource, but only as a starting point. Your customers are your best resources. So, let's say you want to add to your magazine collection. You've visited the local bookstore to raid their zillion-magazine newsstand for ideas; you've used a list query or a *VOYA* article to help narrow down your choices. What to do now? Why not invest in one or two issues of these cool, new-to-you-and-to-your-patrons magazines. Now, find out from your patrons whether they are worth buying!

Start with an established and reliable group, such as your Teen Advisory Board (TAB). A TAB (also known as TAG at libraries that prefer the term *group* to *board*) is an effective way to incorporate youth participation into the way your library does business. By giving the teens of your community a stake in the services, programs, and collections created for them, you generate goodwill, gain credibility, and create a standing focus group on issues of concern to adolescents. Soliciting and considering the input of TAB members is a good way to ensure the success of teen programs, and a natural bridge to increasing teen involvement in the library overall. TABs are increasingly popular, and YALSA (Young Adult Library Services Association) offers support to TAB-hosting librarians through a section on its website (www.ala.org/ala/yalsa/tags/tags resources/tagsresources.cfm) and through its YA-YAAC listserv (lists.ala.org/wws/info/ya-yaac).

Look beyond the TAB kids, too. Because they are proud, veteran library users, we tend sometimes to think only of TAB members when making decisions about teen materials, programs, and services. But these teens are not the only ones using your library, not the only ones in your community, and, we hope, not the only ones you want using the library. So, yes, do confer with them—and then go further. Place the sample magazines in your teen area with a short feedback form (completed forms can serve as contest entries for a prize, such as a year's subscription to a magazine of the winner's choice). Take the magazines along on your next round of school visits. Pass them around, or allow students to come up and browse through them. Note which ones captured teen interest, which were passed along with a glance, and which never made it past the third person before the bell rang. As for those in the library, which one disappeared? Which looks ratty? Which looks brand new? This is an example of soliciting customer input in creative ways, as well as an example of how there is no easy answer, no magical "must buy" list, when it comes to pop culture niches.

So, how else can you find out what's important to your community, pop culture-wise? Let's look at some research methodologies, such as surveys, polls, focus groups, and soliciting customer requests.

Surveys: Real Time and Online

Let's talk about surveys, beginning with survey methodology. When designing a survey, Yann Toledano advises, bear in mind that "the first essential step to conducting an effective survey is to clearly define your objectives. What do you want to learn?"[1] The answer will probably be different for each survey. Once you've clearly defined the information you're after, the questions are easier to pose.

As for the questions, it's not so much the question itself as how you phrase it. As any parent knows, asking "How was school today?" yields one of three responses: "Fine," "Okay," or the ever-popular dead silence. Similarly, if you frame a question too broadly, for example, "What's your favorite area of pop culture?" you may get a response so broad that it's useless ("music"), so narrow that it's equally useless ("Captain America"), or silence.

So, be particular! This is where your skills as a librarian come in: narrowing and defining the terms of your questions. Just as a parent learns to ask specifically about the length and degree of difficulty of Mrs. Slade's geometry test, you need to think of particular questions to glean useful answers. Or, sometimes—just as a parent learns more by overhearing conversations while carpooling because kids forget their parents hear what they say in the car—you have to really listen to what people are saying in the library (more on this in the section on focus groups).

The questions that will give you useful answers relate "to your primary objective … [R]esist the urge to ask questions that don't contribute to your goal."[2] If you find yourself wondering about your role, thinking, "If I just buy what the customer wants, how do library professionals fit in at all?" keep in mind that *this* is part of your role. Doing the legwork and prep work, taking the time, doing the research—all of these tasks will help you phrase the questions well.

Pop culture gives you a chance to have fun, so don't be afraid to make your questions fun! Which survey question would you rather answer: "What do you like best: movies, TV, or music?" or, "What's your favorite awards show: the Oscars, the Emmys, or the Grammys?" This question is fairly broad, but if you want to spend a limited materials budget responsibly and are wondering how much to spend on DVDs and how much on CDs, it will yield valuable information. You can also expand on this idea at awards time with sample ballots. To patrons, it's just a fun way to see who would win the "Library Oscars"; to you, it's a way to find specific titles people are interested in reading, listening to, or watching.

Moving beyond media formats, your survey questions might ask what customers like to do outdoors (giving you ideas for additions to your collections: gardening, landscaping, sports, or beach reads); what their favorite old TV series are (with all the TV shows available on DVD, you need some data to help you narrow the selection); and who their top indie rock favorites are (helping you broaden your music collection beyond the Top 40).

Who should you ask? People coming into the library are your obvious source, but not your only source. Don't exclude them—it's always poor planning to discount your current fan base, and it's great to make the people who are happy with you even happier. But one fantastic aspect of a pop culture collection is its ability to attract new customers, those who would otherwise think, "Nah, they won't have what I like in the library." Now's the time to say, "Yes we do, and we'd love for you to borrow it!" This is, of course, the classic library quandary: How do you get them to come to you, if they're not already coming to you?

Services for teens and kids are an easy answer, not just because pop culture is important to teens and kids, but also because they're a captive audience. Some of them have to come to the library— maybe their parents bring them, or the library is the after-school/before-the-parents-get-home-from-work hangout. Or, if you're a public librarian visiting a school, the kids have to be in class during your visit. If you're the school media specialist, they come to you at least once a week for library class. Whether you're a public librarian scheduling school visits, or a media specialist who sees these kids once a week, we all know where to find them: at school.

In-person surveys with kids can be written, or you can ask kids questions and collect feedback orally. As with any survey, provide some type of reward to encourage participation, whether it is candy for everyone who returns the survey form during a class visit, or the chance to win a library drawing. (It's ideal if you can offer a prize related to the survey, such as movie tickets, a bookstore gift certificate, or an iTunes store card.)

But why should the youth services and teen librarians have all the fun? Brainstorm places your reference and adult services librarians can visit: senior residences; churches, mosques, temples, and synagogues; volunteer groups; PFLAG; Rotary Club ... the list of local groups and community centers is endless. Visiting these groups to introduce the audience to the library's current services can grow boring if you're doing all the talking. But involving the group with questions and answers is fun for people of any age—you engage the audience, let the people know you care about their input, and make your visit (and your library) more memorable. Plus, you're gathering valuable information! You may assume that seniors want "memory lane" TV shows from the 1950s and 1960s, only to discover that what they really want are shows like *Dexter* and *Big Love*, because their limited budgets can't stretch to cover a pricey premium cable subscription.

Don't forget to go online, too! Just as you wouldn't advertise using only one medium (only newspapers, or the radio, or fliers), you have to look at multiple venues for surveys. Your website may be the only way some people interact with the library—and that includes patrons who only come in to use the computers.

Like in-person Q&A sessions and paper-based surveys, online surveys can both expand and limit your response base. On the one hand, you will hear from people who might not bother to respond to a written survey, as well as from Internet denizens well versed in online surveys and polling. On the other, your respondents are likely to fall into a somewhat narrow (although ever-widening) demographic of tech-savvy patrons. In short, we encourage you not to rely exclusively on either real-time or online surveys, but to use both to give you a more well-rounded and accurate picture of your user community. (Find recommended websites for creating online surveys in Appendix A.)

Polls on your library's website are another quick and dirty way of gathering data online. A poll is no more than a very brief online survey, in a format familiar to most Internet users. Because they are so brief—usually just one question—polls are easy to produce and change in response to local and global current events; they provide a snapshot of data, which can be useful as well.

Focus Groups

Focus groups, or group interviews with six to 10 people on a given topic, can yield very useful insights into how community members view current or proposed services and collections. When putting together a focus group, consider the following: Whom do you want to participate? How do you find them? How do you encourage people to give up their valuable time?

The advantage of a focus group over a survey is that focus groups allow for dialogue. Once you create that give-and-take, even though you start out with your own set of objectives and questions, you can end up with something entirely different. You create an opportunity to benefit from serendipitous discoveries. Your job is to get that conversation going, to guide it, to allow it to take on a life of its own without letting it get away from you. What's key here is not only to pose questions that will elicit useful answers, but also to ask questions that inspire quality conversations.

When forming your focus groups, you want to gather a mix of folks, both people who are already using the library and those who aren't. Decide whether you want to meet with current patrons in one group and potential customers in another, or combine them all into a single focus group.

To form focus groups with a pop culture perspective, think about your *potential users*. If you're thinking about adding graphic novels, don't start at the Rotary Club. Go to where your potential users are: the local comic book store. Talk to the owner about holding your focus group there. Do you think there might be an interest in anime and manga? If the local school has an anime club, not only do you know there is interest, but you also have a built-in focus group to work with.

As with surveys, think about going online! In-person focus groups are limited by the assumption that people have transportation to get to the library and a schedule that can be arranged around the library's needs. And while sometimes it's practical for a librarian to go out to the group—to the local comic store, for example—that doesn't always work either. Explore the possibility of conducting a focus group via instant messaging (IM). While you lose the ability to observe body language and tone of voice, you'll gain by increasing the number of potential participants. As those who have participated in online classes and virtual meetings know, using IM can actually encourage conversation; some people who are reticent in a real-life group become quite vocal when participating in an Internet chat session. IM users also have their own ways to express emotion and tone, using emoticons, fonts, colors, and caps to indicate everything from sarcasm to shouting.

If you use IM for your focus group, though, you still require participants to save the same time slot, just for you. Why not try a focus group on a blog, which respects focus group members and their time? To be sure, you'll lose the instantaneous conversational quality to the responses, but as bloggers know, discussions do take place within the comments to individual blog posts. Take a look at any blog post with 10 or more comments; people are talking with each other, reading and responding asynchronously. So use your blog to ask questions, invite responses, and encourage a virtual conversation. This format lets people participate at the place and time that is best for them, and provides them time to think and craft considered responses. As with your other niche-seeking methodologies, mix it up! Not everyone will be comfortable online, so build in time for both online and traditional focus groups.

Statistics

Statistics have always been a librarian's friend. How many people live in your community? How many have library cards? What percentage of kids, teens, parents, and seniors are card holders? How many books are checked out? How many are renewed? Which materials are checked out? How often?

You can't stand by your library's door at all hours, looking at who walks in and observing what they check out. Aside from the privacy issues involved, what we actually see and notice people doing and checking out is only a partial view. No librarian can seriously say, "the teens in my library don't read fantasy," based solely on what the kids in their TAB talk about reading. You also have to check the statistics on fantasy titles to find out what is being checked out and how frequently. Beyond what checks out, what items are constantly stolen? What items are so tattered that it looks like every kid who checks them out passes them along to several friends? This requires us to look at the statistics behind the statistics and to have hands-on knowledge of our collections.

We can cut very precise slices of our statistics: by subject, by genre, by author, by Dewey Decimal or Library of Congress number. We encourage you to collaborate with your colleagues in the IT (information technology) department and create a way to easily track statistics for materials you want to keep an eye on. Statistics are objective, so there's no fear that users will just say what they think you want to hear in a focus group or decide to provoke you deliberately because they had a bad day, or that teens with a silly sense of humor will decide not to take your survey seriously. Now, how you read statistics may be influenced by your subjective opinion; you need to account for external factors that may affect the numbers. For example, low turnout for a given program may seem bad, until you remember that it was the day of the big blizzard or a day when local schools scheduled standardized testing.

If a library stakeholder has questions or directly challenges the value of a collection, statistics can help support your decision to start or add to that collection, as well as to nurture it by scheduling collection-related programming. Alternatively, statistics can show where you may have misjudged; they can help you discover that shojo manga is popular, but other graphic novels are less so. Statistics can help reveal which gaming systems are the most popular. Low statistics may indicate that you've misjudged; but before you give up, ask some key questions: How did you promote the collection? How well are the items catalogued? Where are the materials located in the library? Have you created booklists or cross-media "Recommended If You Like" lists to advertise these items? Are the materials featured on your website? Does your staff support the collection by eagerly promoting the materials? Does your staff even know the collection exists? In short, have you given the collection a fair shot?

Nothing happens in isolation. By creating a pop culture niche (or more than one—aim high!) for your library, you collaborate with the community to meet their pop culture needs. Ultimately, you benefit the community, the groups you're working with, and, of course, your library itself. Target the groups you've worked with and market those materials! When done well, you're not just introducing materials to folks; instead, you're saying, "Hey, remember that talk we had? Here are the results of your input—we hope you like what you see! Please let us know what more we can provide in this area."

Consult Chapter 3, Building a Collection That Really Pops, on matters relating to pop culture collection development. For more information on advocating for and marketing your popular collections, refer to Chapter 4, Advocacy, Marketing, Public Relations, and Outreach.

Voices from the Field

In reading the answers to our survey question "How do you track your patrons' pop culture interests? Do you use this information in the collection development process, and in planning of programs and events at your library?" we were struck by the fact that librarians and library staff *listen*. They listen to what patrons say and observe what patrons do, but they don't always recognize the value of this information or give themselves proper credit for the information they have learned. In other words, chances are you have the data you need to start your pop culture niche; you just haven't identified it, or you haven't brainstormed with the rest of the staff to realize how big (or small) the need is. Taking in and processing information is something librarians do all the time, and perhaps it is such a natural part of our job that we don't always recognize we're doing it.

Why is it important to label these activities, to connect that "just listening" to "collection development?" Because the label gives what you do more power and more respect, because sometimes we do have to state the obvious, and because often our administration needs the buzzwords. They need to hear, "I was gathering information for collection development" or "I've used customer feedback in planning these programs," and they need to know that when you are "just talking" to patrons and customers, you are doing valuable work. Just as we market the library to patrons, remember to market yourself to administration. As you read some of these highlighted responses, we're sure you'll either be nodding and saying, "Hey, I do that already," or thinking, "Hmm, I can do that without doubling my workload."

"Just by talking to them, mostly. It's not formal. We did ask in an online teen survey if they'd be interested in an anime club or attending the vampire prom, but that's as formal as it has gotten. We do use it in collection development. We take suggestions for books and media online and really do try to purchase them. It also does definitely inform our programming. If the teens are all talking about *Harry Potter*, we'll plan an *HP* party, etc." —Laura J., Public Services & Children's Librarian, Davis Library, Plano (TX) Public Library System

"We track all reference questions, and I use this info whenever practical for programming." —Anonymous Public Library Assistant

"I try to develop a trusting rapport with students. School librarians are in a unique position to solicit information that is helpful to understanding their students. We have many opportunities to observe students and hear what is important to them. Staying in touch with what things interest the students in their out-of-school time is a good way to be informed." —Anonymous High School Librarian

"Local papers, conversations with patrons, local radio programming, conversations with staff, especially those involved in community groups outside of the library. Yes, this is a consideration when planning programs and collections." —Anonymous Public Librarian

"Basically I just let the kids and the teens tell me what's hot at the moment. My experience has been that they are very forthcoming once they know a librarian is receptive to their interests and will hear them out about the latest fad. Plus they know I'm into a lot of the same things that they are (gaming, *Veronica Mars*, tattoos) so they know my interest in their discoveries is authentic." —Elizabeth Erwin, Youth Services Librarian, Hunterdon County Library, Flemington, NJ

"We track patrons' interests by word of mouth and by keeping an eye on what they request. We're a small library and everyone works closely together." —Anonymous Librarian Trainee

"The Teen Advisory Board is my eyes and ears as far as what is popular in the community. I also look at what is popular with TV, movies, and music to get a sense of what local teens might be interested in." —Anonymous Public Librarian

"At the moment, because the library is so very small, I simply talk to the young adults. I make certain that they know me by name and don't mind asking me anything. This is the only way that I, at 58, can keep current on popular culture. It's not like I go gaming or hang out at the mall. I write notes and yes, I use this in everything." —Anonymous Public Librarian

"I talk to the kids, I spend a lot of reference desk time online at sites like Boing Boing (www.boingboing.net) and Go Fug Yourself (gofugyourself.typepad.com). I screw around online in general a lot." —Anonymous School Media Specialist *(Authors' Note: That is so not screwing around! It's gathering information you can use, whether it's for programming, collection development, or just being able to understand the lives of your students.)*

"I read ypulse, pay attention to what they're wearing, checking out, etc, and—you know—ASK THEM." —Anonymous Public Librarian

"We have a small library, so it's mostly through conversations in the stacks or over the counter. We absolutely use it for collection development and programming ... that's one of the reasons our needlework collection is growing by leaps and bounds, and we tracked down a crochet teacher for a series of classes this fall." —Anonymous Public Library Director

"Eavesdropping and nosy questions." —Anonymous High School Library Media Specialist

"LISTEN!!!" —Anonymous Public Librarian

"I use my Teen Advisory Board—they are not quite as hip or tech savvy as the teens I see on MTV, etc. For adults, I read *People, EW, Radar*, try to watch a variety of shows, also read some entertainment blogs. Even the local newspaper covers a fair amount of pop culture." —Anonymous Public Librarian

"We don't have a specific formula, but instead rely on library staff and patrons to let us know what's pop and what isn't. You can usually identify someone in the organization who is an expert on music, and someone who does graphic novels, and someone who watches TV incessantly, etc." —Anonymous Public Library Administrator

"We rely on communicating with patrons to find out what they need. This works to varying degrees of success." —James Peek, Librarian, Middlesex (NJ) Public Library

"I talk to my students every day about what they are doing and what they are interested in. I use this information in my collection development and programming decisions. If I didn't, I wouldn't be serving my community of learners. I would be making decisions in isolation. The best way to engage students is to target their needs and interests." —Mary Alice Hudson, Media Specialist, Cape Fear Elementary School, Rocky Point, NC

"We constantly ask the parents, kids, and teens what they want. We want to keep what works of the old, but also incorporate the new. We have a teen advisory group (TAG) that suggests some really great things and we have put [their suggestions] in our programs. We try to involve not only the collection but the programs and events as well. Sort of a multicurricular thing. We keep statistics on all our programs and events." —Liz Sann, Youth Services Department, Programs Assistant, Roxbury Public Library, Succasunna, NJ

"I read magazines, watch TV, and read blogs that discuss aspects of pop culture. I also take note of what teens are asking for when I'm on the reference desk. I definitely use this information when planning programs and dealing with collection development." —Melissa Rabey, Teen Librarian, Frederick County (MD) Public Libraries

"Collection stats are key in determining interests. Also, we have an 'I Want' Bulletin Board for students and teachers to post their choices for purchase. We pay close attention." —Anonymous School Media Specialist

"I don't do a very good job with this part. I read *Entertainment Weekly*, *People*, and try to read new issues of *Time*, *Newsweek*, and *Rolling Stone* as they come in. Some patrons will ask for specific material, but not many teens will do so. I do use this information for collection development, but not for programming (except when I ask teens what movie they'd like to see next)." —Anonymous Public Librarian *(Authors' Note: This is representative of many comments we received: "I don't do anything except check circulation, listen to patrons, etc." Anon, you are doing a heck of a lot! And, yes, it seems that adults are often better at asking for materials that libraries don't have than teens are. Teen advisory boards [and eavesdropping, as noted earlier] are good ways to find out what teens want.)*

"We take note of what patrons request. Patrons can personally request any materials they think we should add to the collection. We have patrons register, and we keep attendance for all the programs that we do. I stay up to date by attending conferences, reading kidlit blogs, keeping up with current events, and interacting and listening to our patrons and what their needs are." —Anonymous Public Librarian

"We have no official process for tracking pop culture interests. Really, it just consists of listening to what they are talking about, watching how they are using the library, keeping track of how your collection is used, even peeking at what they are doing on the Internet (I know, I know, privacy violation). Of course I use this information in my collection development process. When I have 10 kids coming in and asking for Hannah Montana books, well then, I've just gathered some important data that needs to be kept in mind." —Anonymous Public Librarian

"I think it's easy enough to learn those interests just by being around your patrons and serving them at the public desk. You start to pick up on what everyone keeps asking for, or seeing the long waiting lists. Plus, if you pay attention to the media (through TV, radio, magazines, websites) it's easy enough to figure out what the latest interests are and I think it's pretty safe to assume a decent percentage of your patrons would be interested in those things as well. At least, in a public library. Enough to warrant purchasing the popular materials or creating a program." —Anonymous Public Library Paraprofessional

"I try to keep on top of what toys are being sold in stores, what's being shown on the major kids' networks, and what's best-selling on Amazon. I also have a kid-friendly 'Idea Box' in the Children's Room (you can't call it a 'Suggestion Box' if you want the majority of kids to understand what it's for). I get a lot of good suggestions from kids. We also track questions every day and try to talk to each other about things we're seeing more requests for. I do orders every month to try to keep new materials coming in and so that we can be at least somewhat responsive to new demands as they arise. Especially with pop culture stuff, I tend to purchase things in as many formats as possible. So, for an older example, we have *Spongebob Squarepants* books and comics and DVDs and music CDs and games. Everything supports each other, at least ideally." —Adrienne Furness, Children's and Family Services Librarian, Webster (NY) Public Library

"I just listen. I also ask kids what they like, what they're reading. I have often had them fill out surveys on what they do with their leisure time, what kind of reading they enjoy, etc." —Anonymous School Media Specialist

"Our teen librarian has her nose into everything pop culture, and the rest of our programming staff keeps tabs on it as well. The Web librarian and I keep track via blogs and news to see what's current online and in the advertising world. It all gets applied in different ways." —Anonymous Public Library Associate

"I have a survey form on the back of all my teen area flyers, and I ask my patrons to fill those out. It simply asks them what their favorite movie, books, and bands are, and what kind of programming they would like to see at the library. I hold teen advisory group meetings to gather more information, and when I can, I ask my patrons directly what they would like to see more of in the library." —Anonymous Public Librarian

"No—that's an interesting idea." —Anonymous Public Librarian *(Authors' Note: We hope that some of the tips shared by others are helpful!)*

"At the end of the school year, I surveyed the teens about their interests. I felt very lucky to have more than a dozen teens respond about which TV shows they like, etc., and this will factor into the upcoming year's programming. Additionally, with a teen advisory board, I am able to get teen input for many of my decisions." —Anonymous Public Librarian

"I listen to college age students, a variety of radio stations from publicly supported alternative rock to commercial talk radio, read *USA Today* inserts from my local paper, review a few blogs, and listen in on water cooler conversations. Occasionally I'm able to use this information to inform collection development decisions. In my current academic setting I find more leads from NPR relating to my faculty users. My planning of programs is very limited and has not lent itself to being informed by pop culture." —Anonymous College/University Librarian

"There is student input into the selection process through an advisory board, composed of volunteers with an interest in the library. Faculty also request certain kinds of library materials, print and audio-visual." —Anonymous School Media Specialist

"I tend to just ask them. They are very good at expressing what they want and they tell me what they want to read. I use this information for future programs. I want to do more in the future." —Rachel Simmons, Librarian, Atlantic County (NJ) Library System

"I do a recommendation chain twice a year, usually for DVDs and music. It asks students to recommend something they like and they think we should have, and then share that with a friend who then makes an additional recommendation. We usually get lots of good ideas this way." —Anonymous School Media Specialist

"Surveys, direct conversations, Web polls, keeping track of the types of things they ask for that the library doesn't have (you might spot a trend of lots of people asking for different television shows and realize you're deficient in that area)." —John Klima, Access Librarian, Palmer College, Davenport, IA

"I've nurtured relationships with the kids and teens that encourage them to tell me what they're interested in. They've come to understand that if they request it I will definitely buy it. So, if there's something they really like, they'll usually tell me. Also, I give out free paperback coupons at various programs and when the kids redeem them, I get a chance to see what it is they like enough to want to own for themselves. I also have teen volunteers who help me out with ordering by telling me what they think their peers want to read. They know by now that I love horror and realistic fiction, but that I'm kind of weak with fantasy and historical fiction—so they make sure to keep me especially informed of new titles they love in those areas." —Anonymous Public Librarian *(Authors' Note: We love that you've made this a two-way street! That it is not just the librarian telling kids what the "good new books" are, it's also the kids telling the librarian!)*

"We don't invest much into determining our patrons' specific interests, other than accepting suggestions and examining interlibrary loan requests." —Anonymous Public Librarian

"I make note of the things children check out and inquire about. Also, I try to keep track of the popular movies, television shows and music, as well as what children most enjoy talking about. That information is my secondary priority when planning and purchasing, with the school curriculum being first." —Anonymous School Media Specialist *(Authors' Note: Good for you that the children's interests are on your priority list! We sympathize that some schools, due to budget concerns and other issues, wouldn't be able to include it on their list at all!)*

"Still experimenting after six years on the job. So far so good. New Age music does not work." —Anonymous Public Librarian *(Authors' Note: "New Age music does not work" may become our new catch phrase!)*

"Patrons can request things via the website, which helps us know what people want. We also talk to the patrons when they come in, we have a Teen Advisory Board, and we read too many magazines." —Anonymous Public Librarian *(Authors' Note: There is no such thing as too many magazines.)*

"Talking with students about their interests in manga and all things Japanese, for example, has a direct impact on buying." —Anonymous School Media Center Library Assistant

"I track our patrons' pop culture interests by talking to them, watching what is checked out, what is requested, what does not get returned, and what we cannot keep on our shelves. I use all of this information in all aspects of my job." —Alei Burns, Youth Librarian, Grauwyler Park Branch Library, Dallas, TX

"Most of the time, I just talk to the kids and take their suggestions seriously. Now they know that I am open to their ideas." —Michelle Glatt, Librarian, Chiddix Junior High School, Normal, IL

Endnotes

1. Yann Toledano, "Use Online Surveys to Get the Feedback You Need," TechSoup, www.techsoup.org/learningcenter/internet/page5048.cfm

2. Toledano, "Use Online Surveys."

BUILDING A COLLECTION THAT REALLY POPS

So, you've decided on your library's first pop culture niche. Chances are good that you already have some materials to support that niche. Put on your "pop culture" glasses and browse your existing collection to see what your library has that fits your new initiative. Start with your magazines, and continue through your DVDs, CDs, audio books, graphic novels, and, of course, books! Building a collection that goes "Pop!" starts with identifying what you already have, and then moving on to expanding and building your collection. And, while you're doing this, think of all your formats and collection areas! If you've chosen anime and manga for your initial pop culture collection, the easy answer is to buy anime DVDs and manga books. But what about related magazines such as *Shonen Jump*, *Shojo Beat*, and *PiQ*? What about books about how to draw manga characters, and audio recordings or software for learning to speak Japanese? We encourage you to employ a broad-based strategy to develop a well-rounded collection.

Collection Development Strategy

The first step in your collection development strategy is to commit to your collection. Don't hold back! If you're looking to expand your movie collection beyond Oscar winners, don't hesitate out of a concern that DVDs will soon become obsolete. There will always be new formats, and librarians will always have to adapt to them. Committing to your collection also involves consideration of ongoing budgetary issues. Beyond determining how much you need to create your core collection, you need to plan for the cost of maintaining and growing that collection by adding new materials. Having a pop collection that is *so last year*, without anything to reflect this month's highlights, won't keep patrons coming back after their initial "wow, look at that!" reaction. It's one thing not to buy the second season of a TV show because the first season didn't circulate well; it's another not to buy it because you didn't budget for it.

Next, build the collection that your community needs and wants, not the one that the community down the road needs and wants, and not the one you think they should need or want. It's easy to get caught up in playing "Librarian Knows Best," but we *don't* always know best. Do your patrons the honor of believing them when they tell you what they want. See what circulates and consider the population you serve: If your library serves a large population of senior citizens, for instance, you might consider dedicating a substantial chunk of your DVD monies to purchasing classic movies and television shows on DVD. Many films that have long been out of print or unavailable are now being released on DVD, some cheaply and without extras, and some given the deluxe treatment (such as the Criterion Collection). Delight your seniors—and give them a chance to introduce their grandchildren to nostalgic favorites like Fred Astaire and Ginger Rogers, or Frank Capra—with a broad selection of these lost classics. If your community is ethnically diverse, don't look only to Hollywood for your collection. Sophie's library serves two large and growing immigrant populations: Latinos and Indians. Not surprisingly, Spanish, Hindi, Gujarati, and Bengali-language DVDs are among the highest-circulating films system-wide.

We don't mean to imply that you shouldn't use your professional judgment to make additions you think patrons will like—quite the reverse. You have access to a broader range of selection tools than your customers and are in a position to spot trends and be aware of new releases well before the general public. Use that knowledge to get the right materials into the hands of your patrons. Not only will they appreciate it, they will remember it. Every time you provide a library user with something they want (or better still, something they didn't even know they wanted), you gain a powerful ally.

That's it, in a nutshell—make a commitment to one or more areas of your collection that need enhancement, and select the right materials. Sharon Baker and Karen Wallace provide a wealth of strategies and worksheets for developing, maintaining, and marketing a collection that meets customer needs in *The Responsive Public Library* (second edition, Libraries Unlimited, 2002). We highly recommend this title for purchase by every library that is serious about developing appealing collections.

Next, we'll take a look at the tools you can use to develop your pop culture collections.

Pop Culture Materials Selection: Print Tools

Happily, both print and electronic tools for pop culture materials selection abound. When it comes to print resources, we're going to ask you to step outside your comfort zone. We do not expect you to lay aside venerable review periodicals such as *Booklist, Library Journal, Choice*, or *Voice of Youth Advocates*. Rather, we encourage you to supplement your collection development toolbox with popular periodicals that have strong book review sections, such as *People*, *Vogue*, *Vanity Fair*, and our personal bible of all things pop, *Entertainment Weekly*.

When it comes to specific age groups or special-interest groups, it pays to read what they are reading. This meets two needs: your immediate need for materials suggestions, and your long-term need to become generally literate in the interests of, and trends followed by, your targeted group. For example, if you serve children, read *American Girl*, *Boys' Life*, *Discover Kids*, *Sports Illustrated for Kids*, *Chirp*, and so on. If you are a teen librarian, your monthly magazine diet should include healthy doses of *Thrasher*, *Teen Vogue*, *CosmoGirl!*, *WWE*, *SLAM*, *Right On!*, *SPIN*, *VIBE*, *J-14*, and other magazines marketed to this audience. You can find essential magazines for various special-interest niches—from parenting to hunting and fishing to crafts, as well as for a wide variety of demographic groups—in the latest edition of *Magazines for Libraries*. *Library Journal* also provides regular magazine reviews and round-ups.

Bottom line: The magazines you add to your collection serve two important purposes. First, they are there for your patrons to read and enjoy. Second, they are there for you to read and use as a resource for collection development ideas.

Of course, we don't want you to forget the books! Some pop culture interests take up whole books in and of themselves, from zines (*From A to Zine: Building a Winning Zine Collection in Your Library*) to teen-interest collections (*Thinking Outside the Book: Alternatives for Today's Teen Library Collections*). We provide a core list of recommended titles on pop culture for the library professional in Appendix A.

Pop Culture Materials Selection: Online Tools

Online resources for collection development are as vast and varied as print resources. Some print magazines such as *School Library*

Journal (www.schoollibraryjournal.com) have websites that contain all the articles found in the print editions; others, such as *The Horn Book Magazine* (www.hbook.com/magazine), only post selected articles on their sites. Some online-only resources are unavailable in print, such as the monthly Web magazine Bookslut (www.bookslut.com) and children's literature monthly The Edge of the Forest (www.theedgeoftheforest.com). Like print magazines, both of these online resources contain a mixture of interviews, articles, and reviews.

Blogs are another fabulous resource for news and reviews, especially of pop culture material! Pop culture fans love to share and discuss what they are *fan*atic about. Want to know the buzz about a comic book, a band, or a movie? Go to the blogs. Topical email discussion lists are another good online resource.

Online selection tools for pop culture materials fall into various categories. Some are established; some are new. However, with any online resource comes the issue of stability. When a traditional magazine, new or established, goes out of business, the physical issues survive (and the content may also survive in digital form in subscription databases from vendors like EBSCO). Whether new or established, a website can change its internal structure or even disappear completely overnight. But while we cannot guarantee the stability of the online resources we discuss, we feel confident that these sites and resources will continue to be available for some time. How do you find your own online resources? How do you discover that blog or website that is brand new—but awesome? Check out Chapter 6, Information Technology Is Everyone's Job, where we talk about blog-specific search engines such as Technorati (www.technorati.com) and Google Blog Search (blogsearch.google.com).

Pop Culture Resources: The Human Factor

Don't forget about the human experts in your professional and personal orbits. Asking your colleagues what items are on their wish lists can be very useful—and it's politic to do so, as well. You might consider setting up a staff or faculty wish list blog, which is easy enough to do using free software from Blogger (www. blogger.com) or WordPress (www.wordpress.org). Ask your coworkers to leave their suggestions in the comments. (See Chapter 6 for more information and resources on blogs and blogging.) You can then post updates on the blog when you place orders using staff suggestions. If you want to know what collections are particularly popular among your patrons, you can, of course, look at circulation statistics, but it might be even more rewarding to enlist the assistance of your circulation staff. The people who check all the library's materials in and out, day in and day out, have a good two or three fingers on the pulse of what floats your community's collective boat. Ask them what they see crossing their desks, and go from there.

Go beyond your staff, too. Every library plays host to various community groups, ranging from English as a Second Language instructors and La Leche League chapters to movie discussion groups and scrapbookers. Contact the group leaders and ask to take 15 minutes of time on their next meeting agenda to hold a quick-and-dirty focus group; ask group members to list their top five or 10 magazines, movies, books, and musical artists. (See Chapter 2 for more information on holding a focus group.) Hobbyists are experts in their chosen fields, so make the most of the legwork they've done for you and survey them on their areas of expertise. This is a win-win situation: You may find gaps in your collection that you never knew existed; and you may also be able to say to your constituents, "Oh, yes, we already have that here! You should check it out!"

It's also smart to think outside of the library. Soliciting suggestions from local book, comic book, and music shop clerks is a very easy way to glean information about what's popular and good. This method can be particularly useful for discovering new or up-and-coming artists who might not—yet!—be splashed all over the covers of the magazines you read.

If you work in a public library and maintain good relationships with your local school media specialists, try to obtain permission to survey clubs at local schools. Clubs focused on niche interests, such as anime and manga, international relations, music, sports, and so on, are full of youthful experts on their area of interest. The surveys can be conducted in person or by proxy, through the club advisor.

Now, let's think about what kinds of materials you should consider including in a comprehensive pop culture collection.

Beyond Books: Pop Culture in All Its Many Formatted Glory

We need to look beyond the image of the library as a comfortably appointed warehouse for books. Chances are that you already include alternative formats such as magazines, DVDs, and music or books on CD in your collection, but there are many formats beyond the usual audiovisual items that you may not have considered, such as electronic and tabletop games, comic books and graphic novels, and online pop culture resources. Building a pop culture collection gives you the perfect opportunity to start adding other formats. Our friend, colleague, and noted alternative formats expert, C. Allen Nichols, offers a director's perspective on this topic in the sidebar that follows.

ALTERNATIVE FORMATS: A DIRECTOR'S VIEW BY C. ALLEN NICHOLS

Libraries have always been slow to embrace and accept new formats, as well as the content those formats bring to their collections. That content is often related to popular culture, which is creating demand for the new formats in the marketplace. It has been my experience that librarians don't much like the marketplace or pop culture, but we need to remember that our customers do. The most important aspect of our future is to know and provide what it is our customers want.

During my 25-plus years of library service I've realized that this concept is easier to embrace than to implement. I've seen the emergence and disappearance of a number of formats during my career, and the emergence of each new form has caused nothing but consternation and contempt within the community of librarians. Of course they aren't too happy to see the format go once its useful life has ended, because they've spent a lot of time and money learning to catalog, package, secure, shelve, and promote (wait a minute … we don't do too much of the latter), and all that time and effort seems to go to waste. Letting go means all that work disappears. I've seen this over and over again as LPs, cassette tapes, Beta videos, VHS, video discs, comic books, CDs, graphic novels, DVDs, MP3 discs, Playaways, etc., have come, gone, or, in some cases, both. To me though, that is just a basic cost of doing business, and we, as librarians, have to deal with it just as those in the corporate world must when facing similar issues.

Popular culture is for the masses, and the masses are precisely why libraries should add alternative formats to their collections. In what better way can a library provide service to the greatest number of its constituency than to provide that which appeals to the most people? So why do we resist these formats, when they can be vital to increasing a library's customer base and, maybe, circulation statistics?

I believe librarians are afraid of fully embracing the "give 'em what they want" philosophy of librarianship because it erodes the virtuous concept (highbrow quality literature, or "give 'em what they need") of what libraries are meant to be in their eyes. I argue, however, that it is precisely that philosophy that libraries everywhere need to adopt through the addition of new and exciting formats.

Today's world sees the masses answering their own reference questions via the Internet and bypassing our far superior information services, but the masses don't care. This, to me, means that in order to maintain our relevancy as an institution, we must find ways to provide the masses with the services they *do* care about—and often those services incorporate exciting new formats. If we can succeed in this effort to encourage the masses to walk through our doors, we can introduce them to the myriad of other wonderful things we have in our buildings, or even on our websites. Through this we can then promote whatever is near and dear to our hearts.

Popular culture appeals to no group more than the youth of our communities. They are hooked by trends, celebrity, commercial marketing, and whatever is newest and brightest. This group adopts new formats with much greater ease than anyone else. With that knowledge, it shouldn't be a great leap for librarians to understand that the way to continued library success and relevancy far into the future is to provide what it is that appeals to our youth. Yes, this means that the formats will come and go, as youth age and a new generation finds its own new formats to desire, but catering to our children and teens means that libraries will have the opportunity to build relationships that can lead to life-long library users. Isn't this what we all want?

So I say: Embrace these new formats. Deal with the issues of storage and cataloging and *get over it*. Add new formats to your collections and promote the heck out of them. Embrace the new users that come to you for those formats. Be excited about the circulation statistics that will rise because people use them. Lastly, keep your eyes open for the next new format that finds its way to the masses and get ready to begin the process all over again.

C. Allen Nichols, MLS, MBA, is the Director of the Wadsworth (OH) Public Library. With his wife, Mary Anne Nichols, he co-edits the series "Libraries Unlimited Professional Guides for Young Adult Librarians." He also edited *Thinking Outside the Book: Alternatives for Today's Teen Library Collections* (Libraries Unlimited, 2004).

Let's move on and talk a bit about the methods you'll use to select and purchase these materials to get them into your patrons' hands as quickly as possible.

Methodology: Hand Selection and Standing Order Plans

What is hand selection, and what are standing order plans? For the uninitiated, hand selection is exactly what it sounds like: Librarians in charge of materials selection choose, item-by-item, materials to be added to the collection. They use a variety of tools—mostly review periodicals, sometimes supplemented by review copies or galleys of books—to select items for purchase. The process of hand selection is analogous to grocery shopping, where you go to the store and choose each item yourself.

Using a standing order plan is a lot like hiring a personal shopper. Just as a personal shopper knows what you like and will always bring you the chunky black knitted turtleneck sweaters or seersucker trousers you love, a standing order plan ensures that you automatically receive books by the authors, illustrators, and imprints your community loves most. For instance, you can set up a standing order plan so that you always receive titles that have earned starred reviews in *Booklist* or *School Library Journal*— this is an easy way of ensuring that highly recommended titles come to you automatically, on a timely basis, and don't eat into your discretionary spending account. Standing order plans are also extremely useful for collecting all of the latest works by those highly prolific authors who seem to crank out a book every four months or so; for the same reason, they are also the best way to keep up with popular series titles. No matter how much you like hands-on selection, keeping track of popular series and authors can be a headache. Why use your valuable time hand-picking these titles?

Your optimum methodology involves both hand selection and standing order plans. Note that we used *both*, not *versus*, in the previous sentence. We want to avoid the polarizing dichotomy of either employing the time-honored, professional, and subtle art of hand-selecting every item in a library's collection, or mindlessly allowing a far-off vendor to send you items you may or may not find useful—quickly spending all of the money you've allotted them for the year. Materials selection is not an all-or-nothing proposition! Many librarians effectively combine well-structured and periodically reviewed standing order plans (consider multiple vendors to get the best prices on all the formats you want) with the freedom to hand-select items purchased with discretionary funds. Using both of these collection development methodologies gives you the best of both worlds: You have the comfort of knowing that your book vendor will furnish you with a sufficient number of copies of the latest David Baldacci thriller, and also the satisfaction of knowing that your library has the flexibility to purchase books by promising first-time authors or music by artists to watch.

Jill Faherty, Director of Children and Teen Services for Public Libraries, and Katy White, Public Library Service Consultant, both of Baker & Taylor, offer the following advice for setting up a standing order plan: "First find out what the vendor actually has available on standing order. Next, check your collection to see what titles have high circulation, and compare what is available on standing order to what's popular in your collection … If the vendor doesn't have a particular series, author, or award available that you simply must have, ask them if a standing order can be set up for you, even though it's not on the list."[1] Every library wholesaler offers publications and electronic resources designed to help you craft the standing order plan to best suit your library or media center's needs.

A BRIEF WORD ABOUT CENTRALIZED SELECTION

Kathleen Sullivan, the Phoenix Public Library's Collection Development Coordinator, reported in 2004 on her library's success with centralized selection. Sullivan noted that "a growing trend is to make all new materials selection the responsibility of one person or a small group. [...] Many systems find that one of the major benefits of centralized selection is meeting the patron expectation to have access to titles nearer to the publication date."[2] Other advantages of centralized selection include improved access to resources for AV materials, fewer purchasing mistakes, and increased circulation across all formats and age groups.

If you work for a library system that employs centralized selection, you may feel out of the collection development loop. You're a Reader's Advisory librarian, but you have never been encouraged to advise the selectors. Our advice? Offer yours! Sullivan points out that she and her team of central selectors often base selection decisions on input from front-line colleagues, as well as on reviews and other information resources.[3]

If you work for a library that is considering a transition to centralized selection, and you are concerned about losing a highly professional area of responsibility, think about how to imbue your other areas of responsibility with that same expertise. If you work closely with your library's central selectors, your Reader's Advisory skills and services will improve, and you will be free to offer new services, such as roving or virtual reference, or more outreach.

Additionally, due to the built-in nimbleness of centralized selection, this collection development methodology offers the benefit of more customized branch collections. Sullivan highlights a related benefit of centralized selection: It serves the potential customer as well as the dedicated present library user. Both hand selection and standing order plans can work well within a centralized selection framework.

Selecting materials is near and dear to many librarians' hearts; the idea of being kept out of the selection loop can be upsetting. If you are part of the centralized process at your library, do you make it easy for other staff and for patrons to make suggestions? And do you then respond to that input? Do you have forms? Are they available online? Are they easy to find and easy to use? How do you advertise them? (That is, are the forms a secret shown only to those who ask for them, or are they made known to all?) Do you encourage and reward input?

If you work in a library with centralized selection, and you don't see the materials on the shelf that customers are asking about or that you've read about in review journals, magazines, and blogs, be assertive! Speak up. Find that form, paper or electronic. No forms? Send emails. Meet with the materials selectors at your library. Find out what the procedure is to request materials, and use it.

Using a standing order plan for areas where your library's collection development librarians lack expertise or interest, particularly in newly popular genres or formats, can be tremendously useful. Faherty and White highlight the fact that "each librarian on our staff has his or her own genre strength, such as graphic novels, fantasy, or romance. They work with the entire universe of titles available and can pull the ones best suited for the library's collection based on their specific parameters." Standing order plans also offer a great deal of customization. Baker & Taylor, for example, "can perform custom profiling to send you notification lists based on your own specifications. We can recommend what's popular based on your region, overall demand in public libraries, or based on your demographics." In short, once you have provided a library wholesaler with some basic data and your community's preferences, the vendor can draw on deep resources to help you craft a plan that frees you to work with a more narrowly focused set of parameters for your discretionary collection development.

There are disadvantages to using standing order plans, however. This method may feel too hands-off, particularly for librarians used to hand-selecting all materials. In addition, you may need to contend with duplicate materials. For example, if an author is on your standing order plan, and his book gets a starred review, and it also wins a major award, you could wind up with three or more copies of that book, when you only need or have shelf space for one. Weigh this possibility carefully—and ask about the vendor's ability to manage duplication—before making a commitment. Don't be afraid to make mistakes, though; mistakes are fixable, and they help us learn what works. There is no perfect pop culture collection; whatever collection development methodology you employ will present problems, no matter how careful and up-to-date you are. Don't dwell too much on this dilemma, and don't let it prevent you from moving forward with your collections.

Standing order plans are a put-in-time-to-save-time strategy, meaning that you really do have to put in the time to create—and regularly revisit—a standing order plan that works for you and your community. Make sure you have the flexibility to edit and add to the plan throughout the year, and be certain to review and revise it annually. This is a wonderful way to fill in gaps you've missed and to ensure that the plan continues to meet your community's shifting needs and interests. How can you gauge changing interests in your community? Watch circulation statistics, talk to your patrons, and consider conducting annual user interest surveys. (Find recommended online survey sites in Appendix A.) Plus, one of the best things about librarians (if you'll pardon a little profession-wide horn tooting) is not that we know it all, but that we know where to *find* it all. Using a standing order plan, especially one hand-tailored to your pop culture needs, is a great example of finding and using expert advice. You don't need to become a manga expert to offer a first-rate manga collection!

In summary, the advantage of hand-selecting is that you know exactly what you're getting and where your money is going. You enjoy the greatest measure of control over your collections, and you maintain the greatest freedom to tailor those collections to your community needs. The downside of hand-selecting is that it can be very time-consuming. Standing order plans, when created and maintained properly, still let you know a great deal of what you're getting—you are, after all, choosing the specific authors, illustrators, imprints, award winners, chart-toppers, filmmakers, and studios that are useful to your community. You save time because you only make adjustments annually (or more frequently, if necessary), and you don't need to worry about ordering monthly or quarterly. Standing order plans, though, if not monitored and revised regularly, can lead to a surfeit of underused, irrelevant material taking up valuable shelf space. Using both selection methods wisely can save time and money, and will help you build the most relevant collection of materials—pop culture and otherwise—for your community.

The C-Words

We can't talk about collections without bringing in two other C words: catalog and cataloging. Don't worry, this isn't where we complain about library catalogs and cataloging. This is where we ask, what are you doing to help people find the materials in your collection? You can have the greatest collection in the world, chock full of DVDs, magazines, books, and music—but if your patrons can't find what they're looking for, it doesn't matter. Your collections are just taking up shelf space if people go to the catalog, look something up, don't find it, and walk out. Yes, patrons could always ask us. But, if they can't find it on their own, why should we expect them to think, "I must have made a mistake, let me ask the librarian?" This is especially true if you're in a multi-branch library. Even the patron who says, "I didn't find *Firefly* in the catalog, but let me check the DVD shelves to be sure," won't find the DVDs if they happen to be housed in a branch 20 minutes away. And what if the DVD is checked out? The bottom line is, if it is not findable in the catalog, it may as well not exist. You may end up thinking no one wants a given DVD, when, in fact, your patrons do—they've just turned to Netflix or Amazon to get it instead.

Cataloging is your friend—and your patron's friend. Cataloging exists not to ensure a book is put back in its proper place but rather to ensure that your patron finds what your library owns, whether it's a DVD, a song, a magazine, or—well, you get the picture.

We also don't care whether your library uses the Dewey Decimal Classification (www.oclc.org/dewey) or Library of Congress Classification (www.loc.gov/aba), or if you have gone the bookstore route and follow the Book Industry Study Group subject headings (www.bisg.org/standards/bisac_subject/major_subjects.html). Whatever you do, do it well; do it consistently; take it seriously. Take advantage of what your classification system offers. In Dewey, use friendly catalog terms, alternate titles, and series fields. Make sure the terms you use are accurate; when possible, use the terms that customers themselves use.

One way around some of the strictness of Dewey is to create Social OPACs, or SOPACs (more on Social OPACs in Chapter 6). In a nutshell, libraries using a SOPAC open up their catalogs to let users tag items with customer-friendly labels. What better way to make it easier for patrons to find items in your collection than letting them label those items themselves?

It's a Process

Remember: As you make changes to your collection development strategy, selection, weeding, and collection maintenance are a process, not an outcome. You will make mistakes. You will have opportunities to correct those mistakes and make new ones. Handled properly, selection errors are an opportunity to better inform the public about the inner workings of the library. All you can do is continue to educate yourself so that you build the best collection for the community you serve.

Voices from the Field

In Chapter 2, we looked at answers to the survey question, "How do you track your patrons' pop culture interests?" and learned how you found out about what your patrons want in their library. Here, we look at how libraries have taken that information and used it for collection development.

"I don't really track this much beyond reading library blogs. We have an outreach/programming department in our library system that presumably pays more attention to that kind of thing. I know our Collection Development Office also keeps their eye on popular books and titles discussed on TV shows like *The Daily Show* and *Colbert Report*."
—Anonymous Public Librarian

"Our reference tally. We write down every question we get asked, basically. We take that tally every month and apply those requests to our collection development guidelines, and if the materials fit, we will purchase them, assuming they are requested often, and are not just a fluke. We have a lot of patron-input channels like speak-out forms and teen requests, etc."
—Anonymous Public Librarian

"I try to talk to the teens. Ask them what they're listening to or watching. I'm a big TV and music fan, so it's always interesting to get into those conversations with them. Helps them guess my age, which they're interested in knowing. I do use that information in collection development. I try to pass on music and movie selections to the purchasing librarians, and they are usually very open. I use a little in planning programs/events, but I'd like to do it more." —Anonymous Public Librarian

"I don't do any specific tracking, but I have a good feel on what they're always asking for and then pass the information on to the selection people.

Most of their pop-culture interest revolves around Disney shows like *Hannah Montana* or *That's So Raven*. I don't program to TV, mainly because it would involve me having to sit through an entire episode of *That's So Raven* and also because I doubt I could get something like that to fly." —Anonymous Public Librarian

"I am on the reference desk 35 hours per week. I talk to the patrons. I know a high percentage by name. They ask me for recommendations (for foreign films, e.g.) and tell me about their interests and I verbally encourage patrons to tell us what they would like to see the library do or buy or offer." —Anonymous Public Librarian *(Authors' Note: We like how you use your time at the reference desk to do more than wait for the next question, and that you actively ask patrons to find out what they want!)*

"Sorry to sound like a broken CD but I track their interests by talking to as many of my demographics as possible. I also read the magazines they read and try to look at websites where teens share opinions about things. I absolutely use this in my collection development. For instance, not to beat an example to death, but I know *High School Musical 2* will be huge in my community just from talking to them and watching the Disney Channel. Needless to say I am ordering it this week!" —Shari Fesko, Teen Librarian, Southfield Public Library, Southfield Michigan

"Our Collection Manager keeps tabs on the popular press (*Entertainment Weekly, People,* etc.). She isn't always the best at catching "the next big thing" (we were distressingly slow to purchase the Amy Winehouse CD, for example) but she tends to catch the tried-and-true blockbusters." —Anonymous Public Librarian

"I ask our teens what they're interested in and try to order as much as I can (particularly for graphic novels and manga). I pass on teen suggestions for music and movies to those selectors, and I talk to friends and family members who have young children to find out the kinds of music and movies they are listening to and watching in their homes." —Jay Wise, Youth Services Coordinator, Chillicothe and Ross County (OH) Public Library

"We don't have a formal process, as far as I know." —Anonymous Public Librarian

"Pop culture interest is usually targeted through personal upkeep with entertainment news and discussions with students and other librarians. Both are a consideration when looking at materials to purchase. However, with limited budgets, these materials are usually the last on the purchase list." —Anonymous School Media Specialist

"I watch what games the kids play on the computers to see what's popular now. Often we have requests for materials the library doesn't carry, and I make suggestions to the Collection Development Department to purchase these materials." —Anonymous Public Librarian

"I talk to our patrons and pay attention to what seems popular in the community at large (popular movies in my area according to Netflix is one way). I do use this information in plans and purchases." —Anonymous Public Librarian *(Authors' Note: Making use of Netflix to see what your community is interested in? Genius!)*

"I don't keep track, really. I listen to them as they talk in discussions and out at recess. I also look to see what the students order from Scholastic." —Anonymous School Media Specialist

"I gather information through our TAG and we pay close attention to new items that are requested via our consortium's online catalog. If the item is new (last 12 months) and we do not own it or have it on order we generally purchase it (about 90 percent of the time)." —Anonymous Public Librarian

"We try to pay attention to what people request and what circulates. We have a very liberal attitude towards collection development and our patrons have come to expect this. They are not shy about asking for items we do not have or that are checked out." —Anonymous Public Librarian *(Authors' Note: We like how you have created a library culture where patrons are empowered to say what they want from their library!)*

"I try getting teens talking about what they're interested in at the Teen Board Meetings. Although sometimes I just ask them if I know they're interested in a particular area. For example, we're updating our graphic novel collection because that seems to be the type of materials most often checked out. So I got lots of input from teens on what to buy and we just started an Anime Club." —Jennifer Rummell, YA Librarian, Otis Library, Norwich, CT

"I TALK to my patrons. I read professional journals and keep an eye on the other basic tools (TV, movies, magazines, etc.). Of course, this information is integral to collection development and program planning."
—Anonymous Public Librarian

"We have a suggestion box which is well-used, Ask-a-Librarian online, and a suggest-a-title function, also online. We ask right out what they are listening to/watching. We look at their clothes. I look through the teen magazines as they come in and sometimes find gaps we need to fill based on buzz in various publications. I visit bookstores and look at what kids are reading as they sprawl on the floor (lots of manga)." —Anonymous Public Librarian

"We just listen to what the kids are talking about. Who knew that Teenage Mutant Ninja Turtles would make a comeback?" —Anonymous Public Librarian

"In the beginning of the year, I ask my students to list what they would like to see in their IMC (Instructional Media Center) on index cards."
—Anonymous School Media Specialist

"We have a teen advisory board at our library. We also log all reference questions in detail and make purchases based on those statistics, as well as patron suggestions." —Greg Benoit, On-Call Reference Clerk, Webster (NY) Public Library, and Reference Specialist, Nazareth College Lorette Wilmot Library, Rochester, NY

"We simply listen to our patrons and what they want to read, watch, do, etc., and we try to accommodate them if it's in the budget." —Anonymous Public Library Director

"Usually by the circulation records and popularity of items from the book fair. If the pop culture fits what we want to promote, we'll use it. Otherwise, not." — Susan Lescure, Media Specialist, George J. Mitchell Elementary School, Little Egg Harbor, NJ *(Authors' Note: Knowing the mission for your library is so important, and then you can see how and when pop culture meets that need!)*

"I keep track of my patrons' pop culture interests by listening to their conversations (not in a creepy way, of course!) and keeping a sharp eye out for

what they are reading/watching on TV/listening to on their mp3 player. I do indeed use this information in the collection development process by purchasing materials that are directly related to interests of the students."
—Anonymous School Media Specialist

"I keep a binder of requests at my circulation desk." —Anonymous School Media Specialist

Endnotes

1. Jill Faherty and Katy White, email interview with Sophie Brookover, March 9, 2007.
2. Kathleen Sullivan, "Beyond Cookie Cutter Selection," *Library Journal* 129(11): 44, 2004.
3. Sullivan, 45.

Advocacy, Marketing, Public Relations, and Outreach

Great! You've decided to "go pop culture" at your library. You've surveyed the people in your community and examined current borrowing practices and demographics to determine pop culture wants and needs. You've begun to build your collection. The last thing you want to have happen is for no one to check out your new materials or attend your snazzy programs—or worse, to read an angry letter to the local paper, wondering why tax money is being spent on DVDs instead of on "good literature."

In this chapter, we'll discuss advocacy, marketing, public relations, and outreach. We'll speak with experts from the field and provide tips and tools you'll need to build and maintain support for your pop culture collections and services.

You will need support from every part of the library community, from your library board to library staff to current and future library patrons. Leaving out any one of these key players jeopardizes your success. Once the support is in place, you can concentrate on marketing strategies. "If you build it, they will come" may be true for ghost baseball players and Iowa ball fields, but it's not true for libraries.

Avoid disappointment, letdown, and accusations of wasted money and time by realizing that you have to *market* and *advocate for* your collection (including new materials), your programs, and your staff's expertise. Marketing is about the relationships you have with your stakeholders within and outside the library—it involves listening carefully to your community's needs, showing them that you've listened, and then getting ready to listen again. As the authors of *Blueprint for Your Library Marketing Plan* advise, "[y]our task is to zoom in on only the information relevant to the products or services you intend to promote. The categories of information needed are statistics and trends related to your community/campus, your product/service, your chosen target market … and competitive alternatives to your product/service."[1]

On the flip side of marketing is advocacy, which is skillful story-telling. Advocacy goes hand-in-hand with public relations, which is the ongoing dialogue your library has with the press and the public. Nancy Dowd, Marketing Director of the New Jersey State Library, emphasizes that the three elements need to be carefully coordinated, as they are highly interconnected: "An advocacy campaign will help you explain why libraries are essential to your community. A marketing campaign will try to get your community to use the library, and a public relations campaign makes sure that the headlines and public opinion are all positive."[2]

Sometimes you have one of those days where everything clicks. Every reference transaction goes smoothly; every reader's advisory session results in a delighted patron, racing home to read, watch, or listen to their new soon-to-be-favorite book, film, or CD; parents draw you aside after storytime to tell you what a wonderful time their children have at your library. Days like this are the ideal raw material for stories you can share—with your staff, your board, local and national legislators, and the press—about the positive impact your library has on your community. All libraries need to work on telling their stories, because, as Dowd points out, "libraries have an advantage in the trust category, but we sometimes miss out in the exciting, relevant, and important news categories, so it's always important to highlight the unexpected aspects of the library in our conversations"[3] with stakeholders. Sometimes you will need to focus on marketing or public relations more than on advocacy; sometimes the reverse will be true. Most often, though, they work best in concert. Dowd draws an analogy between keeping the three tools in balance and syncing an iPod or PDA with one's computer to keep both up-to-date.

Pop culture is overflowing with examples of people who successfully combine advocacy, marketing, and public relations—they're called celebrities. Few celebrities acknowledge or admit the degree to which they create their own "spin," and not all do it well. And, of course, while celebrities can spin, they cannot control the media. What they can do is decide how and when to release photographs (Suri Cruise's *Vanity Fair* cover) and give smartly timed interviews in magazines like *InStyle*, *Us Weekly*, and *People*. Look at Angelina Jolie: In the early 2000s, she was Hollywood's "wild child," giving interviews about her bisexuality and fondness for S&M (Lindsay Lohan looks tame by comparison!). Now, Jolie is the beloved mother of a growing family, giving interviews about play-dates and humanitarian issues. We're not saying that Jolie is not a loving mother or a dedicated worker for various causes, just that she recognizes how the public reacts to the story of her happy family. With each additional child she has, by adoption or birth, Jolie tells a story about how that child entered her life and how that child adds to and completes her family. This involves advocating and marketing an element of herself that the public reacts to favorably. As for public relations, open almost any popular magazine and you'll see a photo of Jolie as a proud mother walking her smiling child to school or with her children playing contentedly together on the beach. If Angelina Jolie can do it, so can the library.

Think Big, Start Small

As we discussed earlier, a good way to start a pop culture collection is with one discrete area or by building on an existing collection. In this chapter, we'll look at the example scenario of introducing a graphic novel collection for children. This collection will ultimately include graphic novels and comic books, and will support programs ranging from graphic novel book discussions and events with guest authors and illustrators to programs for adult caregivers about the links between reading graphic novels and general literacy. In some ways this is a new collection, but it also builds on the existing graphic novel collection in your teen and adult areas. It also answers a community need: For the past several years, your children's staff have been mentioning the many 8-to-10-year-olds who come into the library looking for comic books. However, the library's only graphic novels are currently in the young adult and adult sections, and are not age-appropriate for younger readers. Your children's staff have also read articles and highlighted research about the positive links between literacy and graphic novel reading. Just like that, you're armed with information you can make work for you: You have both the statistics that document demand and the literacy research to back you up—in case "give 'em what they want" doesn't cut it as a rationale all by itself.

When thinking about marketing, consider the analogy of saving for a child's college education. Parents don't wait until their child turns 18 to begin saving for State U or X Private College; neither should a library wait to market a program, service, or collection until after it's put in place. Market while you are building the collection, or better still, start marketing before you spend a single dime. It's never too early to gather and shore up support for your popular collection, because support for that collection means support for the library as a whole.

Advocate for your pop culture collections just as you would advocate for anything else concerning your library. The American Library Association (ALA) has developed a host of free advocacy resources. Use them! Find a number of these at the ALA Advocacy Resource Center (www.ala.org/pio/advocacy) including a free online advocacy course. Take out your copy of the *Library Advocate's Handbook* (available in PDF format at www.ala.org/ala/advocacybucket/libraryadvocateshandbook.pdf) and follow the steps it outlines for developing an action plan, speaking out, working with the media, and developing relationships with legislators. School librarians should familiarize themselves with the comprehensive *Advocacy Toolkit* available through the American Association of School Librarians (AASL) section of ALA's website (www.ala.org/ala/aasl/aaslproftools/toolkits/aasladvocacy.htm).

Karen Avenick, Friends and Trustees Facilitator for the New Jersey Library Association, looks at advocacy as an essential, if initially uncomfortable, habit you need to develop, just like flossing your teeth. You may not love flossing, but you know it's necessary for your overall dental health. Likewise, advocacy may be difficult for you, maybe because you're introverted or because you find the idea of selling the library a tad distasteful. But, once you make it a daily habit, you "find that each action becomes easier, less intimidating and less time consuming."[4] According to Avenick, advocacy is also "telling the library story, proving the library's value to the community and making the library the least-kept secret in town."[5] It's important to know your audience, to be brief but memorable, and to realize that opportunities are everywhere—on an escalator in the mall, in line at the grocery store, at the dry cleaner's, or on the subway.

The WebJunction article "Demonstrating Impact: Making Your Case" also gives valuable insight and suggestions. "A standard tool for developing funding arguments in the for-profit (and nonprofit) world is the business plan,"[6] the article explains, and it provides several examples and links to resources. More concerned about making your case indirectly? "Your direct message to your funders can be powerfully supplemented by complementary messages delivered to the wider community."[7] The Highlands Regional Library Cooperative (HRLC), Denville, NJ, provides a wealth of advocacy information, articles, workbooks and forms at the website Valuing Libraries— Demonstrating the Contributions Libraries Make to Their Communities (www.hrlc.org/funding/valuinglibs.htm). For example, the Workbook section of the Demonstrating Impact: Making Your Case section offers seven strategizing steps:

1. Assess your resources
2. Identify your target
3. Become a lobbyist
4. Identify what is important to funders
5. Identify what you do best
6. Determine how to articulate value
7. Find the connection

The Workbook then walks you through such helpful steps as identifying library funders and stakeholders.[8]

Local news outlets are quick to run stories about a library director and a board involved in a dispute or to print an angry letter to the editor questioning why a library is doing x or y or z instead of what it's "supposed to do." It may be impossible to prevent this type of conflict, but you can minimize it using techniques to market and advocate for your collection, programs, and services to constituents.

Getting Over Your Shyness: An Interview with Ilise Benun

We sat down to talk with Ilise Benun about shyness, introversion, and developing a two-sentence summary of what you do. The founder of Marketing Mentor, a Hoboken, New Jersey–based consulting firm, Ilise is the author of four books, including *Stop Pushing Me Around: A Workplace Guide for the Timid, Shy and Less Assertive* (Career Press, 2006), and co-author of *PR for Dummies* (second edition, Wiley, 2006). You can find Ilise online at marketingmentor.com.

You have quite a bit of expertise in helping the shy and the introverted stand up for themselves. What are your three top pieces of advice for shy and introverted library employees when it comes to marketing the fine work they and their institutions do in their communities?

1. Know when you are shy. Chances are, you aren't shy all the time. There are probably certain situations where you are in your element and you feel more comfortable speaking to strangers. For example, a patron at the library looks lost and you approach, offering to help. How is that different from introducing yourself to a stranger at a networking event? If you think about it, it's not that different. So try remembering how you feel when you're comfortable and bringing that feeling to a new experience to replace the "fear of unknown."

2. Separate yourself from your business role. Even if you're a shy person by nature, in business there are things you need to do in order to fulfill your role. Try to see yourself differently at work and practice doing tasks that may be uncomfortable. Then, when you get off work, go back to being shy, if you want.

3. Take small steps. Don't expect to automatically change your behavior overnight. Instead, try making small changes. Talk to one new person today, two new people tomorrow, etc. With practice, most of these new behaviors become easier.

Why is it so essential for everyone, not just the extroverted among us, to develop one-sentence, two-sentence, and 50-word self-promotional sound bites? Do you think it's especially important for those representing libraries to do so? If so, why?

The question "what do you do?" is a common starting point for lots of conversations, and your answer can either bring some-one into conversation with you or push them away. That's why it's important to think through your response. If you haven't thought it through, chances are you'll say something that uses jargon, which often alienates others, especially those who don't know your business or industry. If the goal of your "sound bite" is to engage the other person in a conversation, you should say something that both piques their curiosity and gives them openings to say, "tell me more about that."

How can library staff at every level, from maintenance to ref-erence to teen services to administration, develop these essential sound bites? Under what circumstances is each one most appropriate?

First of all, try not to use a label, like, "I'm a librarian." Instead, your sound bites should describe what you do and who you do it for, or who benefits from it. So, for example, if you work in teen services, you might say, "I help the teenagers in our com-munity find the resources they need to do their homework." It doesn't have to be fascinating, just clear and concise.

If you could offer just one piece of advice or encouragement to library employees trying to market their services, programs, and collections to their community, what would it be?

Always remember that it's not about you. People often get nervous and shy because they think the spotlight is on them and they're concerned about what others think of them. As a library employee, you are not marketing yourself. You are sim-ply the ambassador for the library; so any response, positive or negative, is on behalf of the library. Don't take anything per-sonally. If someone doesn't return a phone call, don't take it as a personal rejection. Think instead about what they may be experiencing, how busy they might be, what other issues and projects are on their plate. Then try to take it personally. It becomes almost ridiculous.

External Constituents

How much, or how little, detail you provide to your library board about your new collection depends both on your existing relationship and the types of reports you presently provide. You want to keep the members of the board informed enough so that they don't seem ignorant when they're buttonholed by an irate patron in the supermarket. You want to present the news in such a positive way that those hearing it join in your enthusiasm. Be honest, and don't go overboard—overselling and failing to deliver on your promises is as bad as failing to say anything. Deliver the news of your pop culture collection so that it will be seen in a positive light. At the same time, you don't want to overwhelm the board with data. It's a delicate balance to maintain, but once you've mastered it, you'll be able to do it again with patrons, legislators, and members of the press, whenever the need arises.

Let's return to the example of adding graphic novels to your children's collection. When presenting the initiative to your board, it's probably sufficient to report that "in response to overwhelming requests for age-appropriate materials for children under the age of 12, we're expanding our collection to include graphic novels materials and programming for children." If you are launching a similar collection at a school, and need to provide your rationale to a principal or parents, you may want to begin with information about how graphic novels support literacy, provide proof that children in your community want to read them, and display examples of the many types of graphic novels. If you are peppered with questions, you can use additional data and resources to answer them: You could refer to specific requests for materials by parents and children; offers by children to donate materials to the library collection; and perhaps also complaints from parents who wish the library had graphic novels their 8-year-olds could check out, because the teen materials aren't age-appropriate.

Be ready to distribute copies of articles supporting the literacy-related benefits of graphic novels (see Resources and Recommended Reading for several examples) and circulation statistics of your existing materials: "The library already has copies of *Garfield, Tintin,* and *Calvin and Hobbes,* and their circulation is x." Remember: Questions from your board members are a good test run for the questions likely to be posed by tax-conscious members of the public and the press. You'll be able to anticipate some of these in advance, so prepare succinct, honest, and positive answers ahead of time. This is a dress rehearsal both for your material and for your own ability to stay on message. This can be challenging, particularly in the face of inflammatory questions, so get all the practice you can. Once you succeed in convincing your board that pop culture materials are a valuable part of the library's collections, you will have at your fingertips a cadre of library advocates, ready at a moment's notice to wax eloquent about the value of the library's graphic novels, CDs, DVDs, and more!

Internal Marketing and Advocacy

Don't forget to market and advocate inside the library. Cultivate the support of staff, from pages to library assistants to librarians. Children's department staff may be well aware of the need for graphic novels, because they hear requests, read articles in *School Library Journal* and *Voice of Youth Advocates,* and attend seminars about boys and reading. Don't assume this means the rest of your library staff are aware of this need, or see value in the collection. If you cannot convince your staff, the people who should be on your side from the beginning, how can you convince anyone else to support your collection?

The Value of Cross-Training

In fitness, cross-training is used to improve cardiovascular fitness while building muscle mass and improving flexibility. In libraries, cross-training can be used to broaden and deepen marketing and advocacy skills staff-wide. It can also help you to address potential problems within the ranks before they arise. One of the biggest benefits of cross-training is a reduction of the silo effect, where each department considers itself a small fiefdom within the library. The silo effect discourages staff from being invested in the library as a whole, and encourages an "us vs. them" mentality among the library's staff.

We suggest scheduling at least one cross-training workshop (preferably two or three, but we're realistic) to introduce all members of staff to the juvenile graphic novel collection. The structure and tone of the workshop should be fun and energizing, as well as informative. Arm your staff with the information they will need when speaking with customers, and set a positive tone. Let them know everything from why you're building this collection ("Our patrons asked for it! We are so happy to be able to meet this community need.") to how it will be catalogued and where it will be shelved. Pass around examples of items that will be found in the collection; give a few booktalks about some new comic books and graphic novels. Most importantly, encourage staff to ask questions, and answer them candidly, and with good humor. Consider this back-and-forth a test run, as any concerns voiced by staff will also be voiced by the public.

Don't be discouraged by negative comments and questions by staff. It's not personal, and their point of view can be valuable. You are likely to field questions from the public challenging the literary value of comic books—after all, shouldn't children be reading the classics? When staff raise these issues first, you get great practice in handling delicate questions. Gently remind skeptics that graphic novels appeal to readers for a variety of reasons. Your library has a mandate to serve *all* readers, not just those who prefer the classics. Studies have shown that graphic novels appeal to fluent readers, avid readers, reluctant readers, and readers of English as a Second Language alike. Children are entitled to as varied a reading diet as grown-ups. They have as much right to enjoy *Superman*, *Baby Mouse*, and *Naruto* as your older readers have to read more sophisticated graphic novel fare such as *Maus* and *Blankets*. Your critics may not be aware that graphic novels are a format, not a genre, and that there's as much variety to be found among graphic novels as among any other type of book—so tell them! It might be worth putting in a word about the expectation factor, as well: Children who come to your library expect an experience similar to what they find at major booksellers like Borders and Barnes & Noble. If they see graphic novels on the retailers' shelves, they will expect to see them on your shelves, too.

When designing your workshops, we suggest considering the following questions, drawn from Sharon Baker and Karen Wallace's essential work on building and marketing popular collections, *The Responsive Public Library*:

- How is the business term *marketing* related to the library term *service*?

- What are the library's major products and services? Which are successful? Which bear close scrutiny, further promotion, or elimination?

- What can each department do to decrease inhibitors and increase incentives to library use?

- Whom does the library currently serve well? Whose requirements are being slighted?

- On whom will the library concentrate its efforts?

- How will the library integrate information on targeted groups and individuals with its mission, service responses, goals, and objectives?

- How can the library translate this work into an action-oriented marketing plan?[9]

Nancy Dowd encourages all library staff to be able to respond to tough comments such as the following:

- Who needs libraries when we have the Internet?

- I never use a library; I prefer to buy my books.

- Libraries? There's nothing to do there.[10]

You may be surprised to find you have an expert on staff that you didn't know about, a member of another department who loves graphic novels, for instance. Now you have a recruitable volunteer who can be a cheerleader for the collection and provide expertise: by making collection recommendations, by brainstorming connections to arrange author or illustrator visits, and by spreading the word among his or her social circle, people who may be motivated to visit the library once they know about the new collection.

Continuous Training

Think beyond the initial training sessions. You may find that you and your new cadre of marketer–advocates benefit tremendously from monthly or bimonthly follow-up meetings. The purpose of these meetings can vary—some will provide an opportunity to check in with colleagues on how you've all been using your advocacy moment stories, while others will be set up to preview new materials coming into the library. Holding these meetings on a regular, standing basis makes it easier for staff to plan to attend, and also obviates the need for every staff member to attend every meeting. An occasional missed meeting is not a big deal, and the absent staffer should be keen to get back in the swing of things the next time.

As an alternative to in-person meetings, think about holding electronic meetings—either via email or through a staff blog, which members can read and contribute to on their own schedule. Blogs can host photographs and digital movies as well as text, and could be a valuable tool for connecting busy staff members across a large system. You can keep the blog private and password-protected, or you can embrace openness and transparency and make it public, so your patrons can see what's going on behind the scenes at your library. You may find that your library's users are very interested in how the library markets itself to them!

Not Like a Needle in a Haystack: Connecting People and Materials

How will patrons find this new collection? If you equate marketing with press releases, you overlook the daily advertising that your staff, displays and good signage, programming, and catalog can provide.

Remember, marketing is about relationships and connections, so market the collection by helping your patrons connect with the materials they want. We live in a self-serve society, so people are often reluctant to ask for help. How many times have you heard your customers preface a question with "I hate to bother you, but ... " Help them get over their shyness and give them a reason to come to you by creating "Ask Me!" buttons for your staff to wear. For those highly independent customers, visual merchandising is a godsend. Attractive displays for a new collection are a must. Of course, it can be hard to keep up a display of appealing new items, because popular materials don't stay on the shelf! Don't fret: This is a mark of success. When you run out of graphic novels to display, replace them with related titles, such as books about cartooning and anime, books on the history of comics, films based on comics and graphic novels, and graphic novel-related brochures and posters. Some libraries take photos of their displays and upload them to Flickr (www.flickr.com), annotating them with titles and authors. This way, anyone visiting the site can "see" the complete collection—even when it's all checked out! (Flickr is discussed further in Chapter 6, Information Technology Is Everyone's Job.)

If you prefer to go old school, remember that everyone loves bookmarks. These could contain a short booklist, the subject headings you're using in the catalog, and web addresses for more comprehensive, annotated booklists online.

Programming that ties into your collection is a very valuable marketing tool, so plan a few programs to introduce the new collection: a book discussion, a visiting illustrator, and/or a workshop for parents or teachers about helping kids select appropriate titles and how graphic novels can encourage successful independent reading. Collaborate with teachers and brainstorm ways to use graphic novels in classrooms. Since a school's mission is to support learning, be sure to keep statistics on participation and grades.

Why not offer a raffle to introduce patrons to the new collection? In addition to bringing people into the library, a raffle can be a useful collection development tool. On each ticket, include a question related to the new collection, such as "What is your favorite graphic novel, comic book, or manga series?" Ask participants to place their responses in a festively decorated box designed to look like a graphic novel, or a jar decked out with the names of popular superheroes, and hold a weekly drawing. Invite winners to the library to have their photograph taken with their favorite graphic novels, then showcase the photos in your library's own series of READ posters created with software from the ALA Graphics Store.

Toot your own horn. Send out press releases to the local media outlets and invite all of your press contacts to your in-house training workshop. You may find some local reporters to be comic book enthusiasts—and a valuable resource! Include descriptions of upcoming programs in your press releases, and offer to have a library representative present information about the new collection to any interested community group—tell them to just call the library! If you've included a "favorites" question on the raffle ticket, you now have a reason for a second press release: to announce the winner and report that your patrons voted *Spiderman* the favorite comic book for Your Public Library. Compile and tabulate all the responses, and you have valuable information on titles to add to your collection in the future.

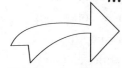

MARKETING TIPS THAT POP: A TOP TEN LIST BY JILL S. STOVER

1. **Open Up (*Your patrons want in!*)** – Marketing is no longer about pushing stuff on unsuspecting customers. Today's savvy marketers know that to be successful, they need to invite customers behind the scenes to participate in all phases of the marketing process, from the earliest brainstorming sessions to the final stages of promotion. How can you include your patrons to make your marketing better?

2. **Staff Need Marketing, Too** – Staff bring your marketing plans to life. Earn their support and enthusiasm by including them in your planning and considering them a vital target market. Make sure they know what you want to accomplish and what your key messages are. If staff need special training or tools to get your plan off the ground, make them available. Remember: Happy staff make patrons happy.

3. **Fear the Status Quo** – Change happens. If you don't see it happening in your library, it's time to shake things up. Changes in lifestyles, technologies, population distributions,

politics, and just about everything else impact libraries. To adapt, librarians need to welcome risk and recognize uncertainty in their marketing plans. Change can be scary, but not nearly as scary as letting the status quo make you irrelevant.

4. **Shh!** – No, I'm not talking about shushing your patrons. Instead, make a point to listen to them to find out exactly what they need and expect. Invite patrons to submit comments and suggestions, and make it easy for them to do so. If you get negative feedback, seize the opportunity to fix the problem so that it doesn't irritate anyone else. Get out of the library from time to time, and keep your eyes and ears open for opportunities to serve patrons better. A lot of useful market research can be accomplished just by listening.

5. **Consider the Source** – Librarians often caution patrons to consider the source of the information they find. When it comes to marketing messages, patrons are skilled at this, and they can easily sort out the insincere from the genuine. Most of the time, they'll trust their friend's or family's opinions over a marketer's. As a result, try letting your patrons do the talking for you. Collect and showcase testimonials, or let patrons write a column in your newsletter or posts for your blog.

6. **Patrons' Success is Your Success** – Patrons expect to do a lot more with information than just read it. They want to create and manipulate it in the form of videos, blogs, podcasts, musical performances, presentations, works of art, and other creative projects. Librarians can endear themselves to patrons by helping them succeed in these pursuits and providing the needed expertise and tools. In doing so, librarians become indispensable partners and fill a niche that few others can.

7. **What's So Great About You?** – Every library is great in some unique way that sets it apart. Maybe you have a close relationship with your community, or superior technology resources, or a rare special collection. Whatever "it" is, embrace what makes you different and tell patrons about it every chance you get. Your special qualities are your competitive advantage and the

reason patrons should use your services instead of someone else's. If you've got it, flaunt it!

8. **"One-size-fits-all" Is for T-shirts** – Despite our best intentions, library services that try to be all things to all patrons usually end up appealing to no one. To create services that are meaningful, target specific market segments and develop your marketing plan based on their needs and preferences. You may be reaching out to fewer people by doing so, but your efforts will yield better results.

9. **Add Value, Subtract Obstacles** – Patrons have an abundance of choices for finding information. How can you add value to this activity so that patrons seek your services? You could help patrons manage information through RSS feeds or send them customized reading recommendations. In removing barriers so that patrons can more easily receive, organize, evaluate, and use information, you add value to your services and earn your patrons' loyalty.

10. **Marketing Mix and Repeat** – Marketing is a never-ending process. Marketing plans, however, have a shelf life. Once your marketing plan comes to an end, evaluate the results based on the goals you established and make any needed changes for the next plan. Incorporate marketing into your daily routine so that it becomes a normal part of your operations. Don't expect that every idea will be a success, but be persistent in your marketing efforts and you'll develop better relationships with patrons and a more innovative workplace. Good luck!

Jill S. Stover is Undergraduate Services Librarian, Virginia Commonwealth University, and author of the blog "Library Marketing—Thinking Outside the Book" (librarymarketing. blogspot.com).

Avoiding Flubs: Practice, Practice, Practice

With advocacy, marketing, and public relations, you control the messages that you are consciously sending to your constituents about your library, its collections, and its programs. You ensure that the first message that your board, your customers, and the public hear is positive. But what about the messages you don't know you're sending—messages that may be negative, or may even be defeating your objectives?

Think about the person who reads your press release, gets excited, and goes to your online catalog to find … nothing. How easy is it for someone to find these materials if they search your OPAC the same way they would search Google? What subjects, keywords, tags, and descriptions do you include to make it easy for your typical patron to find what they want—and what you have? If you lose them now, they won't be back. (For more information on creating a user-friendly catalog, see Chapter 6.)

Many people have narrow views of what a library is for. Sometimes people who don't use their library have the narrowest view but speak the loudest, sending letters to the editor along the lines of: "A library is supposed to promote good literature, so why are you wasting my tax money on that garbage?" Take a deep breath. Don't bite back, no matter how tempting it is! A potential customer has stated what they believe your mission statement to be. Are they right? Do you have a mission statement for your library? If so, does it encompass the materials and programs you have added?

Google "library mission statement" to find a wide variety of results. Hennepin County (MN) Library's mission statement, for example, is "Hennepin County Library promotes full and equal access to information and ideas, the love of reading, the joy of learning, and engagement with the arts, sciences and humanities."[11] The mission statement of the Madison-Jefferson County Public Library, Madison, IN, says it "provides the opportunity: to obtain and use information in a variety of formats; to pursue lifelong learning; to explore recreational interests; and to better understand personal and regional heritage."[12] Ann Arbor (MI) District Library's mission statement reads: "The existence of the Ann Arbor District Library assures public ownership of print collections, digital resources, and gathering spaces for the citizens of the library district. We are committed to sustaining the value of public library services for the greater Ann Arbor community through the use of traditional and innovative technologies."[13] By emphasizing "joy of learning," "recreational interests," and "traditional and innovative technologies," these mission statements reflect libraries that support the inclusion of pop culture materials and programs, such as graphic novels, television shows on DVD, and gaming.

If you haven't examined your mission statement in a while, and your new initiative does not fit under your existing statement, now is the time to revise! If your statement isn't inclusive of your new pop culture collection, chances are that other library initiatives aren't covered by it, either. So update your mission statement if you need to, and then tie it in when responding to naysayers; make it clear that this collection is needed to fulfill your mission.

Your pop culture collection *does* fit within a library's mission. We know it's not a matter of "good literature" vs. comic books; we know a well-rounded library has both. So, why does our hypothetical letter writer present it as an either/or matter? Have you unintentionally sent that message by completing a big weed right before you announced your new collection? You don't want to create the perception that "they discarded the *Nancy Drew* books to add the *Nancy Drew* graphic novels." Timing is your friend, as is transparency: What are your weeding guidelines? Are you following them? Are they available online for the public to read and comment on? Do you provide space for a public conversation on the importance of weeding in keeping a collection up-to-date, relevant, and attractive to the community you serve?

Maybe it's not a matter of weeding, but of placement. In selecting a great place to put your new comic books, did you move your large-print books to an impossible-to-find area? When selecting an area for your new materials, think not only about where they will go, but where existing materials need to be shifted. Work with staff in deciding the placement that works for your entire library and your entire collection. Let staff know why things have been rearranged so that they can answer customers; then let your customers know where things are! Post clear signs directing people to where things are now, as well as signs to help people find where things will be in the near future. The Youth Services Department at Sophie's branch library has been reorganizing its layout to cluster materials by each age group it serves—babies and young children, grade schoolers, and teens—which will help patrons find the materials they want more easily. They have been producing new signage on a biweekly basis to keep patrons and colleagues in the loop.

Wegmans, a supermarket famous for its selection and excellent customer service, recently opened a store near where Sophie lives. The new store is enormous, easily twice the size of the supermarket where she usually shopped, so Sophie was gritting her teeth in anticipation of a steep learning curve as she adjusted to the Wegmans layout. Imagine her delight when, on every visit during the store's opening month, she was handed a map showing the items in each aisle. Based in part on this thoughtful gesture, Sophie hasn't shopped at the other supermarket in months! Why not follow the Wegmans example and create a few maps of your new library layout, photocopy them on brightly colored paper, encourage your staff to hand them out to all patrons coming through your doors, and make them available at your main service points? People will see that their favorite materials aren't missing, and they'll be made aware of other items in your collection they might not have realized even existed.

How do you usually market your collection and programs? Press releases, fliers, and posters? A public service announcement on the radio? Think beyond your regular route of newspapers and schools. Be more specific; instead of just sending fliers to the school media center, find out about school clubs or classes that may be interested in your collection. Visit the high school anime club, or make a contact with the middle school art teacher. What other clubs and organizations could you contact? If you're starting a graphic novel collection, why not stop by the local comic store? Take your show on the road—don't just send out a press release and fliers, make personal visits! Yes, this takes time, but you don't have to do this alone. Remember those staff-wide workshops? Seek out volunteers among your cross-trained staff members to assist with outreach. This is good for morale, as you give people the opportunity to incorporate their own pop culture interests into their work, and you don't saddle any one person with the entire burden of marketing the collection. During your initial promotion, you may need to either budget for extra staff hours to cover that out-of-library outreach or make do with fewer people on the public service desks.

Maintaining Your Pop Collections

It can be more difficult to maintain your collection than to create the initial media blitz announcing it to the community. Customer input is critical, so start by tracking the obvious: circulation statistics and program attendance. To maintain accurate circulation statistics, you may need to ask your colleagues in the IT department if they can track the popularity of a particular subject heading or Dewey number in your ILS. Try to elicit comments and feedback from customers at programs, at the information desk, and even online. Ask specific questions so that you can get specific answers. In each new item, tuck a small piece of paper that says "rate me" to be filled out by the patron: "loved it, liked it, hated it." When the item is returned, remove the completed response form and put in a new one. Track the responses to get insights into what people like, then use that input to create displays. (Learn more about soliciting and using customer feedback in Chapter 2.) Show off your staff members' areas of expertise and empower them to exercise their creativity by encouraging them to create displays of their favorite reads, CDs, and

DVDs. The displays can be themed, or not, depending on what strikes your staff's mood.

Once you have developed a feel for your community's tastes and needs (you may be surprised at the sorts of things people ask for!), you can consider using a standing order plan tailored to those tastes. Learn more about creating and using standing order plans in Chapter 3.

Pop Reach (Pop Culture Outreach)

In the pop culture equation, collections plus programs does not necessarily equal success. You need to engage people in your community in a conversation about what you are doing. Outreach is about venturing out into the community and bringing your library to the places where patrons live, study, work, and play. At its simplest, outreach involves telling people why they should come to your library. Good outreach increases door counts, circulation statistics, and program attendance, all numbers that you can proudly present to your director as measures of success for your pop culture initiatives.

Pop culture can help inject a "wow" factor into your library's outreach efforts, helping you go beyond glorified in-person advertising. Successful pop culture outreach can serve many purposes, from promoting the new pop culture initiative to introducing the library to new people to gathering support by demonstrating new dimensions to the library. Using bookmobiles and enticing, interactive websites, you can bring the library to wherever people are. By building partnerships, you create community connections; people and organizations become invested in the library and its success. Those kinds of outputs may not be as easy to prove, and it may take longer to show their results, but it's well worth the effort to recruit new community partners who will champion the library.

In addition, outreach can and should play a major part in the development of your pop culture initiative and the planning of related programs. Your community involvement helps you both create relevant programs, collections, and services and build relationships with new constituencies. Visiting the local high school anime club to ask fans for titles of "must own" anime DVDs? Outreach. Working with that club to plan quarterly manga/anime events in the library? Also outreach. Maybe you make an annual visit to the local historical society to speak about the library's genealogical resources. Imagine how much more effective those visits could be if the same librarian made them bimonthly, building ongoing awareness of library resources and crafting responses to the society's wants, needs, and plans.

Taking the Pop Approach

When you built your pop culture collection, you didn't start from scratch. You used existing collection development staff, policies, and resources to create a collection that fits your community's interests. Now use the same strategy for outreach. Pull out your library's current policies, guidelines, and other existing outreach tools. Consult resources such as the tipsheets provided by ALA's Office for Literacy and Outreach Services (www.ala.org/ala/olos/out reachresource/outreachtipsheets/outreachtipsheets.htm). Look at your pop culture initiative and start brainstorming groups, people, events, and places to visit. Start with the ideas you had when you launched the initiative, but think bigger! Think about where your patrons gather besides the library. You're establishing a comic book collection, but your town is too small to have its own annual comic convention. (We can't all live in San Diego!) Ask yourself, where do your comics-loving patrons go? Is there a county, state, or other nearby convention that they look forward to? Add that gathering to your "to-visit" list. Remember: You don't have to do this alone. Sit down with staff to brainstorm outreach possibilities and preferred outcomes. Do you want to make connections with parents, so that they know that reading comic books can actually improve literacy scores? Do you want to generate excitement about the new collection among kids and teens? Do you want to develop a mechanism for soliciting collection input and book reviews from patrons? Do you want to establish a relationship with a local comics shop? Write it all down, and don't censor yourself. We understand there are only so many hours in the day, someone has to stay in the branch, and it takes time to plan all those programs. Still, we encourage you to shut off your inner naysayer. For now, just brainstorm: The sky is the limit. Put down as many ideas as you can think of. You can prioritize later.

Continuing with our comics collection example, your list of outreach possibilities could include:

- Public and private schools, including art teachers, English teachers, reading specialists, related school clubs, activities, and publications
- Parent-teacher organizations
- Parenting groups
- Homeschoolers
- Local art schools
- Art galleries
- Comic book shops
- Bookstores
- Comics and manga conventions and associations (local, county, or state)
- Authors, artists, and illustrators

We admit, that's a pretty long list. Now think about *why* you want to talk to each group, using this process to help you determine your top outreach priorities. If you're hosting a contest to help promote the collection, talking to art teachers may be your first priority—not only could you ask the art teachers to promote the contest to their students, but you could invite them to judge the contest, too. If your main concern is letting parents and concerned adults know the value of comic books (beyond the obvious—readers love them!), then target parent-affiliated groups first. When brainstorming with staff, ask them about any connections they might have. If you have a comic book lover on staff who visits the local comic shop weekly to pick up new titles, use that connection to build your relationship with local experts (and maybe negotiate a discount on bulk purchases!).

One Word, Multiple Possibilities

Outreach affords you so many possibilities for building and deepening the library's connections to your community. Given all these different possibilities and purposes, don't forget that one size does not fit all. Vary your standard presentation and handouts based on your audience. Are you bringing copies of articles about the comics-literacy connection to groups of teachers and parents? Or copies of comic books?

Because your pop reach will vary based on the pop culture area you are highlighting, start with some global ideas:

- Prepare an outreach toolkit, including basic handouts (books, library cards, business cards, bookmarks, personalized pencils)
- Recruit, train, and recognize volunteers
- Personalize fliers for outreach events with the names, dates, and locations of the events
- Compile a list of media contacts and create a basic template for press releases
- Create a call sheet for each organization you reach out to, including names and contact information for the lead people, their areas of interest, and their library needs

Mine other works for outreach ideas, as well. Because outreach is such a prevalent libraryland activity, you can find a number of books that either offer suggestions specifically related to pop culture or provide ideas that can be tweaked for use in the field. For example, Julie Bartel's *From A To Zine: Building a Winning Zine Collection in Your Library* includes outreach ideas for zine collections, while *5 Star Programming and Services for Your 55+ Library Customers* by Barbara T. Mates includes outreach ideas specific to over-55 patrons, which will be useful if your pop culture initiative targets Baby Boomers. We provide a list of these and other outreach-rich resources in the Resources and Recommended Reading section at the end of the book.

Since outreach is about going to where your patrons are, don't forget the patron at home. We don't mean instituting door-to-door outreach projects! Just don't forget the person sitting in front of his or her computer. Knowing that your website reaches a sizeable portion of your audience, why not view it as an outreach opportunity? At the simplest level, it can promote your pop culture collections and programs; at another level, it can be part of the collection—or even be its own program. (For more ideas on the various technologies you can incorporate, see Chapter 6.) For example, if part of your promotion for your new comic book collection involves running a "create your own comic book" program, include images from that program on your site, perhaps through Flickr. Better yet, make your participants' original comic book creations available online! *Weaving a Library Web: A Guide to Developing Children's Websites,* by Helene Blowers and Robin Bryan, includes other recommendations for using the library's site to connect with children, including collaborative ideas that librarians and children can work on together.

Of course, not everyone is Internet savvy, and not everyone has a computer. If your patrons get their information about the library via the radio or local paper, why not use those venues? Ask if your local paper will carry a regular "From the Library" column that talks about what is happening at the library. This can be written by any-one—your director, children's librarian, reference staff. In fact, we suggest that you rotate authorship on a regular basis, so that your authors don't burn out, and so that community members meet and become familiar with a variety of library voices. If radio, particu-larly locally produced radio, plays a large role in your community's information-seeking habits, invite your teens to create a podcast about new programming and get your local radio station to broad-cast it. Also make it available online at the library's website and the radio station's as well.

Ultimately, outreach isn't about telling people what the library can do for them. It's about opening and sustaining a dialogue, ask-ing people what they need and then figuring out how the library can meet those needs. Successful outreach, tailored to community needs, helps libraries work with community members to reach mutually satisfying goals.

A library is only as successful as its relationship with its patrons. Introducing something perceived as "new" can be threatening. But if you think ahead and treat your pop culture collection like other library initiatives, practicing advocacy, marketing, public relations, and inventive outreach, you will see letters to the editor—thanking and supporting the library!

Voices from the Field

The following quotes are selected responses to the survey question "How do you market your collections and services to your com-munity? Have you had to defend or advocate for the inclusion of pop culture programs or materials to library staff, board members, customers, or others? What specific steps, if any, have you taken in so doing?"

"We're working on new ways to market our stuff, using more 2.0 applications (our first YouTube video is coming soon). Luckily, our board is very supportive of pretty much everything we want to try, and have never asked for a justification. Neither have our patrons or community at large. The more we do, the happier people are." —Anonymous Public Library Director

"I review Information Literacy Standards and the 40 Developmental Assets to see if these programs fit into these standards. That is the best way to convince staff, boards, and others to support the program." —Gaye Kulvete, YA Librarian, Groton (MA) Public Library

"I have been fortunate not to have had to defend or advocate for the inclusion of pop culture programs or materials, as part of our library's mission statement is to provide materials for the entertainment of the individuals we serve. Within our library system is a core group of librarians interested in popular culture, and we are advocates to each other and our peers in a non-direct way. Marketing the collection is usually done through displays, or can also be done through booklists, newsletter articles, or word of mouth from librarian to patron." —Heidi Andres, Teen Librarian, Cuyahoga County Public Library, Middleburg Heights, OH

"Our marketing is done primarily by our communications department, and yes, we have had to defend our choices. However, before we launch any new activity, material, or service, I am required to complete a thorough background search to be able to defend and support our choices." —Judy T. Nelson, Youth Services Coordinator, Pierce County Library System, Tacoma, WA

"A couple years ago, we started a special comics section for kids in the Children's Room. We recently started a Series Binder Wiki (seriesbinder.lishost.org) to start giving patrons and staff easier access to information about series books, especially pop culture tie-in stuff, which can be very difficult to figure out. We are big on displays and bulletin boards that tie in to movies, television shows, and the like. We have a blog for the public (wplkids.wordpress.com) that we're also trying to use as a way to get information out there for folks. I am very seldom asked to defend my pop-culture-loving ways, although I did have something of a fight on my hands when we started stocking PS2 games. At the time, I just gathered all the info I could to show the cognitive benefits of gaming, and that PS2 was, at the time, the leader in games—most games available, most systems sold. It worked, and our PS2 collection is one of the highest-circulating collections in the library." —Adrienne Furness, Children's & Family Services Librarian, Webster (NY) Public Library

"We market in several ways. I'm personally in charge of print marketing: everything from standard event guides and brochures, flat screen ads in the branches, newspaper advertising, ads in local magazines, website advertising, and even ads that display at the movies prior to the previews. We've had to do some convincing regarding things like instant messaging, message boards and blogs, and other forms of social marketing. The hardest thing, I think, is convincing the administration to trust that the staff can effectively handle those kinds of marketing platforms without damaging the library's reputation." —Anonymous Public Library Associate

"We have seasonal program guides that people can pick up at the library, and we have listings on our website, and fliers that we distribute to bookstores and the community center. Our library is very open to all kinds of programming, and our board and friends of the library group are incredibly supportive." —Anonymous Public Librarian

"We attend community events (churches, community groups, City Hall). We also have bulletins and fliers in all of these places. I am in the process of advocating for gaming in the library. I have spoken to my Director and shown her many articles from magazines and other media." —Anonymous Public Librarian

"My web page is my primary means of communication. I have not had to justify any programming or purchases because I make sure that everything I purchase, promote, and/or do is supported by the standard course of study for elementary school students. Luckily, development of a lifelong love for reading is part of that course of study. That covers a lot of ground." —Mary Alice Hudson, Media Specialist, Cape Fear Elementary School, Rocky Point, NC

"Our marketing consists of a marquee outside the library, a bimonthly newsletter mailed to each home in the community, and fliers at the local schools. I also maintain a website and blog where I post information, and our local school district allows me to have PDF versions of fliers massemailed to parents. The staff and board have been quite receptive to pop culture programs." —Maryellen Liddy, Teen/Reference Librarian, Kinnelon (NJ) Public Library

"I market to the teachers, who pass it along; I integrate it into lessons about information literacy skills; I provide a welcoming environment in which the kids are comfortable coming to the library media center and always are looking for what's new. I also offer open access for parents once a week for them to select items to introduce to their kids." —Stephanie Rosalia, School Library Media Specialist, Eileen E. Zaglin School PS22, Brooklyn, NY

"We market with PSAs in newspaper and on radio, fliers posted in schools and around the community, notices in school papers. A few customers have questioned why we show movies, etc. I generally point out that many movies are based on books, talk about the need for safe activities for teens in our community, explain that attracting kids to libraries in today's multi-media world takes more than books. We have had a fair number of complaints about kids "just playing games on computers"; other than viewing pornography, we allow patrons full access to the Internet. It's hard to convince some adults that the kids using the computers to play games is just as valid as adults using the computers to check their email." —Mary Neuman, Youth Services Librarian, Asotin County Library, Clarkston, WA

"All of our branches have been through merchandising training and we put together a lot of web based promotion and lists to circulate at the branches. We have a procedure for dealing with complaint items, many of them pop culture (graphic novels, anime, celebrity bios, YA novels, etc.). They go to a committee for review, the committee makes a recommendation to the director, and letters are sent to the complainants. Many of the complainants are staff members." —Linda Stevens, Media Specialist, Harris County Public Library, Houston, TX

"Our community is pretty progressive. As far as I am aware, there was almost no resistance when we began circulating Play Station 2 games." —Greg Benoit, On-Call Reference Clerk, Webster (NY) Public Library

"We wrote an article for the school newspaper and set up a display near the puzzle/board game area where students relax at the front of the library, with simple signage and front-facing DVDs." —Emily Barney, Assistant to Library Director, Chicago-Kent College of Law

"We market our services through monthly calendars, newsletters, community bulletin boards, email, Google Groups, and press releases. We have an extremely supportive Board and Director, so having to defend programming ideas is never an issue." —Anonymous Public Librarian

"Originally, I marketed in-house with posters and a monthly newsletter, which I also sent to the schools. We also post our programs on our web page, but it is a static web page, and we have to send all of our information to the city for it to be posted. I wanted something a little more real time that I could update myself, and felt a blog would be the next step. I had to fight very hard for a very long time at every level to get a teen blog started at our library. It got stuck at just about every level, as the decision-makers just really did not understand what it was about or the logistics of it. I had to work very hard for six months, but we finally received permission for the blog. Materials and programs are not as difficult to defend at our library." —Anonymous Public Librarian

"We market through our newsletter (which gets distributed via bulk mail to the village), our website, press releases. No one has objected to me personally about the inclusion of pop culture programs or materials in my collections. If anything, people complain if you don't get Barbie Fairytopia fast enough. We also have in-house marketing such as bibliographies and posters." —Anonymous Public Librarian

"I do many things to advertise what we have: 1) I fill my 3-D bulletin board cases with new arrivals that interest the students; 2) I bring new interesting books to faculty meetings monthly. I get on the agenda and booktalk the ones I think will interest the teachers for their lessons; 3) I give booktalks on the new books I have read to the classes monthly as they come down to borrow books with their reading teachers." —Laurie Belanger, Library Media Specialist, Paul Harrison Memorial Library, Lakeville, MA

"We have a monthly newsletter, web page, and monthly lists of programs. Our local newspaper runs a weekly column of library events. A large screen TV in the lobby runs a constant program of what's happening on a daily basis. We have not had to advocate for or against any programs, either to our board or the public, in my recollection." —Anonymous Public Librarian

"Word of mouth and other teens telling their friends has been the best way for me to let teens and children know about our programs and our resources. Our PR department creates fantastic fliers, and we are well established in our city/county, so parents tell other parents about the library. We have begun a great partnership with our local Department of Job and Family Services for a structured play and parenting program that has been a great success as well." —Jay Wise, Youth Services Coordinator, Chillicothe and Ross County (OH) Public Library

"The school monthly newsletter has been the way that all programs are marketed. We are building a new library media center this year, and we plan to have a library media center web page. A monthly report to Head of School, staff, and board of directors explaining activities, new materials, etc., is also provided. This may become electronic in the new library media center. I attempted to launch a library media center newsletter a couple of years ago; however, the school newsletter was seen as competition so the LMC information became part of the school newsletter. We may launch a newsletter for the new library media center this year." —Anonymous School Librarian

"Our marketing is rather poor. I made signs to hang in the library to advertise our graphic novels and their location. I have not had to defend the inclusion of pop culture programs since most of what we've held has tied into books or education in some way." —Anonymous Public Librarian

"The most successful marketing tool so far has been direct contact with students, teachers, and parents at the library and at the schools. Thankfully, my director and the board are fairly open to new and exciting program ideas and I've yet to defend a program because it encountered resistance." —Anonymous School Librarian

"We recently unveiled an 'Ask a Librarian' campaign that featured/played with stereotypical images of librarians, visual puns, etc. Response has been good from undergraduates and faculty. The only people who seem to dislike this more 'casual,' self-deprecating approach are other librarians." —Anonymous Academic Librarian

"We have a well-maintained website, a monthly newsletter, and periodic features in the local weekly newspaper. We don't have what I would call 'pop culture programs'; in terms of collection development, our graphic novel and DVD sections have grown substantially in the last 3–5 years. We've added graphic novels for grown-ups and children (previously the collection was only in the YA room)." —Anonymous Public Librarian

"We did at first have to justify our pop culture programs but the statistics speak volumes. How can you argue with a program that attracts a thousand people?" —Anonymous Public Librarian

"It's very difficult. We advertise through print and in the library. We also try to put our events on cable TV and our website but just don't have the staff to keep up with it." —Anonymous Public Library Director

"[We use our] website, calendar of events, bifolds for teens and children, school visits (playing book bingo), PR in newspapers and on county cable channel. Some programs have gotten very minor objections, but nothing serious (ghost hunting, Body in the Library Halloween program—from parents primarily who think we are teaching the occult; these same folks also object to *Harry Potter*). The biggest problem is parents wanting to attend teen programs, which we are required to allow, but which puts a damper on things, as you can imagine. Staff-wise, one major problem is getting the selectors and administrative staff for the system to understand the special requirements to entice teens into the library and to programs. They are very slow to grasp that teens are different. We share interesting items found in journals, newspapers, and online with the selection/administration staff, and find we are slowly acquiring the technology (still can't use flash drives!), like downloadable books, that will bring them in. The Library Board continues to allow MySpace and Facebook access despite some calls from staff to block them." —Anonymous Public Librarian

"We're always defending the purchase of non-print materials. The people in power now grew up with the libraries of the '50s & '60s, which were all about books, and they cannot fathom why we need to provide anything other than 'classic' literature. We try to achieve a balance of pop with classics, particularly in DVDs and novels. We could definitely do a better job of marketing our pop collections to specific audiences." —Anonymous Public Librarian

"I produce a library brochure I distribute to all parents in their orientation packs. I also give a brochure to students during their first library visit of the year. I have a library web page. I do lots of announcements in our daily bulletin. I write articles for our parent newsletter." —Anonymous School Librarian

"Library newsletter, posters around town, table tents in the coffee shop and the restaurant where all the oldsters eat breakfast (they're the ones that talk the most, good or bad!), ads and news releases for programming in the local newspaper—we have gotten really great support from the local newspaper. We've been lucky that way. We have only rare complaints about the collection development and inclusions—although we have one crabby old buck who complains about scantily clad women on magazine covers and argues that yoga is a religion, so we should also have more conservative Catholic materials to counter the yoga. There's one in every crowd, isn't there?" —Anonymous Public Librarian

"If a student, teacher, or administrator has suggested a special title or kind of book, I take that book to that person and show that is available for their use. I also pass out new book bibliographies. I have new book receptions with food and soft drinks for faculty." —Anonymous School Librarian

"In anticipation of responses to our new adult graphic novel collection, I made a presentation to our board before the collection launched, about the literary value of these books and the fact that the images are important in telling the story/artistic merit, etc." —Anonymous Public Librarian

"Our mission statement allows for the inclusion of pop culture or 'entertainment' activities and materials, and we're extremely fortunate to have strong support in the community for what we do. I think that because we haven't ditched cultural programming and traditional collections for pop culture, we haven't had to 'sell' folks on it." —Anonymous Public Librarian

"Our management and board are *very* supportive of the teen department, so I don't really have to advocate for programming. I think that where I really need to fight is in using technology to reach teens (podcasting, having a kick-butt website, making the website more interactive, etc.). We have a teen calendar that goes out, we try to make school visits, we send out postcards, we have posters in the branches, etc." —Anonymous Public Librarian

Endnotes

1. Patricia H. Fisher and Marseille M. Pride, *Blueprint for Your Library Marketing Plan: A Guide to Help You Survive and Thrive,* Chicago: American Library Association, 2006, 12.

2. Nancy Dowd (Director of Marketing, New Jersey State Library), email correspondence with Sophie Brookover, March 2007.

3. Dowd, March 2007.

4. Karen Avenick (Friends and Trustees Facilitator, New Jersey Library Association), email correspondence with Sophie Brookover, December 2006.

5. Avenick, December 2006.

6. WebJunction Staff, "Demonstrating Impact: Making Your Case," *WebJunction*, January 4, 2004, www.webjunction.org/do/PrinterFriendly Content?id=1204

7. "Demonstrating Impact," 2004.

8. Highlands Regional Library Cooperative, "Valuing Libraries—Demonstrating the Contributions Libraries Make to Their Communities," www.hrlc.org/funding/valuinglibs.htm

9. Sharon Baker and Karen Wallace, *The Responsive Public Library*, 2nd ed., Englewood, CO: Libraries Unlimited, 2002.

10. Dowd, March 2007.

11. Hennepin County Library System, "HCL Mission and Vision," www.hclib.org/pub/info/HCL_mission_vision.cfm

12. Madison-Jefferson County Library System, "About Us," www.mjcpl.org/index.php?c=About-Us&s=Your-Library

13. Ann Arbor District Library, "Who We Are," www.aadl.org/aboutus

TRENDSPOTTING

The difference between spotting a trend and getting sucked into a short-term fad is often only visible with hindsight. However, whatever type of library you are in—public, special, school, academic—you use someone else's money to build your collections and provide services. This requires you to meet certain written and unwritten obligations. You have a heightened obligation to be responsible, and you must answer to someone about how you spend these funds. Especially when it comes to pop culture, you want to know if what you're considering is merely a short-term fad whose popularity will flame out quickly and thus be difficult to defend. Will you ultimately regret collecting certain materials as wastes of time and money that would have been better spent elsewhere? Or are you looking at a nascent long-term trend? The gamble of purchasing *High School Musical*–related materials in 2006 would now have proven to be a canny move, ultimately resulting in congratulations, happy customers, and good publicity. How can you balance an investment in popular culture materials and services with the need to avoid falling on your face—whether by picking the wrong trend, missing out on a trend altogether, or, worst of all, jumping on a trend so late that it is (in the immortal words of pop tart Hilary Duff and noted YA author Scott Westerfeld) *so yesterday?*

Trendspotting draws on all that you've already accomplished—through finding and pushing your community's pop culture buttons and creating a niche for yourself and your library; by building a collection that goes pop; by advocating for and marketing the pop collection; and by engaging in pop reach—and allows you to take all of that one step further. Most of what we've discussed so far involves going to your community and asking, listening, and building on that knowledge. Savvy information professionals, though, take this one step further by monitoring and anticipating trends *before* our patrons ask about them.

You can spot trends based on what you know about pop culture and what you know about your community. As with many library-related activities, this is an art, not a science. There are no ironclad rules to guarantee success every time you match up your intuition and knowledge. That's scary, we know—as obsessive planners ourselves, we feel your pain. To master your anxiety, we recommend the three Fs: Be fearless, be flexible, and embrace the possibility of failure. Okay, maybe not "failure." No one likes "the other F-word," as we like to call it. How about this: Be prepared for a lack of success. Better still, be prepared to *change your definition of success.* If a staff member spends 15 hours playing with the *technology du jour* and ultimately recommends that the library not adopt it, don't view this effort as wasted staff time. This kind of exercise is a success, because: (1) You've determined what works (and what doesn't work) for your library; (2) you've empowered staff to pay attention to trends and how, if at all, the library could use them; and (3) you've shown that you are truly paying attention.

Be fearless. If your survey data shows that patrons crave a top-notch collection of TV shows on DVD or an anime collection, now is the time to marshal your data, your research, and your gut feeling that this is a good idea. Present your case to the budgetary powers that be and see if you can muster a small budget for a pilot collection.

Be flexible. When considering a new anime collection, we encourage you (nay, challenge you!) to look beyond review periodicals written for the library market, and invest some time and money in reading reviews from *Anime Insider* or *Otaku USA*, periodicals aimed at the anime fandom market. You can find a tremendous variety of anime titles and series, so you may need to play with the items you carry and the age group you're targeting. Tinker with the ways in which your library catalogs and promotes these materials. For example, does your OPAC use the term "anime" as well as the Library of Congress Subject Heading "Animated television programs—Japan"? If your library has a blog, are your staff members blogging new items? Is the teen librarian loaning new titles to the local high school's anime club members? Bear in mind that even when you've done all you can do, it's possible that your shiny new venture may not be the right collection for your library, after all. This is why a pilot program, with a specific start and end date, is a trendspotter's best friend; instead of ending something ("failure"), you simply decide not to make it permanent.

Embrace the possibility of failure. Part of embracing the possibility of failure is freeing yourself from the burden of comparisons. Let's use this new anime collection as an example. Don't look at the statistics for your library's anime collection and compare them with the circ statistics at a neighboring library that has had a similar collection in place for a couple of years. Don't compare your anime collection to other collections within your library (at least, not at first). Realize that you need to give it room and time to grow. So, your first anime night drew only 10 kids. That is 10 kids more than you would have had in the library on any other given night! What's more, those 10 kids are going to tell their friends that the library hosted an anime night. Congratulations! You just bought yourself some credibility with teenagers in your community. What are we saying here? Give yourself the room, time, and support to build on your successes, no matter how modest they may seem.

Identifying Resources, Extrapolating Ideas

What resources can you use for pop culture trendspotting? The answer is endless and changing, ranging from blogs and lists to magazines and newspapers. How can you apply what you find to the task of connecting with your community? There is no one magic bullet of pop culture resources; the key is to be aware of many sources, combine them with your knowledge and skills, and add insight and imagination. You may remember the 1988 comedy *Working Girl*, in which Melanie Griffith starred as Tess Gallagher, a helium-voiced but dead savvy Wall Street secretary from Staten Island. Tess impersonates her incapacitated, shrewish boss, Katherine (a deliciously nasty Sigourney Weaver), to collaborate on a brilliant business deal with Jack Trainer (Harrison Ford). Katherine tries to claim Tess's idea as her own, but Tess proves it's hers by explaining how she came up with the idea:

> This is *Forbes*. ... It's just your basic article about how you were looking to expand into broadcasting. Now the same day ... I'm reading page six of the *Post*, and there's this item on Bobby Stein the radio talk show guy. ... He's hosting this charity auction that night—real blue bloods. Now I turn the page to Suzy who does the society stuff and there's this picture of your daughter ... and she's helping to organize the charity ball. So I started to think, Trask, radio. Trask, radio. And then I hooked up with Jack, and he came on board with Metro. And so now, here we are.[1]

Tess has been reading everything from serious business magazines to local gossip columnists, and her imagination (honed by work experience and education) leads her to put together disparate facts and ideas and come up with a winning, profitable solution.

This is where your attitude toward technology and popular periodicals comes in. Anyone can do what Tess did, but does your library culture support that style of far-ranging information gathering? If colleagues see staff members reading blogs, do they frown at them and instruct them to do that on their own time? Or do they smile, knowing that the staff member is acting like a professional and staying on top of trends?

When you look at the wide variety of resources available, you realize: This is a lot to read and digest! (See the resource list in Appendix A to seed your list of bookmarks or feeds.) First, remember that you may already be reading several of the resources mentioned. Second, trendspotting is not done in isolation: This is not a job that you take on all by yourself. You may even want to establish a formal trendspotting committee, as the Ocean County Library did (see sidebar on page 102). Or, you may organize an informal group that meets weekly for lunch to share what they've found and brainstorm ideas. Whatever system you use, spread the reading and researching responsibilities among several people and have a system in place for brainstorming. Finally, we recommend that you regularly mix up and vary your diet of trendspotting reading, viewing, and listening—choose one or two sources as your staples, and rotate different resources in and out of those you use to develop ideas.

Developing Tie-Ins and Establishing Trust

Christine Matteo (see sidebar on page 102) highlights two things that are so important we think they bear repeating. First, she notes that members of Ocean County Library's Trendspotting Committee are "voracious consumers of news events, and could apply or extrapolate a potential trend to a service that the library was either already offering in a more traditional way, or an entirely new service opportunity." This ability lies at the heart of the value of trendspotting. Being able to identify a trend in the making is one thing; extrapolating it to library service is much more significant. Forecasting the popularity of a new recording artist, author, or format is wonderful, but marrying a new format to a service the library already offers—for example, loading audiobooks onto circulating iPods, as one Long Island library did—is brilliant, newsworthy, and shows the library in a very flattering light.

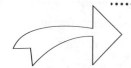

TRENDSPOTTING AT OCEAN COUNTY LIBRARY: AN INTERVIEW WITH CHRISTINE MATTEO

Liz sat down with Christine Matteo, Chief Librarian at Ocean County Library, Toms River, New Jersey, chair of her library system's Trendspotting Committee, to get some insights into how the committee works and its role in the Library.

Ocean County Library has a Trendspotters Committee. Please share with us—why Trendspotters? And why a committee?
The idea originated during the development of the Ocean County Library's Strategic Plan. We were brainstorming ways to achieve one of our Objectives: "Everyone looks to the Library for the Next Big Thing."

We thought that a group of interested staff members could do ongoing research about how the corporate sector tracks trends. We knew that in order to remain relevant to our customers, we had to look beyond the roles traditionally offered by public libraries and consider the entire scope of world trends, from science to education to culture and beyond, and to apply the trends we were "spotting" to library service. We needed a committee to dedicate work time towards consciously doing the research using futurist societies and publications, sharing the ideas with management, and proposing actual service initiatives that addressed the trends we were seeing. We have, since the inception of the committee, proposed several viable strategies for Ocean County Library to remain in the forefront of library programs and services available to the whole spectrum of the community.

What was the process involved in starting the committee? Did you need to do any internal marketing to get people to support the committee? What has been the staff reaction?

Typically, when we are ready to begin a new committee, we talk it up at our biannual series of Administration Forums. All staff are encouraged to attend these biannual events, where library management shares information about the direction the Ocean County Library is taking, and how the staff can play an integral role in furthering the library's Strategic Plan. Once a year, we send out a "call to committee," advertising all of the various opportunities for staff to be engaged in the library's initiatives. Staff volunteer based on their knowledge, skills, and abilities. The staff who worked on the first Trendspotters Committee had natural tendencies to ask "What if?" They were voracious consumers of news events, and could apply or extrapolate a potential trend to a service that the library was either already offering in a more traditional way, or an entirely new service opportunity. Some of the members also attended the annual World Future Society conference, and we've been sending representatives to this conference ever since. The first year we went, we were the only library represented, and attendees would ask, "why is a library interested in future trends?"

The first five trends we identified were then presented to the entire staff, again at a series of Administration Forums. All of the trends included proposals for how Ocean County Library could apply them to service initiatives. This generated even more excitement among the staff for the following year.

What has OCL done to make Trendspotters a success? What are some of the results of having the committee?

Trendspotters has been successful because at least one idea every year is translated into an actual initiative, funded by the Library

Commission. The Trendspotters see that they make a real differ-ence, and this keeps up the level of commitment from the group.

Why do you think it is important for libraries to think about trendspotting?
This is such a cliche, but the library isn't just about books anymore. According to some futurists, the written word will be gone in 50 years anyway! So what will libraries do in the future to continue to effectively serve their communities, providing them with educa-tional, recreational, viewing, listening, reading opportunities, provid-ing a level playing field so that the less advantaged members of the community can achieve a high quality of life, so that our future will be bright and hopeful? Trendspotting is the closest we can come to having a crystal ball—the trick is to see how a trend can possibly apply to our service goals for our communities.

Being willing to experiment with anticipating trends is a wonder-ful way to build trust capital with your many constituents, both within and outside of the library. This is essential, because capital, once built up, can be reinvested in a process of more experimenta-tion and capital-building. Remember, your experimentation can be small- or large-scale, depending on the amount of risk involved, the number of staff members working on the project, and the time it will take to roll out the initiative and evaluate it.

Christine also mentioned the methodology Ocean County Library uses to build excitement for, and trust in, the value of spot-ted trends: "The first five trends we identified were then presented to the entire staff, again at a series of Administration Forums. All of the trends included proposals for how Ocean County Library could apply them to service initiatives. This generated even more excitement among the staff for the following year." OCL uses both bottom-up and top-down communication to establish the trends it will track and apply to the strategic plan and library services.

Members of the trendspotting committee generate ideas, then share them with staff at all levels of the library to build system-wide buy-in.

Some questions to pose to yourself and to the trendspotters in your library include: How will you encourage staff-wide trendspotting? You may want to have a committee or roundtable, but how will nonmembers share knowledge of trends that they have spotted? Will you use staff meetings as a brainstorming zone? Will you create an internal blog or wiki to function as an electronic idea room? How will you ensure that one really creative person isn't made to be both the idea generator and the workhorse? These are all issues to consider, and every library's approach to working them out will be slightly different.

Voices from the Field

Here are some selected responses to the question: "How do you keep abreast of new developments that could be useful to staff and patrons? How do you publicize your finds?"

"I read everything—papers, magazines, and the Internet. I pass information along via email or post it on our web page. Mostly email." —Ellen Jennings, Young Adult Services Coordinator, Cook Memorial Library District, Libertyville, IL

"We keep abreast by belonging to a number of listservs, and [through] membership in our local association, as well as ALA. We can publicize our finds either through the local newspaper, by fliers, and promotions within the library, or via the radio, where we often will booktalk some titles." —Geri Dosuala, Youth Services Librarian, Artesia (NM) Public Library

"I try to read journals and other information sources to stay abreast. I also try to attend workshops or seminars, which introduce new ideas. I try to turn-key that information to my staff through memos, direct contact, or through in-services that I provide." —Pat Slemmer, Librarian, Williamstown (NJ) High School

"Home pages of popular teen and/or news sites; collaborating with the student services sector of the school staff; and watching what the teens really do online when they are supposed to be working on school assignments. Publicity right now is word-of-mouth, one-on-one assistance with students, and disseminating information through classroom teachers." —Arlen Kimmelman, Librarian, Clayton (NJ) Middle/High School

"I read [celebrity gossip Web sites] Oh No They Didn't (community.livejournal.com/ohnotheydidnt) and Perez Hilton (www.perezhilton.com) because those are the celebrities and clips the kids and teens are talking about. I also rely on magazines such as *VIBE* and *Entertainment Weekly* to get a sense of what is on people's radar." —Elizabeth Erwin, Senior Youth Services Librarian, Hunterdon County Library, Flemington, NJ

"Read, read, read." —Michael A. Golrick, Director, L.E. Phillips Memorial Library, Eau Claire, WI

"Talking to the customers and listening to what they have to say, what they like, what they don't like, what they want to research, what they are interested in. Word of mouth in my small hometown, and now word of mouth in my small store." —Anonymous Bookseller

"I just read the news and watch entertainment shows on TV to see what is hot. However, by the time something gets on those shows, it is sometimes already on its way out." —Anonymous Public Librarian

"I use the information I learn at conferences and on blogs and in articles. I will copy and send to the teachers' mailboxes, I will speak to whole classes, I will address faculty at meetings, and sometimes I get permission to speak to the kids in the cafeteria while they eat. (The assistant principal frowns on this some because it is their only free time.)" —Laurie Belanger, Library Media Specialist, Paul Harrison Memorial Library, Lakeville, MA

"I attend [my state's library association] meetings, subscribe to listservs, and read magazines for what other libraries are doing. I also scan TV/movies/books/whatever for ideas, and I listen a lot to what the teens are saying." —Saleena Davidson, YA/Reference Librarian, South Brunswick Public Library, Monmouth Junction, NJ

"I read a lot of local publications to stay on top of what is happening with popular culture in my city and community (films that are playing, bands coming to town, etc.). I publicize these finds through email, newsletter articles, and one-to-one interaction with library patrons." —Heidi Andres, Teen Librarian, Cuyahoga County Public Library, Middleburg Heights, OH

"This is a tough question. My ability to find new developments is far greater than the public's or the staff's ability to understand them. I tend to show people things on an ad hoc basis. In the future I may create a blog-type thing on our website, but I'll have to make sure it's sufficiently used to warrant the time required to maintain it." —James Peek, Librarian, Middlesex (NJ) Public Library

"I read blogs and subscribe to listservs. Because this community isn't very tech-savvy I am slowly teaching them the ways I keep in touch with new developments, and I write about them in my monthly column." —Annie M. Wrigg, Director, Pelican Rapids (MN) Public Library

"By reading journals. Attending Book Expo, ComicCon, and AnimeFest. Communicating with teachers and curriculum supervisors. We share on various listservs such as YALSA, ALSC, and Mays, a local group of youth services librarians." —Liz Sann, Youth Services Program Assistant, Roxbury Public Library, Succasunna, NJ

"We discuss new ideas and trends at monthly staff meetings. We also have a staff specific blog for sharing new tools and ideas. This blog is updated daily by all staff members." —Amy Thurber, Director, Canaan (NH) Town Library

"We have a fairly small staff, so things tend to spread personally, either in conversations or emails, with small discussions at our weekly reference meetings if something seems useful to everyone." —Anonymous Academic Paraprofessional

"Reading blogs, watching TV, reading *EW*—having an 11-year-old daughter helps, too." —Michelle Glatt, Librarian, Chiddix Junior High School, Normal, IL

"Read, read, read, and listen, listen, listen. From the cover of *Us Weekly* on the newsstand to *Rolling Stone*, nightly news, CNN, Oprah, MTV, VH1,

Bust magazine, blogs, websites, etc. I suppose we publicize our finds by getting them into the collection. IMHO, libraries aren't the best at 'publicizing' our collections." —Daniel Barden, Technical Services Administrator, Alachua County District Library, Gainesville, FL

"I'm sort of a pop culture junkie, so it's not too hard. I attend a lot of punk shows and comic cons, which are great places to stay ahead of the curve." —Maryellen Liddy, Teen/Reference Librarian, Kinnelon (NJ) Public Library

"I read professional journals and newspapers. I talk to the kids all the time. I attend conferences, notably, the Internet@Schools conference regularly. I read listservs, and stay in touch with other librarians and library school educators to see what is new and to share ideas. I make what I find part of my teaching and staff development." —Stephanie Rosalia, School Library Media Specialist, Eileen E. Zaglin School PS225K, Brooklyn, NY

"Reading the literature from our state and professional journals keeps me aware of new trends. A monthly written report goes to the Head of School and Board of Directors for the monthly board meeting. This report is part of the minutes, and some or all of it is included in the school newsletter and any flyers about upcoming events. Daily announcements are also used to promote programs when possible." —Anonymous School Librarian

"I follow a couple of dozen blogs, from technological blogs to book review blogs. I publicize my finds by either posting them to my library's blog and/or del.icio.us account or speaking of them to the particular staff and/or patrons that would be interested." —Anonymous School Librarian

"I read a lot of blogs and websites. I usually email individualized notes to my fellow faculty." —Anonymous School Librarian

"Professional reading, general reading of magazines and books, especially teen books, surfing the net for program ideas, going to continuing education workshops, and my listservs are lifesavers! I publicize through word of mouth, MySpace, etc." —Anonymous Public Librarian

"I read all that I can in print and online publications. I listen to the patrons and teens. You name it." —Anonymous Public Librarian

"We have monthly service level meetings where things like that are discussed. We also have online and face-to-face reading groups where the public and staff are encouraged to mingle. Soon we will have a database intranet that is designed to be a better forum for the staff to share ideas than the current email system." —Anonymous Public Librarian

"I like surfing the Net myself, checking out things I hear about from my high-school age brother. I subscribe to LM_Net as well as print based journals like *SLJ* and *LMC*." —Anonymous Public Librarian

"Read. Read. Read. I read the library journals online. I read library blogs. I read newspapers. I post on a blog. I love facts and figures. I use email, my blog, the YA librarians' blog in my county, and I love to talk to people." —Anonymous Public Librarian

"It's very hard. I read blogs, like Pop Goes the Library, Librarian Avengers, Library Marketing—Thinking Outside the Book. We have several librarians on staff who serve as excellent filters (those early adopters) who report on useful things they find. Often it's a matter of talking to student workers to try and see what they (and their peers) are using and are interested in." —Anonymous Academic Librarian

"I read magazines like crazy (things like *VOYA* as well as *Seventeen* and *Bitch*). I also read a number of online news sources that help with this." —Anonymous Public Librarian

"Blogs are the best! I read and try to get my staff to read a whole variety of blogs on different topics. Marketing blogs like Advergirl.com (leighhouse.typepad.com/advergirl), Creative Think (www.creativethink. com), Ypulse, Seth Godin's blog (sethgodin.typepad.com), and Totally Wired; trend-watching blogs like Lifehacker and Smart Mobs (www.smart-mobs.com); and even PostSecret (postsecret.blogspot.com) and Cute Overload (www.cuteoverload.com) often provide tremendous inspiration and clues to what's happening." —Anonymous Public Librarian

"I check IMDb for film updates, also Walden Media. I read the magazines. I talk to my students constantly! They are probably my best source of information. If they say, *Toy Story 3* is not going to have the original stars so it won't be any good, I won't purchase any books or promote the media I have. I find that a sidebar conversation in computer or library time is the

best way to spread news. That way, it's almost like gossip and kids get excited taking ownership. A week later, I post on bulletin boards."
—Anonymous School Librarian

"I read blogs like Pop Goes the Library." —Anonymous Public Librarian *(Authors' Note: Awwww! We love you the most!)*

"If any staff member finds an interesting article or something they feel should be included in the collection, they'll send out an email to everyone in our department or we pass the journal or article around the department until everyone has gotten a chance to look at it." —Anonymous Public Librarian

"I'm awful at keeping abreast. Really I do my best, but we are in the day and age of information overload." —Anonymous Public Librarian

"I mostly read articles and news on websites—specifically, I keep up-to-date regarding horror films and library news in that manner. I take advantage of RSS feeds to make it easy, and it's when you have everything gathered in one place that you really start noticing trends!" —Anonymous Public Librarian

"I'm a big pop culture consumer, and I also like knowing about the businesses that produce what I consume, so I read all kinds of pop culture stuff online and in magazines (*Entertainment Weekly*, Salon.com, *NY Times*, *Premiere*, TelevisionWithoutPity.com, *Spin*, *Rolling Stone*, *Publishers Weekly*). My job puts me in face-to-face contact with most of our collection developers, so if I see something they've missed, I have a chance to catch them up on what I've seen." —Anonymous Public Librarian

Endnotes

1. Katharine E. Monahan Huntley, "'Working Girl' Review," Dramatica.com, www.dramatica.com/story/film_reviews/reviews/WorkingGirl.html

INFORMATION TECHNOLOGY IS EVERYONE'S JOB

The days of Information Technology (IT) as a department completely separate from front-line library services are over. Gone, too, are the days when everyone's booklists, calendar information, updates, and other library content disappeared into the Technology Funnel, seemingly forever, while the IT department formatted it, added HTML, and, finally, uploaded the content onto the library website. In this model, if the IT department had someone out sick or was busy with computer updates or other priority technology projects, your content sat. And sat. And sat ... until it was no longer current or useful.

Now, not only are emerging technologies—hardware, software, and web applications—available to all library staff and customers, they are also increasingly easy to use, even by those of us who (unlike Liz!) weren't computer science majors. Our customers use these technologies. Library staff use these technologies. Some libraries, though, are "old school." They maintain the Technology Funnel, worry about control, and want to preserve oversight of every department. They micromanage any content going online, and are reluctant even to consider social networking applications for fear of what staff and customers may say or do. The result? IT departments distracted from true technology concerns (such as computer upgrades and open source catalogs), delays in publishing timely content, outdated content languishing online, and frustrated staff who have to wait for things to be done when they know they can do it themselves. "New school" libraries, on the other hand, trust staff and customers by creating guidelines and then launching blogs, wikis, and other online applications consistent with their mission statement.

Right now, you may be thinking, "OK, guys, but this is all about technology. Where does the pop culture come in?" (Yes, you can call us guys: We're from Jersey—"guys" is not gender-specific in our neck of the woods.) Technology can both *be* pop culture in itself, and can be *used* in innovative ways to provide pop culture library services such as materials, programming, and outreach. One need look no further than the wild popularity of photo-sharing sites such as Flickr (www.flickr.com) and video-sharing sites like YouTube (www.youtube.com) to see how quickly and completely technology has become intertwined with and can drive popular culture. This is an opportunity no member of our profession can afford to miss. The good news is that you don't have to know how this technology works at a code level in order to use it effectively!

Technology: Fun and Easy

We will provide you with a few ideas and examples of ways to utilize technology. But one of the great things about today's technology is that because it's designed for anyone to use, anyone can, and does, use it. The learning curve is very short, meaning that once you make your way through the "how do I do this?" phase, you can play with the technology and use it in innovative ways to meet your library's service goals. What follows is a heavily annotated list of current (as of early 2008) technologies to familiarize yourself with and to consider using at your library. This list isn't complete, and technologies change, but we hope that there is enough here to pique your interest and get you started. Try to embrace at least one idea from the following sections.

Flash Drives

Liz likes to say she studied computer science back in the days when they still used computer punch cards. (To be totally honest, though, she only used punch cards during a high school summer session; she watched other people use them her freshman year.) Still, personal storage of computer data and information has evolved from punch cards and tapes to 5.25" floppy disks (which, as Liz can attest, were easily destroyed) and 3.5" floppy disks to CD-ROMs and now USB flash drives. (A recent viewing of the 1998 version of *Lost in Space* showed that future space explorers stored data on ... CD-ROMs. That sound you hear in the far-off distance is us cackling.)

Today's preferred method of storing data is the USB flash drive, also called a pen drive or thumb drive. Compact and solid state, these devices are more durable than CDs and floppies. They won't scratch and can't be trashed by shutting them in a three-ring binder (which was how Liz ruined a final project back in college!). With storage size ranging from 512 MB to 32 GB, flash drives can be used to store photos, music, presentations, documents, and even computer applications.

What does this mean for you? Many public library staff don't have their own dedicated workspace or computers. Flash drives make it easy to carry work from computer to computer—a handy feature in today's multi-computer workplace. Not only are flash drives small and easy to carry, they can also be fun. Some are attached to a lanyard or a key chain; others can take the form of bracelets, teddy bears, or lipstick—just about anything. Vendors of promotional materials can also personalize flash drives with your library name. What a great giveaway! If you are presenting a program to the library board about your new pop culture collection, in addition to paper handouts (or instead of handouts), why not store all the information on personalized flash drives that you hand out at the end of the program?

Portable Media Players

Portable media player (or PMP) is "an umbrella term for a variety of handheld devices that play back audio, video or both. The device may also serve as a portable photo album and display still images such as GIFs and JPEGs."[1] PMPs such as Sony's Playstation Portable (PSP) and Apple's iPod and iPod Touch not only play music and display still images, but also allow users to play games, download television episodes, and watch movies. Apple's iPod, which was introduced in 2001, is perhaps the best-known PMP. According to Apple's press release at the time:

> Apple® today introduced iPod™, a breakthrough MP3 music player that packs up to 1,000 CD-quality songs into an ultra-portable, 6.5 ounce design that fits in your pocket. iPod combines a major advance in portable music device design with Apple's legendary ease of use and Auto-Sync, which automatically downloads all your iTunes™ songs and playlists into your iPod, and keeps them up to date whenever you plug your iPod into your Mac®.[2]

Less than five years later, Apple announced:

> The new iPod®, the best digital music player and most popular portable video player in the world. The new iPod features a 60 percent brighter and more vibrant 2.5-inch

color display perfect for watching TV shows and now Hollywood movies right in the palm of your hand. The new iPod features seamless integration with iTunes® 7 and the iTunes Store (www.itunes.com) which now includes over 75 Hollywood movies, 220 television shows and popular video games designed specifically for the fifth generation iPod. The new iPod is available in a 30GB model at the new low price of $249 and an 80GB model, which holds up to 20,000 songs or 100 hours of video, for $349.[3]

We include these details because they show how quickly technology advances and how many improvements an innovative company can make to a product in a brief period of time.

While iPod may be the most popular brand name, many other MP3 players are available. What do these devices have to do with your library? You can allow users to download audiobooks, from sites such as ListenNJ (www.listennj.com) powered by OverDrive (www.overdrive.com), to their personal computer or MP3 player from the library's website. (Because of copyright protection on the audiobook files, Apple's iPods cannot be used with this service at this time.) If your library provides books that are downloadable to certain devices, why not promote this service with a portable media player giveaway—being sure to select a model that is both easy to use and supported by your provider. And why not have a public computer in the library dedicated to audiobook downloads?

We've recently seen exciting developments in PMPs designed for ebooks, which, love 'em or hate 'em, are now here, and here to stay. Some people complain that it can't be a "real" book, or a "real" reading experience, if you can't read the book in bed or in a bath, or if you can't physically turn the pages. Other people, though, are eager for a small, portable device that is easy on the eyes. At the time of this writing, the Sony Reader (www.sonystyle.com) and the Amazon Kindle (www.kindle.com) were the two hottest digital readers around—so hot that neither Liz nor Sophie could do anything but lust after them from afar. What can libraries do? Forward-looking ones say, "How can we be part of the revolution? Isn't it part of our role to make sure our patrons aren't left behind when new technology comes out?" The Sparta Public Library in Sparta, New Jersey (www.spartalibrary.com), purchased two Amazon Kindles to loan to its patrons when the technology was introduced.[4]

Another option for providing audiobooks to customers is the Playaway (store.playawaydigital.com). Playaway is designed for your non-techie patrons: It's smaller than a deck of cards and comes with the audiobook already loaded. Just put on the earphones, hit play, and listen! Libraries are buying these so that customers who don't own a portable MP3 player can enjoy audiobooks on the go, too, without checking out CDs or cassettes. Playaway offers library packaging, so libraries just have to decide how to store the device, what to do about earphones (supply them? sell them? tell users to buy their own?), and what to do about batteries (replace after every check out? use rechargeable batteries? tell users to buy their own?). The Playaway is great because it introduces portable media devices to people who might be iPod-phobic; by providing Playaways for free, the loaning library also narrows the digital divide, so that those who cannot afford a portable media device can learn how to use one.

Apple's store for music, books, video, and podcasts for the iPod is called, naturally enough, iTunes (www.itunes.com). While most of the content is fee-based, some of the software tools are free, including the iMix (tutorial at www.apple.com/support/ilife/tutorials/itunes/it6-2.html). The iMix is a tool that anyone can use to create a personal playlist, which can then be accessed through iTunes or published on a website. Why would a library create a playlist? Say you have a performer coming in a few weeks. You display the artist's CDs, and have posters and fliers in your library as a matter of course. Why not tap into your website's potential as a publicity machine and host an iMix playlist online, as well?

There's no reason to limit your library's iMixes to visiting performers, though. During Women's History Month, for example, you might post an iMix of women artists, as varied as Bjork, Madonna, Blossom Dearie, Emmylou Harris, Sheryl Crow, Asha Bhosle, Yeah Yeah Yeahs, Lily Allen, Missy Elliott, the Go-Gos, and Etta James. And that's just to start! We didn't even include stars of Broadway and opera!

Does your library have a book discussion group? Use iMix to prepare a soundtrack to accompany their next book. It's fun and easy; just check out the short iMix we threw together for Michael Chabon's *Wonder Boys*. Sophie chose songs from her own music library, using some of the themes and plot points from the novel. The result?

- Elvis Costello, "Everyday I Write the Book"
- Beach Boys, "In My Room"
- Rufus Wainwright, "Cigarettes and Chocolate Milk"
- Flaming Lips, "Waitin' on a Superman"
- Ella Fitzgerald, "Embraceable You"
- The Bangles, "James"
- The Cars, "Just What I Needed"
- John Prine with Dolores Keane, "In a Town This Size"
- The Faces, "Ooh La La"

(We would love to provide a link, but iMix links are only good for a year, so we decided to take a pass on that multimedia tie-in opportunity.)

RSS

The acronym RSS has gone through a number of iterations, among them Rich Site Summary, RDF Site Summary, and our favorite, Really Simple Syndication. All About RSS, at Fagan Finder (www.faganfinder.com/search/rss.php), explains that "RSS files (which are also called RSS feeds or channels) simply contain a list of items. Usually, each item contains a title, summary, and a link to a URL (e.g. a Web page)."[5] Basically, RSS provides all of the current information from a website, without any of the formatting. To illustrate, while the website for Pop Goes the Library (www.pop goesthelibrary.com) reflects the vision of the website designer (AKA, Sophie, well, only to a degree—this is a template from Blogger), with various font sizes and colors as well as sidebar information (Figure 6.1), the RSS feed for the site is stripped of all the "extras" and contains only the content (Figure 6.2).

Figure 6.1   Pop Goes the Library website

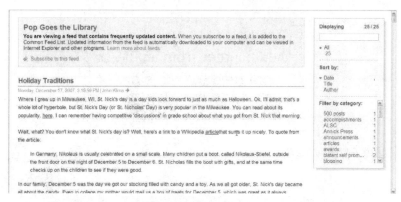

Figure 6.2   Pop Goes the Library feed

RSS is important to you as a user and as a provider. A user may be a deliberate end user, someone who uses a feed reader or aggregator (explained in the next section). Or, if a website you visit uses content from another site's RSS feed, you may be using RSS feeds and not even know it!

To illustrate, Liz blogs about libraries and pop culture at Pop Goes the Library. She also blogs about books, movies, and television at A Chair, a Fireplace and a Tea Cozy (yzocaet.blogspot.com). These blogs have two different audiences, with two different interests—but sometimes readers at Tea Cozy may be interested in one of the posts on Pop Goes the Library. Rather than constantly creating new posts at Tea Cozy to point out posts of interest at Pop, Liz uses a built-in "Feed" widget from Blogger (www.blogger.com), her blogging software, to automatically add the content from Pop to Tea Cozy (Figures 6.3 and 6.4). Liz simply added Blogger's Feed widget to her template. Now, whenever Pop is updated, the links to Pop are updated on the main page at Tea Cozy (Figures 6.5 and 6.6). Thus, every reader of Tea Cozy, whether they know it or not, is using RSS—all possible because Pop has an RSS feed.

If your library had RSS feeds, who could use them? Anyone with a website! Imagine: Through RSS, you can offer a constantly

Figure 6.3 Adding RSS content to a blog

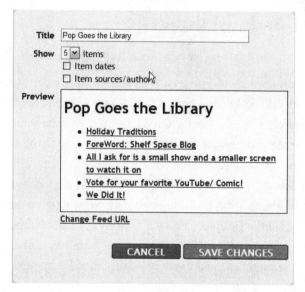

*Figure 6.4 Adding content from Pop Goes the Library to A Chair, a
Fireplace, and a Tea Cozy*

updated, timely, mini-advertisement for your library's site. For
example, if your library catalog creates a new book feed, you can
use that feed on the library website to keep patrons updated about
your new books. If your online calendar produces an RSS feed for
events, community groups and organizations can use that feed to
promote your events on their own sites.

Figure 6.5   Tea Cozy displaying Pop Goes the Library content via RSS

MOST RECENT POSTS FROM POP GOES THE LIBRARY

Holiday Traditions

ForeWord: Shelf Space Blog

All I ask for is a small show and a
smaller screen to watch it on

Vote for your favorite YouTube/

Figure 6.6   Content from Pop Goes the Library as seen on Tea Cozy

Let's say that a local high school anime club has a web page. Traditionally, libraries would be happy if the club page simply linked to the library's site and noted that "Manga and anime materials and programs are available at the local library." Perhaps the anime club site could even provide links to the library catalog and calendar as well as the main website. With RSS feeds from the library, though, the club's page can include a constantly updated list of new anime and manga titles, as well as a list of new anime- and manga-related library programs. All the anime club has to do is make a one-time addition to its web page template.

The library can also use the feeds of other sites to add content to its own web page; just be sure to check each site's terms and conditions. The online edition of the *New York Times* (www.ny times.com), for example, says in its terms for NYTimes.com RSS feeds: "We encourage the use of NYTimes.com RSS feeds for personal use in a news reader or as part of a non-commercial Web site or blog. We require proper format and attribution whenever New York Times content is posted on your Web site, and we reserve the right to require that you cease distributing NYTimes.com content. Please read the *Terms and Conditions* for complete instructions."[6] The site goes on to mention other ways to display *New York Times* headlines: "NYTimes.com also offers a free headline feed for displaying headlines on personal or professional Web sites, for noncommercial purposes. For more information and instructions, see *Add New York Times Headlines to Your Site.*"[7]

Ask your community members what they want to see on the library's site. Instead of worrying about creating or recopying news content, government meeting minutes, or the weather, find the relevant feeds and add them. Also, don't forget to provide permission on your site for those who wish to use library feeds on their sites. Make sure you offer easy, step-by-step instructions, along with a help number, so that community members can follow up if they run into problems using your feeds.

How do you create RSS feeds? Most blogging software and other dynamic online applications, including Flickr, del.icio.us (del.icio.us), and Facebook (www.facebook.com), automatically create RSS feeds whenever a user updates his or her account. Talk to your IT people; ask your vendors. How do you add RSS feeds from another source? Again, talk to your IT people (this is why they should be freed from the job of adding content to websites—to concentrate on technology issues!). Sites that can help you with the coding include RSS2Java (www.rss2java.com) and RSS to JavaScript (www.rss-to-javascript.com).

Feed Readers/Aggregators

When we discussed RSS channels, or feeds, we mentioned that RSS is important to you as a user. While RSS feeds are often associated with blogs (largely because blogging software automatically produces RSS feeds), any site can have an RSS feed: a news site, a weather site, a library's home page.

One of the easiest ways to waste ridiculous amounts of time on the Internet is by going to your favorite websites and blogs to see whether anything new has been posted, and finding out that nothing has—or at least, nothing you're interested in.

The solution? Feed aggregators. As Wikipedia explains, "In computing, a feed aggregator, also known as a feed reader or simply as an aggregator, is client software or a Web application which aggregates syndicated Web content such as news headlines, blogs, podcasts, and vlogs in a single location for easy viewing."[8] This means that you can use an aggregator to read multiple feeds. So, instead of having to remember many URLs to visit many websites, you visit one website (or piece of software), your aggregator. Via that aggregator you can read all the latest posts and news from all your favorite sites—you've created your own mini–*Reader's Digest* version of all your favorites.

Why is this important? And how is this pop? If your users like to keep on top of websites with aggregators, rather than viewing the sites themselves, you're losing a valuable opportunity to reach patrons if you don't provide RSS feeds to your content. If your concern is that staff spends too much time online, RSS aggregators help minimize time spent keeping up-to-date with news, ideas, and technologies. Feed readers can also be a way to keep up with who is talking about your library. Bloglines (www.bloglines.com) is one of the best-known aggregators; you can create a permanent Bloglines search on any phrase (or set of search parameters) to let you know whenever a feed contains a certain phrase, such as "pop goes the library" or your library name. What a great way to stay on top of what patrons, other libraries, or visitors write about your library! Bloglines also lets you know how many people have subscribed to your site's feed, which can be helpful data when advocating for your library. Other widely used aggregators include Google Reader (www.google.com/reader/view) and the Friends page of LiveJournal (www.livejournal.com/support/faqbrowse.bml?faqid=219).

Blogs

Blogs are one of the easiest technologies for a library to use. A blog is simply a frequently updated website. Entries appear in reverse chronological order, with the newest post on top, making blogs especially appealing for highlighting new materials, programs, services, or anything else new or noteworthy. Blogging software generates RSS feeds automatically, and most importantly for many users, it offers precreated templates and a WYSIWYG ("what you see is what you get") editor. Basically, if you are a reasonably proficient user of any word-processing program, you will be a successful user of most blog software. You can create a website without knowing HTML or doing any fancy coding. (Are you drunk with power yet?)

You can find a lot of information about blogs and blogging. Start with Aliza Sherman Risdahl's *The Everything Blogging Book: Publish Your Ideas, Get Feedback, and Create Your Own Worldwide Network* and Michael P. Sauer's *Blogging and RSS: A Librarian's Guide.* Also check out online resources such as the handouts and resources from Michael Stephens's program "Community Building Through Your Web Site: Library Blogs and RSS" (www.sjrlc.org/web20/handouts).

Why use blogs? Again, because it's easy. Instead of sending content to your technology department and waiting for it to appear on your website, you can publish that content yourself, with one click of the mouse. Blogs, even those written under library guidelines, tend to have a warm, human voice, making your site inviting and personal. People can publicly comment on blog entries, so you can start a conversation with patrons and staff—and can get valuable feedback on collections, programs, materials, and pop culture initiatives.

The Web can be a scary place. News stories abound about online predators, cyberbullying, and private photos and supposedly private messages being made public in humiliating ways. What better way to create a teachable moment in your community, for patrons of all ages, than to have them participate in blogging and other social software applications? When people actually use the technology, it becomes less scary—users also become more responsible when they learn what is, and is not, appropriate online behavior. Offer hands-on learning experiences, rather than one-time training sessions. Giving people the opportunity to use Web 2.0 technology in the library is yet another way libraries can help level the technological playing field.

Wikis

A wiki is a "collaborative website which can be directly edited by anyone with access to it."[9] The most famous example of a wiki is the source this book uses for many definitions: Wikipedia (en. wikipedia.org). Library-related examples include Library Success: A Best Practices Wiki (www.libsuccess.org), the YALSA Wiki (wikis.ala.org/yalsa), and the Children's Series Binder Wiki (series-binder.lishost.org). Tools for building your own wiki can be found at MediaWiki (www.mediawiki.org/wiki/MediaWiki), Google sites (sites.google.com), and PBwiki (pbwiki.com).

When we teach technology classes, our students often ask us about the differences between blogs and wikis. Why choose one over the other? Why use both? After all, both blogs and wikis are easy to use, provide simple ways to create attractive and easily updated websites, and can have multiple users.

We like to reframe the question in terms of what you want users to get out of the site. Is it primarily for news, upcoming programs, the latest books, and library happenings? Or are you looking for a place to store information, such as booklists, topical links, and other resources? A blog is best when your patrons are most interested in the newest things you have to say, and don't mind searching through posts, which are arranged by date order or category. If, however, you want to store and organize your information, collecting all like information together, then a wiki is what you want.

For example, are you looking to keep your patrons informed about the latest anime news, releases, and programs? Start a blog; recruit patrons to post content. But, if you want to create a manga resource, with sections on original Japanese manga, original English language manga, anime, characters, and conventions, then start a wiki. One good example of a library that uses both blogs and wikis to maintain two-way communication with its customers is the Saint Joseph County Public Library in Indiana. The library's main blog (www.sjcpl.org/ blogs/lifeline) provides daily updates on new items and programs at the library, while the library's subject guides have been transformed using a wiki format (www.sjcpl.lib.in.us/subject guides/index.php/ Main_Page). This format makes the guides easier to update and maintain.

Tagging/Folksonomy

We're a bit scared by the number of people who secretly want to be catalogers. They may deny it—but how else to explain the popularity of folksonomy and tagging? Of course, Wikipedia doesn't use the term "catalog" in its description of folksonomy:

> A folksonomy is a user-generated taxonomy used to categorize and retrieve web content such as Web pages, photographs, and web links, using open-ended labels called tags. Typically, folksonomies are Internet-based, but their use may occur in other contexts. The folksonomic tagging is intended to make a body of information increasingly easy to search, discover, and navigate over time. A

well-developed folksonomy is ideally accessible as a shared vocabulary that is both originated by, and familiar to, its primary users.[10]

One of the main differences between tagging and cataloging is tagging's lack of a controlled vocabulary; as individuals tag (create keywords for) pages, photos, or links, they use terms that make sense to them as users of the content. A patron might tag a book with "manga," while a cataloger would use "Comic books, strips, etc.—Japan—Translations into English." Which term will lead a patron to the materials she wants to find? Which speaks the language of the user, rather than insisting that the user learn library jargon? And which method will adjust faster to changing popular terminology?

Especially interesting is the fact that people tag voluntarily. Tagging is a common component of web applications, especially social software. The act of labeling itself becomes a conversation, as people not only tag items they use, but also look up items with similar tags. When tagging, first check the FAQ of the particular application to see how to use multiple words or phrases in an individual tag. Some allow you to group words together between quotation marks, while others insist on CamelCase (produced by removing the spaces between two or more capitalized words, a practice common in wikis) or the use of underscores between words to create a multiword tag. If more than a few people are going to be tagging blog posts and photos with a tag referring to a conference or event, suggest a universal tag (for example, Midwinter_2010 or mw10). Pop Goes the Library contributors have used tags (called "labels" in Blogger) to be serious *and* funny (Figure 6.7).

Tags not only help you find items online, but can also give you a clear visual representation of the main themes of a website or blog. You can create a "tag cloud" to add to your website or blog with ZoomClouds (zoomclouds.com) or New Blogger Tag Cloud (phy3blog.googlepages.com/Beta-Blogger-Label-Cloud.html), both

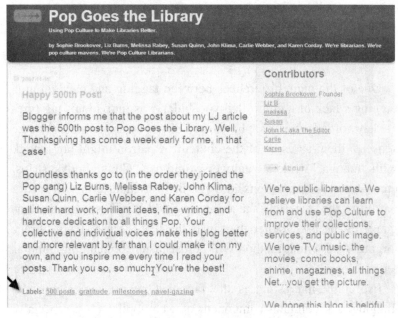

Figure 6.7 Labels (tags) as displayed in Blogger

of which will continually update as you add new tags. (You can even use SnapShirts [www.snapshirts.com] to create a T-shirt with an image of your current word cloud.) The words are random in a tag cloud, but their size indicates the frequency of use. You may be surprised at the tags you use a lot! Take a peek at the tag cloud (called "label cloud" in Blogger) from Tea Cozy (Figure 6.8). Certain terms and phrases such as "Buffy Quote of the Week," "poetry Friday," and "reviews" jump out, letting you know that these topics are most frequently talked about on the blog. Words that appear in a smaller font are used less frequently. Click on any one of these terms to get a list of all the posts labeled with that tag.

LABEL CLOUD

1st Annual Kidlitosphere Conference 48 Hour Book Challenge ALA articles awards **Best Books of 2006** Best Books of 2007 best books read in 2007 Blog Of the Day bloggers blogging blogs books Buffy Quote of the Week Carnival of Children's Literature cybils fantasy fiction GN graphic novels Harry Potter historical fiction humor Internet Fun interviews Kidlit Conference kidlitosphere Meme middle grade non fiction not a blog but hey I like the label picture books poetry poetry Friday Printz realistic reviews Robert's Snow: for Cancer's Cure sbbt summer blog blast tour TV YA YA books for adults YALSA

Figure 6.8   Label (tag) cloud from Tea Cozy

Social Networking Sites

At the time of publication, MySpace (www.myspace.com) and Facebook are locked in a battle for supremacy among social networking sites. Both sites allow members to customize their profiles by uploading photos and music, and both encourage networking by giving users the ability to designate other users as friends and to join a wide variety of interest groups. At present, MySpace's popularity seems to have peaked, while Facebook is enjoying continuing increases in membership. Sophie personally prefers Facebook, where her list of friends includes colleagues, family members, friends from college and high school, and even some of her teen patrons from the public library. We encourage you to explore both options (as well as whatever new networking sites emerge in the coming years) to market library collections, services, and programs to your users, as well as to maintain a presence where your users live online.

Photo Sharing

Photo-sharing sites are both fun and powerful—in large part because they are so easy to use, particularly for those who love to take photos and don't want to spend time writing. No writing, no proofreading—just upload your photographs, add some descriptive captions, and you're done. At a personal level, your great aunts who live a thousand miles away can now see your kids' cute Halloween costumes *on* Halloween. At a professional level, your patrons can watch the decoration and transformation of your children's department in almost real time.

We're going to talk specifically about Flickr because we both use it, and so do many libraries. Flickr is a massive photo-sharing community. Members can upload a maximum of 100 photos for free, or pay to upgrade to an unlimited number of photos. (In 2008, the upgrade cost $24.95 a year.) Other photo-sharing sites include Photobucket (www.photobucket.com) and Picasa Web Albums (picasaweb.google.com); Picasa also has a free software download for organizing and editing photos.

When you create an account to easily upload your photos, all of your images are stored (and backed up!) somewhere other than your personal computer or server. You can tag photos with labels reflecting their content, such as "Whoville Public Library," "storytime," or "author program." You can also determine the privacy setting on a photo-by-photo basis. Maybe your teens love to see photos of themselves whooping it up at a lock-in, but are shy about sharing them with the world; or, maybe you're using Flickr to help educate them about the different levels of privacy (or lack thereof) on the Internet. Tag all of your teen photos with "teen advisory board," mark them as accessible only by Friends, and then add all of your teen advisory board members as Friends in Flickr.

If you already showcase photos on your library's website, you may be wondering what benefits Flickr offers that you don't already enjoy from your current arrangement. Some of the more interesting uses of Flickr by libraries include:

- **Tours** – Grab your camera, walk in the door of your library as if it's the first time, and take a ton of photos. Upload them to Flickr, arrange them into a set called "Tour," and provide a virtual tour to your community! The next time you go on a school visit or other outreach event, you can take the entire group on a tour via the magic of Flickr.

- **Programs** – Document everything from storytimes and author visits to impromptu celebrations and gaming events using Flickr. Allen County Public Library in Indiana has a wonderful variety of photo sets showcasing their programming. We are particularly fond of their Talk Like a Pirate Day photos (www.flickr.com/photos/acplinfo/sets/7215760219 6843961)

- **Transformations** – In 2006 and 2007, Georgia State University Library underwent massive changes, and the savvy librarians who work there decided to track the changes and progress using Flickr. You can see the results by browsing their sets (www.flickr.com/photos/gsulibrary/sets). Be sure to look at the Grand Opening Event set to see how it all turned out!

- **Displays** – A common problem with that display of new books or films is that your artfully arranged materials fly off the shelves! Patrons are always asking for new items. In addition to posting lists of new items to your website, you can upload photos of your displays and new items before anyone has a chance to check them out. Patrons can now see at a glance all the new books, CDs, and DVDs, and can place holds immediately (especially if you provide a link to the items' catalog records in the captions to their photos in Flickr).

- **Student projects** – Teachers and school librarians have embraced Flickr in a big way, from a second grader's Flat Bobby (her version of Flat Stanley) project, starting in New Hampshire and traversing the globe (www.flickr.com/photos/tracylee/sets/1749585) to Lewis Elementary School's 2007 Community Care Day in Portland, Oregon (www.flickr.com/photos/lewiselementary/sets/72157601655549404) to Osage Middle School's Bluebirds project in Shamong, New Jersey (www.flickr.com/photos/srussell/sets/72157600938116644). What a fantastic way to show parents and administrators what their children are learning and doing. Brilliant!

- **Read a book** – Invite patrons to take photos of themselves reading books and share them on Flickr. Hennepin County (MN) Library often invites customers to share photos of themselves reading books. Their book for summer 2007 was, unsurprisingly but appropriately, *Harry Potter and the Deathly Hallows*. You can see the results at www.hclib.org/pub/bookspace/hpphotos.cfm.

- **Library promotional material** – Create attractive, collectible calling cards for your library using Flickr's partnership with MOO (www.moo.com/flickr). You can select a variety of images or just one iconic image (such as a parent and child reading together, or your library's logo) to print up on the cards, which come 100 to a box.

Of course, we urge you to be mindful of your existing library guidelines on copyright and permissions. You wouldn't use other people's content without permission in your library newsletter, so don't do it on your blog. Likewise, you wouldn't use a photo without copyright permission on your website or on posters, so don't use those photos in your Flickr account. If you require signed releases from patrons and parents of storytime toddlers before using their photos on your website, then yes, you'll also need releases for those photos you make public via Flickr or another online photo-sharing service.

Social Bookmarking

We've all saved favorite websites on our computers. But if you move from computer to computer at work, or sometimes bring work home to tinker with on your personal computer, keeping track of all those links can get a little confusing. It's even more confusing when multiple people use the same computers, and it can be frustrating when your favorites don't move with you.

Enter social bookmarking tools, such as del.icio.us (del.icio.us) and Digg (digg.com). A del.icio.us account stores and shares bookmarks on the Web, so you're not tied to one computer. Basically, you save a web address to your account and use as many tags as you want to label it—del.icio.us is a great way to practice tagging. Because it's quick, easy, and free, you can easily share bookmarked sites with both patrons and staff. Digg takes bookmarking and adds community. Digg users can submit favorite websites ("Digg It"). Based on the number of people submitting, a site becomes "popular," perhaps even gaining front-page status to bring it to the attention of other Digg readers. Readers can also comment on and discuss bookmarked stories.

One possible library application: Add an official "Digg It" button to your library website, or to particular pages or content, to make it easy for customers to "Digg" library programs, posts, and news. The Cleveland (OH) Public Library (www.cpl.org), which uses blog software to update its site quickly and easily, includes buttons for del.icio.us, Digg, Google, Yahoo!, and Technorati at the bottom of each blog post, so that patrons can quickly use any of these Web 2.0 applications for library news. What does this mean? You're not only letting people know the library is aware of these applications and uses them; you're easily enabling people to promote your library.

As with most Web 2.0 technologies, once you rev up your imagination, you can apply social bookmarking in many different ways. Reference providers at multiple locations can share their favorite resources with colleagues and patrons, while children's librarians can share review sites with parents. The City of San Mateo (CA) Public Library (www.cityofsanmateo.org/dept/library) has a del.icio.us page (del.icio.us/SanMateoLibrary) organized by the Dewey Decimal System, while the Ocean County (NJ) Library took one of their local school's summer reading lists and turned it into a tagged del.icio.us page (del.icio.us/srms_summer_reading_list).

Gaming

Gaming has exploded in the library world! The Gaming section on Library Success: A Best Practices Wiki (www.libsuccess.org/index.php?title=Gaming) has a wealth of helpful information, and new and forthcoming books for librarians include *Gamers... in the Library?! The Why, What and How of Videogame Tournaments for All Ages* by Eli Neiburger and *Game On! Gaming at the Library* by Beth Gallaway. What does this mean for pop culture? Neiburger and Gallaway have responded to what their patrons wanted and what their colleagues need to know. Sophie has based gaming programs for teens at her library in part on the model provided by Neiburger's wildly successful gaming programs (co-hosted with colleague Erin Helmrich) at Ann Arbor (MI) District Library (AADL). Full coverage of their ongoing tournaments can be found at AADL's teen blog Axis (www.aadl.org/axis). We're aware that your library may not have many patrons who are interested in gaming. Regardless, don't assume gaming is just a teen thing. There are gamers in every age group—what do you think your grandmother's weekly bridge get-together is?

If you are considering introducing gaming programs, we encourage you to think creatively about your available space. It is never fair when one group seems to take over the library and makes it impossible for other patrons to do what they came in to do. Some libraries are fortunate in having the funding and space to create a separate area for gamers, so that gamers and other computer users can both do their things in peace. If you only have one computer lab or one large meeting room, we suggest that you host dedicated gaming nights on a monthly basis. The computer lab can be dedicated to MMPORGs (massively multi-player online role-playing games), such as RuneScape (www.runescape.com), and the meeting room can be given over to Wii Bowling or Guitar Hero III. That way, the gamers will feel welcome, and the non-gamers will know what nights to avoid if they prefer peace and quiet.

Social Catalogs

According to Wikipedia, a "social cataloging application is a web application that allows users to catalog items (i.e., books, CDs) owned or otherwise of interest to them. Once cataloged, such applications generally allow users to share their catalogs with others, and interact with others based upon shared items."[11] In other words, people use these applications to catalog their own private collections of music, books, and/or DVDs. The "social" aspect comes in when they share their catalog with other users.

LibraryThing (www.librarything.com) allows people to not only create their own catalog of titles, but also to add tags, create reviews, and see what other people say. In a nutshell, LibraryThing is a community centered on books. Hmm ... does that sound familiar? Sadly, most actual library catalogs don't provide the same community-building capabilities. However, more and more libraries are realizing that OPACs are not just tools for cataloging books, but also a way to open the door to user input and create community. LibraryThing and libraries both see value in not reinventing the wheel, and LibraryThing now offers LibraryThing for Libraries (www.librarything.com/forlibraries). This application helps you and your library be community centered. Other online social catalogs include Shelfari (www.shelfari.com) and Goodreads (www.goodreads.com).

Social OPACs

Take a traditional online public catalog. Add social networking tools such as tagging, commenting, and reviewing. What do you get? A social OPAC, sometimes called a SOPAC. Examples include the AADL catalog (www.aadl.org/catalog), Hennepin County (MN) Library catalog (www.hclib.org/pub), and PennTags through the University of Pennsylvania (tags.library.upenn.edu).

Why mess with your OPAC? Why let patrons mess with it? If pop culture is about truly listening to patrons and providing the library experience they want and need, then social OPACs are pop culture OPACs. SOPACs let users, both patrons and staff, customize their experience by allowing tags, comments, and reviews. They create a shared, user-friendly folksonomy. And, finally, social OPACs create ownership of the catalog: ownership by the users.

Podcasting

Wikipedia defines a "podcast" as a:

> ... series of digital-media files which are distributed over the Internet using syndication feeds for playback on portable media players and computers. The term podcast, like broadcast, can refer either to the series of content itself or to the method by which it is syndicated; the latter is also called podcasting. The host or author of a podcast is often called a podcaster.
>
> Though podcasters' web sites may also offer direct download or streaming of their content, a podcast is distinguished from other digital media formats by its ability to be syndicated, subscribed to, and downloaded

automatically when new content is added, using an aggregator or feed reader capable of reading feed formats such as RSS or Atom.[12]

The mechanics of podcasting, along with technology and software requirements, are addressed in books such as *Listen Up! Podcasting for Schools and Libraries* by Linda W. Braun.

Interested in listening to podcasts yourself, either for fun or with a view towards creating one for your library? Check out podcast directories such as Podcast.net (www.podcast.net), Odeo (odeo. com), or the NPR Podcast Directory (www.npr.org/rss/podcast/pod cast_directory.php). Free podcasting tools include Odeo Studio (studio.odeo.com/create/home), Audacity (audacity.sourceforge. net), and PodOmatic (www.podomatic.com).

Podcasting can be pop culture, if your patrons are listening to podcasts. Library podcasts can range from short interviews with local authors and performers to announcements of upcoming library events and staff picks of books and DVDs to the library director sharing updates with the community. Alternatively, the pop culture aspect may lie less in the content than in the creation; you can set up mini recording sessions and help users create their own podcasts at the library. Other ideas for podcasts include library news, patron and staff spotlights, author readings, storytimes, oral histories, and booktalks and reviews, created both by staff and patrons. You can also re-purpose the microphones you purchase for podcasting by using them for online meetings with Skype or other Voice over Internet Protocol (VoIP) telephony.

Video Sharing

YouTube (www.youtube.com) was created in 2005, and was purchased by Google in 2006. Your eyes do not deceive you—it seems to us, too, as though this video-sharing site has been around forever. Once again, we see a simple concept explode into worldwide popularity. Like other social software, YouTube encourages content creation and sharing; it allows tagging and comments, it's easy to use, and it's free!

What can libraries and librarians do with video sharing? Library commercials and booktalks are obvious choices. The Ubiquitous Librarian (known in real life as Brian Mathews, librarian at the Georgia Institute of Technology) blogged about YouTube and libraries in a post called "Do You YouTube?: Creating a Content Channel":

> I wanted to experiment with creating a video community, rather than just a listing of tutorials on the library web site. From observation, students don't use or know how to navigate the library site, so why bury video clips on there? [...] I am promoting the channel concept. Whenever I respond to student email, I include a suggestion that they check out the videos I created to help them do research. I've also had it added to the ME [mechanical engineering] orientation materials (from the school, not the library.) And of course, I've promoted it to faculty. The initial reaction was favorable. The faculty like that it is tailored toward their discipline and I'm hoping they will suggestion future topics or searches.[13]

One obvious application for the content channel approach is to create booktalk videos hosted by staff—these could include retrospectives of a major author, showcases of award-winning titles, or read-alouds of outstanding picture books. Another approach takes advantage of YouTube's analogue to comments on blogs: the response video. If a library patron reads a book based on a library YouTube video, and then posts a response video, you've just started another great, public conversation about library services. Just as with blogs and instant messaging (see the next section), this is about using technology to meet your customers where they live online.

Instant Messaging (IM)

Instant messaging, or IM, "is a form of real-time communication between two or more people based on typed text. The text is conveyed via computers connected over a network such as the Internet."[14] IM programs include AOL Instant Messenger (AIM; www.aim.com), Windows Live Messenger (get.live.com/messenger/overview), Yahoo! Messenger (messenger.yahoo.com), and Google Talk (www.google.com/talk). Wow! That's a lot of IM services. When different people use a multitude of IM programs, what do you do? How to choose? You can aggregate your IM accounts with IM aggregators such as the web-based Meebo (www.meebo. com) or the free download Trillian (www.ceruleanstudios.com).

Why IM? Because your patrons are using IM. Why insist that reference assistance be provided on library terms—in person, or not at all? IM success stories, along with tips, can be found at the Chat Reference Libraries section of the LISWiki (liswiki.org/wiki/List_of_libraries_providing_virtual_reference_services).

Other Technologies

Once you begin adopting and adapting the technologies your patrons use as a pop cultural approach to library services, the possibilities become endless. Take, for example, roving reference. The idea of getting staff out from behind the reference desk and into the library stacks to answer questions and help isn't new, but big barriers have long stymied librarians and administrators' longings to make such a service as efficient as possible. How does the staff person answer the question in the stacks if he or she requires a computer with Internet or catalog access to do so? As more and more libraries provide wireless service, and as smartphones, laptops, and tablet laptops decrease in size and price and improve in the quantity and quality of applications they offer, roving reference becomes much more affordable, practical, and user-friendly. Until now, a roving reference librarian had to drag a customer back to the reference desk and wait for a free computer. Today, the librarian may pull out a PDA and quickly answer the question while strolling the stacks. Roving reference is a great example of how not to fall into the "we tried it before and it didn't work" trap.

Another customer-friendly pop culture technology is text messaging. You want quiet in the library? Texting is an answer! This can be particularly useful when marketing reference services and programming to teens, because teens love to text. Why not create short, text-friendly book reviews to send out to all TAB members? You could also use texting to remind patrons of meetings or to advise them when the library suddenly closes because of a water main breakage or inclement weather. Services such as LibraryElf (www.libraryelf.com) offer the option of sending text messages to users to notify them of due dates and items on hold. To further add to the fun, host an intergenerational program where teens teach "how to text" and point out when it's best to text, when to email, and when to phone.

Voices from the Field

Here are selected responses to the survey question, "How do you incorporate trends in technology—for example, PDAs for roving reference, social networking sites like Flickr, MySpace, Facebook, IM reference—into your library's services? If you do, what do you use, and why? If you don't, why not?"

"Our teens like using MySpace, Facebook on the public access computers. We have wireless access now. We are also working on establishing our web page." —Geri Dosalua, Youth Services Librarian, Artesia (NM) Public Library

"We have a MySpace account, and a Flickr site, but they haven't been well publicized yet so I'm not sure yet of their effectiveness." —Ellen Jennings, Young Adult Services Coordinator, Cook Memorial Public Library District, Libertyville, IL

"Our district has a technology supervisor who sets the tone, and a district technology plan and policy dictates what can be done. We do not have access to social networking sites from the school campus, due to filtering. Our network is for curricular use only and so is limited in that way. We do provide our students with distance learning opportunities and we incorporate several databases to enhance their learning resource environment." —Pat Slemmer, Librarian, Williamstown (NJ) High School

"It has to be budgeted first and approved by the tech department. They push for new technologies—we have a strict policy for Internet use." —Susan Lescure, Media Specialist, George J. Mitchell Elementary School, Little Egg Harbor, NJ

"Our school is using Smartboards, Intelliwriters, document display cameras, teacher websites, and podcasts. Being a new school, we are expected to introduce new technology and keep abreast of emerging technological ideas. All rooms have mounted projectors that are connected to both a TV tuner and the teacher's computer." —Tracey Suits, Media Specialist, Charles S. Rushe Middle School, Pasco County, FL

"We are trying. While I as the director have a personal blog and Facebook, it has been hard, so far, to integrate that into library services. The new website has potential, but I cannot get many staff to even use our intranet." —Michael A, Golrick, Director, L.E. Phillips Public Library, Eau Claire, WI

"We know that the majority of computer users, mostly Young Adults, are going to MySpace and similar sites or are going to sites for music, videos, or games such as Runescape and DarkThrone. We allow this and don't have any restrictions." —Anonymous School Librarian

"Although our children's department has a blog, we do not incorporate any other Web 2.0 applications in the patron communication/marketing process. This is a major failing on our part. I believe every library that is serious about communicating with teens should be on MySpace or

Facebook." —Greg Benoit, On-Call Reference Clerk, Webster (NY) Public Library

"I allow my students to visit MySpace when they have free time in my library. I believe that it provides teachable moments if I can watch the kids on MySpace and tell them how to use it safely." —Anonymous School Librarian

"They [social networking tools] do not belong in a school. They cause too much trouble (for instance, bullying) during the school day. I try to educate students about technology and the role it plays in their life." —Patti Keller, Library Media Specialist, Grafton (MA) Middle School

"We have roving reference with handheld PCs. We use Flickr, MySpace, and a blog. We also have virtual reference and more. We use it because our patrons want it." —Sarah Cofer, Teen Librarian, Worthington (OH) Libraries

"I am on the technology committee and we are speaking about using blogs. Rather, I am speaking about the use of blogs in school. At this time we take time with the local police to warn the students about giving too much information out on the Internet. I give lessons on how to save data on memory sticks or thumb drives. I am always showing classes how to access information through the state-provided databases for research. I want to do more, but the older established faculty is slower to try new things." —Laurie Belanger, Library Media Specialist, Paul Harrison Memorial Library, Lakeville, MA

"I can't use everything because of federal filters in school libraries, but I have found ways to use Ning [www.ning.com], MySpace, and educational blogs and wikis." —Sue Crowther, Librarian, Chicope (MA) Comprehensive High School

"I have a blog—check it out! (zanettimontessori.blog-city.com)—and a link there to another blog (pfeifer.edublogs.org) where I review books of interest to the Montessori community. On the first blog I have links in sup-port of the curriculum and student postings. We aren't allowed to blog in our school system but they are letting me go since it is a library 'informa-tion portal.' Students cannot put their names and we have an incredibly limiting filter through the district that prevents all of social sites from acti-vating—like the link 'student artwork' cannot be viewed when we are at school because it's hosted on Flickr. It is very frustrating to me! Students aren't allowed to blog. I would change this in a heartbeat. What better place to learn about safety and ethics of social sites than at school?" —Teresa Pfeifer, Librarian, Alfred Zanetti Montessori Magnet, Springfield, MA

"I have an unofficial blog and Flickr account, for discussing teen services. I'm hopeful to have these become official in the next few months, and utilize this technology to reach more teens. A roving reference project is in the works, and I'm hoping to advocate for IM reference in the coming year. We have one gaming program planned for the fall, and I hope to have more in the future." —Melissa Rabey, Teen Librarian, Frederick County (MD) Public Libraries

"I teach classes on MySpace and I have a MySpace page for my teen library that has library information, lists of programs, new books, a catalog widget, programming pictures, games, and more. Our library also has a Flickr page for countywide programming. We also have IM reference. I use these services as a sort of 'virtual outreach' to go out into the virtual communities in which the teens inhabit." —Matt Roach, Teen Librarian, Public Library of Charlotte and Mecklenburg County (NC)

"So far, we have found using blogs to be an easy way to share information in-house and with our patrons. We are just at the beginning stages of investigating if any of these trends would be beneficial to our library." —Amy Thurber, Director, Canaan (NH) Town Library

"Our reference desk uses IM reference as well as other online sources to answer questions. We have Refworks and a text-messaging feature on our OPAC so that students can easily make notes on titles outside the OPAC. We also have librarians active in Second Life, providing reference help to InfoIsland and researching ways for the school to participate in this online world. We don't use MySpace, Facebook, or Flickr yet, as we haven't found a use for these sites that would merit the committees and red tape needed to create sites for the library, as it is part of a large institution that keeps control over its name." —Anonymous Academic Library Assistant

"I use Flickr to post photos of school activities, maintain a blog for my library, and use del.icio.us for making hotlists. These are excellent, efficient ways to communicate with digital natives." —Michelle Glatt, Librarian, Chiddix Junior High School, Normal, IL

"We are in the process of creating a Flickr page for the library and hope to have a week or so when students take pictures in the library to appear on the site. We have used Trillian for IM reference for almost a year and it's going fairly well. We're considering how we could incorporate Meebo widgets into our newly reconfigured wiki. We do not have a presence in MySpace or Facebook. Personally, I'm skeptical about the worth of being a part of these social networks as an institution. I see more value in individual librarians making themselves available via Facebook or MySpace on their own terms." —Anonymous Academic Librarian

"We have a MySpace page, which has been quite useful. Patrons message me with programming ideas or items they want us to order. We have talked about doing a MySpace program, to help parents understand why social networking can be positive and to inform the kids about how to safely use the Internet and social networking sites." —Alei Burns, Dallas (TX) Public Library

"We are about to launch our library's Learning 2.0 program modeled on the PLCMC program (ours is iHCPL: a Learning Experience) to train staff and the public on these technology trends. We hope that this will encourage ideas for incorporating these tools into group work life, instead of just some individuals using them personally." —Linda Stevens, Media Specialist, Harris County Public Library, Houston, TX

"I am trying to work with teachers on using aspects of Web 2.0. For example, this past spring I collaborated with a science teacher on a project in which the students used blogs and created class wikis." —David Bilmes, Library Media Specialist, Schagticoke Middle School, New Milford, CT

"We have a relatively new position, 'ebranch librarian,' who will be working on most of this. We offer free and completely open access to the Internet, so patrons can use all of the above-mentioned sites. We have a MySpace manga club, but that is about it." —Daniel Barden, Technical Services Administrator, Alachua County Library District, Gainesville, FL

"I have a blog through LiveJournal that I use for announcements and book reviews. During the summer, teens who report hours for the summer reading program must complete a short book review form. I then upload those reviews into the blog. It's been very successful, as has our teen website. I

like being able to disseminate teen reviews to a wider audience."
—Maryellen Liddy, YA/Reference Librarian, Kinnelon (NJ) Public Library

"I am limited by Department of Education filters and rules as to what I can do. Much of the social networking technology is blocked, but the kids are learning how to blog in a controlled situation and they will use wikis this year to share their work on class projects." —Stephanie Rosalia, School Library Media Specialist, Eileen E. Zaglin School PS225K, Brooklyn, NY

"I personally am pushing for more use of blogging software to make it easier for all of us to keep our website fresh. We have done IM reference, but some of the less-techie librarians were not comfortable with it. (It makes reference interviews harder.) And there was a cost concern, among other things, not just the technology cost, but in human hours. I do think we also have to be careful that we don't alienate our older patrons by over-technologizing. I'm sure we are walking a fine line, because I know that computer savvy, usually younger, patrons appreciate us being hip to new stuff."
—Anonymous Public Librarian

"We don't because organizational policy doesn't accommodate it."
—Anonymous Public Librarian

"I use Flickr to blog with other media specialists. We do not use any social networking sites within our school. However, I have used certain videos from YouTube and information from school library listservs. We do not allow IM because our students are young and there are no controls over whom they may contact. The same is true of social networking sites. I have used both to create lessons, provide links to pages that I create on the computer through the wonderful site Filamentality. This allows me to control the information students utilize and helps protect them from inaccurate and inappropriate resources." —Anonymous School Librarian

"As a small school library, I use del.icio.us to create easily accessed (and easily modified!) link lists for student projects and student interests. I also use LibraryThing to generate dynamic lists of new books in the library on the library blog." —Anonymous School Librarian

"We have a library website but it doesn't get a lot of traffic. We tried a secure discussion board with some of the book clubs and the kids really liked it at first, but eventually got tired of it. I think it was the limited audience reading their posts. Worries about security precluded us opening up the board to the Web as a whole. Security is a big stumbling block. That and the fact that our kids are pretty young (and our population is relatively low on the socio-economic scale—only about half, if that, have computers and Internet access readily available)." —Anonymous School Librarian

"Our library has just put their MySpace up. At the moment, the teen volunteers at the main library are posting. They also created the space. We felt that the larger community 'space' was occupied by young people, and it is a great way to be where they are without going to the mall. The teen volunteers are excited about it and teens are excellent word-of-mouth marketers. We are in the process of discussing the use of RSS feeds and whether they will be a useful tool in getting specific information to teens quickly. We are opening the YA librarians' blog to teens chosen by us. Our patrons have been very active in posting comments to our blogs, so we decided that they should have the opportunity to post on our blog. If not ours, they will be posting somewhere else. We have Live Homework Help and a general virtual reference. Virtual learning is great because the teens feel comfortable with the technology, it's one-on-one, and it's private." —Anonymous Public Librarian

"Our library created a group in Facebook and many of the librarians on staff have individual profiles. We have a notebook PC for providing roving reference and more portable IM/chat reference. Indeed, our IM/chat reference seems to be quite popular. Just last night I spent nearly 30 minutes guiding a student through the research process—while he sat in another library on campus. The kids today like their technology." —Anonymous Academic Librarian

"I teach students about Creative Commons, Fair Use, and Flickr; we make a magazine cover using Flickr tools and pictures from Flickr." —Anonymous School Librarian

"We have worked with podcasting before at our library and we do have a website. Unfortunately, we don't do much more than that because our community is definitely on the 'have not' side of the digital divide. Many patrons do not own home computers, DVD players, etc. and struggle to use these materials even in the library." —Anonymous Public Librarian

"We use Meebo at our Youth Services desk so kids can IM us anytime the desk is open. The youth computers have access to some, but not all, gaming and social sites, due to filtering in the kids' computers. All adult computers can access these sites, and kids can use those computers with parent permission/supervision. We do roving reference, but not with PDAs. One of us is scheduled to roam every weeknight. We will use Flickr for the first time with a silly pet photo contest. We use a blog for our teen advisory board. Our new website interface will also have a blog feature on our teen page, for information only. We opted not to create a MySpace teen page due to the advertisements and their unpredictability." —Anonymous Public Librarian

"Currently, our district board is discussing the use of what they deem as questionable media in the school. Last year, we had an experience with a student filming a teacher without his knowledge and posting a humiliating MySpace video about him. A lot of progressive online technology has come to a halt." —Anonymous School Librarian

"This is the realm of the young. I resist any attempt to institutionalize these trends." —Anonymous Public Librarian

"The library has a blog and an integrated IM interface via AOL on its front page. The reference librarians preferred the AOL interface to the Meebo widget. This service is still in testing." —Anonymous Public Librarian

"We use our library's MySpace very seldom because we feel it is not worth the effort. We have had very little interest from our community in the fact that we have a MySpace. To my knowledge, we have not used Facebook at this point." —Anonymous Public Librarian

"We do it very slowly. If one staff member wants to do it, everyone must give buy-in and be trained in it. IM reference came about for us very quickly—within 6 months from ideation to training to adoption to publicity." —Anonymous Public Librarian

"I did try Facebook, briefly. I felt as if I was spying on the kids—maybe because my own daughter is their age and we live in the town I work in. It seemed too personal for me to be on there as the librarian (and someone's mom). Kids know they can email me when they want to chat and that is usually how I use technology to communicate with them. I would use IM and might consider doing that if others find it very helpful." —Anonymous Public Librarian

"Much of the problem I've encountered with getting libraries to incorporate new technologies comes from fear of the unknown. Many of them believe these technologies are dangerous, not in tune with what public libraries 'should be doing,' expensive, and time-consuming to learn and use. To combat this, I've offered educational programs and encouraged colleagues to attend regional programs as well. The libraries that do send reps to these sessions have come to use blogs, Flickr, and MySpace. I don't know of anyone doing IM reference or using social bookmarking." —Anonymous Public Librarian

Endnotes

1. "portable media player" (definition), PCMag.com, www.pcmag.com/ encyclopedia_term/0%2C2542%2Ct%3Dportable+media+player&i%3D556 96%2C00.asp (accessed August 5, 2007).
2. Apple, "Apple Presents iPod," Apple, October 23, 2001, www.apple.com/ pr/library/2001/oct/23ipod.html
3. Apple, "Apple Introduces the New iPod," September 12, 2006, www.apple.com/pr/library/2006/sep/12ipod.html
4. Norman Oder, "A New Jersey Library Starts Lending Kindles," *Library Journal*, December 13, 2007, www.libraryjournal.com/article/CA651 2445.html
5. Fagan Finder, "All About RSS," Fagan Finder, February 19, 2004, www.fagan finder.com/search/rss.php
6. "RSS: Terms for NYTimes.com feeds," *New York Times*, www.nytimes. com/services/xml/rss/index.html
7. "RSS: Other ways to display New York Times headlines," *New York Times*, www.nytimes.com/services/xml/rss/index.html
8. Wikipedia, s.v., "Aggregator," en.wikipedia.org/wiki/Aggregator (accessed August 5, 2007).
9. Wikipedia, s.v., "Wiki," en.wikipedia.org/wiki/Wiki (accessed August 1, 2007).
10. Wikipedia, s.v., "Folksonomy," en.wikipedia.org/wiki/Folksonomy (accessed July 29, 2007).
11. Wikipedia, s.v., "Social cataloging applications," en.wikipedia.org/wiki/ Social_cataloging_applications (accessed August 5, 2007).

12. Wikipedia, s.v., "Podcast," en.wikipedia.org/wiki/Podcast (accessed May 2, 2008).

13. Brian Mathews, "Do You YouTube?: Creating a Content Channel," The Ubiquitous Librarian, theubiquitouslibrarian.typepad.com/the_ubiquitous_librarian/2006/07/do_you_youtube_.html

14. Wikipedia, s.v., "Instant messaging," en.wikipedia.org/wiki/Instant_messaging (accessed August 1, 2007).

PROGRAMMING THAT POPS

Great programs lie at the heart of a pop culture library's services, especially because they serve so many varied purposes. Programs provide an opportunity to cross-market your collections of books, music, and films. Programs give you the chance to attract a new audience to your library. Programs are a way to tell stories about your library's engagement with your community, its sense of fun, and its awareness of pop culture trends. Most of all, programs let you connect effectively with your community members in ways that are meaningful for them.

We view programming as the ultimate expression of our pop culture philosophy, because programs showcase your collections and services *and* integrate them with events that reach out to *and* bring together members of your community. In other words, not only do they let you walk the walk, but they encourage you to get out there and really strut your stuff.

In Chapter 8, Pop Programming Year-Round: Pop Goes the Year, we suggest some pop-inspired programs for each month. You can replicate these suggestions step-by-step, select and adapt pertinent parts, or use them as a leaping-off point to go in an entirely different direction. Everything is scalable, and of course, we encourage you to make changes to create the best fit for your community. As we've said before, what plays in Poughkeepsie might not fly in Boise, Orange County, or Winnipeg. You may notice that some of the programs we've developed are related to rather serious observances—Patriot Day, Yom HaShoah, and Ramadan, for example. We have included these as an expression of our view that pop culture truly encompasses all areas of human interest and endeavor, not just what shows up on PerezHilton.com or in the pages of *Entertainment Weekly*. Certainly pop culture can be fluffy and frivolous, but it's just as often challenging and thought-provoking; we selected and crafted some of the programs in this and the next chapter to reflect that belief.

Finding Inspiration, Valuing Preparation

Inspiration doesn't just happen. Thomas Alva Edison once said, "Genius is one percent inspiration, ninety-nine percent perspiration." The pop twist on this: "Pop culture programming is one percent inspiration, ninety-nine percent preparation!"

For example, let's say you have a bunch of board games in your library, whether for the after-school crowd or for grownups. You notice that Monopoly is the most popular game, and decide to host a Monopoly tournament. Your preparation involves getting the board games, and doing the organizing to make an all-ages tournament a success. Oh, and don't forget—preparation involves checking the official rules! Just as it is important to know your public performance rights for movies, television shows, and sports events, you need to ask the right questions before creating any program. Take, for example, your Monopoly tournament. You guessed it: If you want to call your program a "Monopoly Tournament" and advertise it as such, there are rules to follow. Check out the Monopoly section of the Hasbro site (www.hasbro.com/games/kid-games/monopoly/default.cfm?page=News/tournament) to find a registration form, an FAQ, and the option to send for a Tournament Kit.

Preparation for successful pop programming includes capturing ideas when inspiration strikes. We encourage you to brainstorm ideas for programs throughout the year and to journal these ideas. If you work for a library system that schedules its programming and events several months in advance, you may have a great idea, but not enough time to meet a newsletter deadline. Don't shrug it off and forget about it! Jot down the theme and some planning notes and throw them in your Outlook or Google calendar (www.google.com/calendar) to use next year.

Sometimes, pop culture is *now*—in response either to current events or to the newest craze (knitting, decoupage, or board games). It's also hard to guess when the Big Celebrity News Story will happen. This could involve a baby, a marriage, a death, an arrest, or a photo. But it will happen, and it will be talked about. Handy news services for celebrities include Defamer (www.defamer.com) and E!Online (www.eonline.com).

Has a celebrity baby been born recently? Display baby name books, as well as books on how to take digital photographs (to take all those baby pictures) and knitting (to make those tiny clothes). Celebrity babies don't need much, other than normal names and privacy, but why don't you contact local shelters and other groups that help less-fortunate parents and babies and, with library board permission, collect needed items? Maybe your crafters can knit booties or sweaters.

What about celebrity marriages, divorces, and deaths? These can provide an opportunity not only to display legal books, forms, and resources such as FindLaw (www.findlaw.com), along with various etiquette and planning books, but also to have programs about financial planning to cover significant life events.

What do you do when your schedule must be finalized two months ahead of time, and you (and your patrons) want to do it *now*? Our suggestion: Build in a little flexibility when you draft your programming calendar to allow for just this type of thing. Instead of scheduling a program every Saturday, for instance, always block out one free Saturday (or weekday night or afternoon). This serves the express purpose of leaving a meeting room open for a program that is perfect for *now*, yet didn't make your library's PR deadline. Of course, you'll have to be aggressive about publicizing it, since you won't be able to rely on your usual methods. What a great time to utilize some of the technology we talk about in Chapter 6, such as the insta-publish appeal of blogs and podcasts!

When you are thinking about program ideas, find inspiration among your collections. You can showcase an enhanced foreign-language DVD collection with a film festival, complete with discussion groups after the screenings. To build excitement for your graphic novel and manga collections, consider an all-ages extravaganza on Free Comic Book Day (the first Saturday in May; www.freecomicbookday.com). Promote your library's magazine collection (and encourage increased circulation) by hosting an open house. There are as many possible programs, in as many shapes and sizes, as there are library collections.

When you think about who will host or lead your programs, employ a healthy mix of homegrown and imported talent. You have intelligent, passionate, and creative people on your staff who can be resident experts or event hosts—but also look beyond your immediate staff to colleagues at other libraries, and even outside librarianship. To meet the seemingly bottomless appetite for manga and anime-related programming at her branch library, Sophie offers a monthly anime and manga club, as well as manga illustration workshops and information sessions for parents intended to demystify the topic. Of these, Sophie leads only the first—the illustration workshops are led by a member of the anime club, and the information sessions are conducted by an expert from Diamond Comics Distributors. Sophie's role is to scan the landscape, paying close attention to trends (both emerging and entrenched) and responding to them appropriately. She doesn't need to run herself ragged trying to become an expert in anime and manga, when she's more into Brad Bird and Dark Horse comics.

Finally, don't forget to ask your patrons what kind of programs they'd like to attend. You can do this by using a quick online survey, placing a suggestion box at the circulation desk, or through simple face-to-face conversations. Sometimes the best ideas will come from the most casual interactions, so keep your idea-harvesting antennae up!

If a library hosts a program and nobody attends, did it really happen? When you are launching new programs aimed at drawing in new patrons, this is definitely the time to be creative—don't rely on tried-and-true promotions alone. By all means, continue to use methods that have worked for you before, such as posters, fliers, and announcements in the Community section of your local newspapers. Be sure, however, to push the envelope a bit. Who are you trying to reach with your programs, and where can those people be found? The supermarket? Local daycare centers? Comic shops? Schools? Online? Be inventive! Promotion ideas can include publicity in local papers, on blogs, through podcasts, at school libraries, during morning announcements at schools, and in daycare centers, YMCAs, or JCCs.

As you brainstorm ideas, one point bears repeating and remembering: Read the fine print. This book is not a legal guide, nor do we know all of your library policies and local and state laws. Just because we, or a "Voice from the Field," mention a program, that doesn't mean we've included the full legal "to-dos" for running that program. Find out about the permissions you need to have a program—any program. What you have to do (or don't have to do) may vary, depending on factors such as whether you're watching a TV show via your local cable company, viewing it on DVD, or accessing it via an Internet download. Also, don't assume that just because you saw a program done at another library that it means it's OK for you. You don't know what went on behind the scenes, what licenses the library paid for, or what permissions they sought. Often, an "OK" to use something is just an email or phone call away. This is important, because it models copyright compliance behavior for your staff and patrons, it shows respect for professionals in the entertainment field, and, well, it's the law. Besides cultivating a general awareness of the issues, we suggest using such resources as Mary Minow's LibraryLaw Blog (blog.librarylaw.com) and the "Carrie on Copyright" column in *School Library Journal* (www.school libraryjournal.com/community/Copyright/47058.html).

GET THEIR ATTENTION!
BY DEBRA KAY LOGAN

Veteran school media specialist Debra Kay Logan of Mount Gilead (OH) High School shares her experiences in putting a popular ad campaign to work in school libraries.

Got books?

Take the dairy industry's "Got milk?" and milk mustache promotion and combine it with ALA's READ posters, and you've got a successful, legen*dairy* reading promotion that has been used across the country. After all, one of the best ways to foster reading is to have young people see role models reading. The very first "got books?" week happened in Ohio and brought enthusiasm, reading, community involvement, and two cows to a middle school.

Community involvement started well before the week began. A local photographer donated his time and arranged to have nearly 80 8x10 color photographs developed and printed for a token fee. A local frame shop owner mounted the photos and ultimately donated nearly a thousand dollars worth of work and materials. The milk mustache READ photos featured alumni, faculty, staff, choir members, and community leaders. Even local celebrities—athletes, DJs, judges, television anchors, teachers, and then U.S. Treasurer Mary Ellen Withrow (a hometown native)—were among the people who donned milk mustaches, picked up favorite books, and munched cookies for photographs that were displayed throughout the school during the week-long celebration. Even the community canine officer posed with his dog—they were pictured with cookies and dog biscuits on their plate while reading Peggy Rathman's *Officer Buckle and Gloria*. Many participants took a few moments to write statements on why reading is important in their lives. The reading statements were posted with the photographs, and students were encouraged to read them as part of one of many contests that week.

Cookies and milk were not found only in the milk mustache reading pictures. We invited each grade level to participate in a Cookie and Milk Read-In. A local dairy provided flavored milks, and a nearby cookie factory donated cookies. Students spent part of their afternoons reading, drinking milk, and eating cookies. Students were also invited to early morning read-ins in the library. As well, the whole faculty and staff helped to distribute "Caught Reading" coupons to students. Local businesses donated movie passes, ice cream coupons, personal pizzas, roller skating passes, and innumerable other prizes for students who were "Caught Reading." There were enough prizes for every student in the school to win at least one, although many students won several. Even the most challenged reader could be a winner!

English teachers helped track student reading throughout "got books?", which received radio and front page newspaper coverage. We set—and met!—a school-wide reading goal. The culminating event was a visit from A-1 the cow and her calf. Students at the former Taft Middle School in Marion rushed to the windows to catch a glimpse of A-1. During their lunch period, students were treated to the real reward: The vice principal, a true city boy, milked A-1. Students clustered around and petted her calf.

Media coverage was not limited to the community press. Before the week began, members of the middle school student morning news team were sworn to secrecy. They worked in advance to plan and tape a special extended broadcast to launch the week's events. During each morning newscast that week, students and teachers were updated on the day's contests and events. Students from the high school media department helped record and promote the event, and also taped all of the special events. These recordings, along with an interview segment, were used when "got books?" was featured on an extended version of the superintendent's weekly news program on the school's local community access channel.

After the event, the American Dairy Association & Dairy Council Mid East invited me to write a turnkey "got books?" kit, which was originally distributed to all schools in a region that stretched over three states. Several years later, the California Teachers Association arranged to temporarily make the kit available online during their annual Read Across America event.

For me, the true indicator of the success of this promotion occurred during the last few days of that school year. A student with a history of being disenfranchised and uninvolved sought me out to tell me that he had seen A-1 the cow on the district's access channel the night before. The usually silent student spoke fondly and enthusiastically of the cow and beamed as he commented on how nice A-1 was. He concluded that "got books?" week had been the best thing that had happened to him all year.

For more inspiration, make sure you check out the "Voices from the Field" sections at the end of this chapter and Chapter 8. The questions that solicited the best programming ideas were: "Please describe your favorite or most successful program of the last twelve months," and "What kind of pop culture programming do you offer at your library? For what age groups do you offer it? Do you offer programs tied to current events (for example, a *Harry Potter* book-launch party)? Do you create programs to match your collection and community interests as they arise?"

The responses were varied and creative. Needless to say, since we conducted our survey in summer 2007, also known as the summer that the last *Harry Potter* book was published, we had many, many people respond that yes, they held various and sundry *Harry Potter* events, including a lot of "Wizard Rock." Interestingly, some people seemed surprised that *Harry Potter* was included as "pop culture." To them, the boy wizard is now firmly in the "classics" arena. As one school media specialist said: "I do sometimes feature a book that is being made into a movie in as one of my literary club selections. I select books that I would never purchase as my 'free books' from the book fair. I do not consider *Harry Potter* as pop culture. The *Potter* series will continue to be read, just as *The Chronicles of Narnia, Lord of the Rings*, etc. They are classics already." Another public librarian chimed in: "*Harry Potter* as pop culture? Interesting."

Other popular programming ideas centered around manga and anime, ranging from clubs to film festivals, as well as gaming, from Wii to old-school board games. Television shows that inspired programming ranged from *CSI* to *American Idol* to *Amazing Race*. Liz likes to say, "Why reinvent the wheel?" Why, indeed? Here are some ideas to use as inspiration for programming that will work at your library:

- Anime and manga clubs
- Body art
- Book groups
- Car culture (NASCAR, Formula 1, World Rally Cup, Paris–Dakar Rally)
- College preparedness
- Crafts
- Financial planning

- Food and cookery
- Gardening
- Movie/DVD discussion groups
- Regional events (state and county fairs, food, horticultural, and cultural events)

But at My Library ...

Three concerns cropped up over and over again: budget constraints, time constraints, and mission constraints. In one way or another, respondents voiced the concern that "well, that may work at your library, but at my library ..." We hope these suggestions inspire you and show that not all exciting, quality programs involve a lot of money. When you find yourself thinking "but at my library ... " that doesn't mean you cannot do it; it just means that you need to tweak the idea or use it as inspiration for a version that does work at your library.

Librarians are always mindful of just how much something costs. Our suggestion to those libraries with budget concerns (aka: everyone)? We have three letters (and one classic Peter Gabriel hit single) for you: DIY (aka Do It Yourself). Children's and teen librarians are used to doing things themselves, reducing the cost to "only" the time spent in prep and materials. We have done children's and teen's programming ourselves and fully realize how much is involved in DIY programs, but sometimes staff outside these areas don't get it. We've heard horror stories of YA librarians with a teen program that starts at 7 PM who are scheduled on the reference desk until 7 PM. The adult services supervisor is used to programs that just require unlocking the meeting room door, making sure the seats are set up, and saying "Hi, what do you need" to the outside presenter. In many cases the YA (or children's) librarian *is* the presenter, and so needs time to create the program, get supplies together, and set up the room. Look at the talent in your library, and give them support for DIY by allowing them the time they need to create and run quality programs.

Beyond DIY, make use of local experts who might be willing to donate their time and expertise. Pull out the local business listings to see who may be able to provide interesting programming. A local dance studio may agree to a one-time free class. Professors and teachers from local universities, colleges, and schools probably have talents and interests to share. Also look to your local, state, and federal government, which have their own outreach and education goals. For example, the New Jersey Department of Banking and Insurance Office of Public Affairs has an Education Section that offers various Consumer Awareness Programs such as "Identity Theft—It Could Happen to You" (www.state.nj.us/dobi/division_consumers/pdf/educationprograms.pdf). When compiling your list of experts, include people in the library who you may not think of at first, such as the student page whose passion is film. Teens are a fabulous resource and often have a lot of fun planning and running special children's programs around *Harry Potter*, Lemony Snicket, and *The Lord of the Rings*.

Work with your local Friends group to get additional funds for big-ticket items. If you are concentrating on teen services, why not have your teen librarian (or better yet, one of your teenage customers) attend the Friends meetings? This way, when you ask for money, the Friends can put a face to the person asking, and you can draw on an ongoing positive relationship. Liz ran a big anime night that involved collaboration not only with local experts (the high school anime club) but also with the Friends group, who helped out both by providing funds and by attending. The Friends had just as much fun as the teens! Don't have the money to buy a Wii or games like Dance Dance Revolution and Guitar Hero III? Ask your Friends! Be ready to demonstrate how the console and games will benefit your library's programming popularity—and be ready to allow the Friends to play when they see how much fun it is!

When it comes to time constraints, we agree—having to create program calendars two to six months ahead of time can be problematic! We hope that the year-round calendar in Appendix B will be a useful tool to inform you of pop culture events before they are reported in the paper. As we mentioned earlier, we do encourage you to leave some free time in your meeting room schedule to gain some flexibility in your programming. Worst-case scenario when you have a great idea but no time, room, or money for a flashy program? Displays! Book and material displays, along with posters, can be put together on the spur of the moment and can be as big or little as space allows. Those displays can also include fun quizzes, such as "match the superhero to the movie."

Time constraints may also mean that you just don't have time to do it all. It seems like every month, every week, every day even, could inspire an amazing program. Yes, we give you a lot of food for thought here, but think of this as a buffet. You don't have to eat everything; you don't have to do everything. Sometimes, it may simply be a matter of dressing up an old program in new threads. Sometimes, being a librarian seems like spinning plates—you know you can only manage so many plates, er, programs, at one time. The hardest thing isn't saying "no" when you want to say "no," but saying "no" when you want to say "yes."

We've also heard that library mission statements do not support or incorporate pop culture. Chapter 4 talks about looking at your mission statement to see if what you are doing fits, and about updating your mission statement to fit the library you have now, not the library that existed five or 10 years ago when the statement was drafted. A few school librarians we surveyed flatly stated that the mission of schools is separate from pop culture and that pop culture has nothing to do with school libraries. With that in mind, we were particularly impressed with those who found ways to make pop connections to their curriculum, such as supporting assignments with fun, attention-grabbing exhibits, or calling tests "Who wants to be a

Millionaire/Infoaire." We especially liked Sue Crowther's (Chicopee [MA] Comprehensive High School Library) idea of using social networking sites to get teenagers interested in *Romeo and Juliet*. Other inventive uses of pop culture are found in the "Voices from the Field" sections of this and the next chapter.

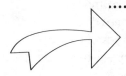

FANWHAT? STORIES BEYOND THE BOOKS: AN INTERVIEW WITH CARLIE WEBBER

Sophie chatted with Carlie Webber, Young Adult Services Librarian, Bergen County Cooperative Library System, Hackensack, New Jersey, and contributor to the Pop Goes the Library blog, to find out more about "fandom."

What is "fandom?"
Fandom is the community, usually found online, that revolves around mutual admiration of a book, movie, TV series, band, or even a Broadway show. Within fandoms, there are often events like conventions (called "cons"), essay or fanfiction writing festivals, vidding competitions (creating fan-made music videos), or chats about certain episodes of shows.

What is your fandom?
I'm involved in the *Harry Potter* and *Numb3rs* fandoms. They're not as diametrically opposed as their central plots might lead one to think, but they operate very differently. *Harry Potter* is a large, splintered fandom where you get thousands of opinions, stories, and pictures. There are probably millions of *Harry Potter* fan works and discussions. *Numb3rs*, although it is a popular show, has a much smaller, cohesive fandom. It's not even in the top five of the most popular TV show fandoms. (Those, I would have to say, are *Supernatural, Buffy, Smallville,* the *Stargate* franchises, and *Battlestar Galactica*.) There aren't as many discussions and you often see the same players at many fan "events." The best analogy I can think of is comparing a small

liberal arts college to a Big Ten school. You'll get an education in both, and write papers and go through all the standard academic and college life motions, but your influences and environment are very different.

What does fandom have to do with libraries? For example, we clearly get it that libraries will have *Harry Potter* books, movies, and related books. But is there anything else that libraries do that can reach out to their patrons who are fans? What types of programs or other materials can we provide? Do fandom-involved folks even want to be reached out to by their libraries?

Fandomers, although we're generally quiet about our activities except to fellow fandomers, are often very knowledgeable about popular culture and want to see our favorite TV shows, books, and movies get shelf space. We always know when the next season of our show will be out on DVD. We always know where the actors from our favorite TV shows appear in other series and movies, and when we find a new actor whose work we enjoy, we'll often seek him or her out in other roles. For example, I didn't watch *Serenity* (the movie based on Joss Whedon's one-season TV show *Firefly*) until I'd been a *Numb3rs* fan for a while and learned that David Krumholtz played Mr. Universe!

To appeal to library patrons who are fandomers, I think the most important thing to do is be aware of the movies, books, and TV shows that have a cult following, that is, a smaller following of very loyal viewers. (*Harry Potter* is the exception to all fandom rules because of its enormous popularity.) A cult following can have a huge influence on a TV show or movie's staying power and place in popular culture. The best example of this is *The Rocky Horror Picture Show*. It died quickly in the theaters and would have faded into obscurity had it not been for cult fans who turned it into an interactive experience. Movies and TV shows that gain a cult following often have longer staying power, and therefore more circs for your collection, even though they may not have huge numbers of fans. Cult shows and movies usually appeal to those who like to watch with their brains as well as their eyes, and may even appeal to people who are big readers but who don't watch a lot of TV.

As far as programming, fanfiction workshops can work, but when planning one you'll have to decide if it will be open to all fandoms or just one or two of the big ones, like *Harry Potter* or *Star Wars*. One program that might be fun would be to have a *Rocky Horror*-esque viewing of popular fandom films, where the audience is encouraged to laugh and talk back to the movies. Book-and-movie discussions are always great for hardcore fans. You could even run an ongoing TV viewing series, in which you could take something like *Star Trek: The Next Generation* and watch one season two episodes at a time over the course of a number of weeks.

The most important thing to remember when planning fandom programs is that everyone's level of participation in a fandom is different, and not everyone participates the same way. Some people in the *Harry Potter* fandom, for example, are essayists. They will write pages on the Moony-Wormtail-Padfoot-Prongs relationship but never once write a work of fanfiction in which Harry and Hermione fall in love. Some people read fanfiction (works written by fans exploring that which does not happen "on stage" in the book, movie, or TV show) and enjoy writing it. Some read it but never write. Some participate in discussions on boards and blogs. Some are fans of the canon and just want to lurk and view other people's spin-offs of the original creation. And although many fandomers take a *Fight Club* stance on their fandom involvement, i.e., "The first rule of fandom is: You don't talk about fandom," you can still hold programs that will appeal to fans of a work and will not force people to reveal their level of fandom involvement. *Harry Potter* fanfiction writers will come to your book discussions and movie showings, but they might never talk about their writing for any number of reasons. Whether or not they talk, though, they always appreciate your library's making an effort to recognize their interests.

Voices from the Field

We received some great program suggestions that failed to tie in neatly with the calendar of pop in Chapter 8, Pop Programming Year-Round: Pop Goes the Year. So, here are great pop culture programming ideas you can use any time of the year!

"Health class collaboration. Health students come to the library (or us to their classroom—each student has a tablet/laptop) and we provide instruction/program for the following topics: magazines, fiction, database searching, consumer health info, and a 'Who wants to be a Millionaire/Infoaire' for their final exam (review of health and information literacy issues)."
—Anonymous School Media Specialist

"My personal favorites are craft programs. I love that the 'learn to knit' programs of two years ago have evolved into a group that meets here weekly to knit and crochet together. Travelogues remain a successful choice for seniors." —Anonymous Public Library Assistant

"We had a scavenger hunt during last year's Teen Read Week, in partnership with the local middle schools. The point was to familiarize the teens with the adult reference and young adult literature sections of the library. The teachers made it an assignment and we provided motivation by entering those who participated into a drawing for an iPod, donated by the Friends of the Library. We had almost 400 students participate that week. It was awesome!" —Ellen Jennings, Young Adult Services Coordinator, Cook Memorial Public Library District, Libertyville, Illinois *(Authors' Note: We like that not only does this reflect the needs of your teen customers, and show a great collaboration with the schools, but bonus points for using the pop culture interest of the kids—an iPod—as a further draw.)*

"Students in my public middle school actually set up and run the fall book fair. We have dollar value goals, where teachers in the school volunteer to do crazy things at the pep rally if we reach certain goals. This raises money for extra library programming, gets the students involved (some students otherwise do not have a place), and promotes unity with the staff. It is a lot of fun!" —Anonymous Public Librarian

"Hard to miss summer reading, but one of our newest programs is our 'Active Afternoons at the Library.' It's a gaming afternoon for teens, once a week. We have a Wii and a PS2, teens with library cards in good standing can come in to play, and we are organizing tournaments as well as offering board games around the perimeter of the room if they want to play something else while waiting for their turn. Has been very successful, organized by our Adult and Children's services librarians." —Anonymous Public Library Administrator

"Feng Shui; Lebanese Dancing." —Anonymous Public Librarian *(Authors' Note: We just want to jump in and note that many, many people offered suggestions that involved the food and dance of various cultures, from Lebanese dancing to Irish step dancing.)*

"Sixties. Popular children's stories published in the 1960s such as *Very Hungry Caterpillar* and *Where the Wild Things Are* and associated 'hippy' stories. Crafts centered around a sixties theme, e.g. flower headbands, peace necklaces, tie-dyed butterflies, god's eye weaving, paper bag vests decorated with sixties insignia such as smiley face, peace symbol, yin and yang. Sixties music playing in the background. Lots of fun for kids, staff, and parents." —Anonymous Public Librarian

"Most successful is our teen magazine. We produce it two to four times a year using Microsoft Publisher. Teens are involved in all aspects—content, design, layout, production, and distribution. Lots of teens can be involved in one way or another." —Anonymous Public Librarian

"My favorite program immediately prior was a two-part program that brought in staff from a local makeup counter followed by a hairdresser/colorist for styling/beauty tips. Girls were very happy and their mothers wanted to come, too. It is being repeated regularly throughout the system." —Anonymous Public Librarian

"Nintendo Night (and I'm not just saying that because of the topic of your book!) It was a two-hour program on a Friday night this summer, and permission slips were required. Forty-two kids were there … I could have used another adult and a bigger room! Kids entering grades 6 to 12 brought their GameBoys (any version). We also set up my original NES on the TV with a selection of games, and hooked a kid's GameCube up to the library's projector for four-player *Super Smash Bros Melée*. While those were going on, I ran a *Pokemon* tournament for both SP and DS (different versions of the game for different systems). It was a huge success, and they are all asking when we will do it again!" —Gretchen Ipock, Young Adult Librarian, Sellers Library, Upper Darby, PA

"Knitting for Peace day! Library welcomed knitters of all ages for the whole day. One of the most successful adult programs I've seen. Knitters everywhere! Plus, famous knitter/author Betty Christiansen."
—Anonymous Public Librarian

"We've had *American Girl* offerings for the younger children, and I did a Teen Food Fear Factor last year. I've also done *Jeopardy!* style trivia contests. Periodically, I'll run a 'Win Your Favorite CD' or 'Win Your Favorite DVD' contest, which is a great way to gauge teen interests and shape collection development accordingly. Most of the teen programs are offered to grades five and up." —Maryellen Liddy, Teen/Reference Librarian, Kinnelon (NJ) Public Library

"All my programs are planned by asking myself 'What will hook my teens?' We have an anime club. We have henna parties. We had *Harry and the Potters* five days after the release of the last book in the series. We've done several duct tape events, knitting, and for Teen Read Week we had a program called 'booktalks and a chocolate fountain.' So basically most of my events have a tie into pop culture." —Tammy Imel, Teen Librarian, Kanawha County Public Library, Charleston, WV

"Since our community is primarily Hispanic, we offer computer classes in English and Spanish. During the Spanish computer class, we offer a bilingual kids' fun zone so that parents can attend the computer class and not worry about arranging for a babysitter for their children. In conjunction with the Central library, we are involved with a large Quinceañera event."
—Alei Burns, Youth Librarian, Grauwyler Park Branch Library, Dallas, TX

"We host a week long 'Library Arts Café' each spring. Each day has a theme: Rock Band Day, Theater, Visual Arts, etc. On that day, students perform each class period to English classes and study hall students that arrange to visit. For example, on Rock Band Day, student bands truly rock the library. We also have a refreshment area, our 'coffeehouse,' during this week, which is our fundraiser for the year (instead of a book fair). Every student in the school visits at least once during the week; many are able to come several times because of their study halls." —Anonymous School Media Specialist

"We have … put on *Whose Line Is It Anyway?* We've also had forensic science programs, relating back to the TV program *CSI*, some of whose TV series DVDs are located in the Teen Section. Some branches host anime over lunch for teens in the summer. We've also offered 'Steppin' because of the movie *Stomp the Yard*. And we done a few knitting programs because it seems to be becoming more popular. I also put out a display every year for '*American Idol*: Who's Goin' Down?' Kids vote each week on who will get voted out, and we write sarcastic remarks about each one kicked off who was especially bad. Prizes are awarded, but many aren't picked up because the kids just like to vote and then see what we write on the poster about the losers." —Anonymous Public Librarian

"Orientation of newly assigned airmen at [the air force base where our library is located]. We sign them up for a library account, hand out informational materials, i.e. guides to electronic resources, CLEP/DANTES study materials, access to local public libraries and their materials, and [we] give them a quick refresher on how to use the library. … Because we have an emphasis on leadership/management/Air Force history in our AF Chief of Staff Collection and our newly created Wing Commander Collection, we'll be introducing lunchtime book discussion groups for those collections." —Anonymous Special Librarian

"We celebrated National Candy Month in June. We had a life-sized Candyland game, candy craft, and a bubble gum blowing contest interspersed with candy-themed books. I only had a handful of kids but it was so much fun!" —Anonymous Public Librarian

"We had Charlotte's Web Country Fair this past spring that drew 35, which was good, considering it was not in season. We had different activities going on at the same time, and despite the lack of staff, we managed pretty well." —Anonymous Public Librarian

"A Spa program (middle school pop culture seems very oriented around body image)." —Mary Neuman, Youth Services Librarian, Asotin County Library, Clarkston, WA

"A series of Armchair Travel programs co-sponsored with the community education department. This attracted people of all ages to the library." —Anonymous Public Librarian

"The Antiques Appraisal, which the library did not sponsor—our local Historical Society used our meeting room to host it. The library was just the venue." —Anonymous Public Librarian

"We do a lot of costume character programs geared toward families, with characters from popular books/series (*Curious George, Mudge, Peter Rabbit*, etc.). This summer, my co-librarian set up a couple programs where folks from a local *Star Wars* fan club came to the library in costume to talk about *Star Wars*, sign autographs, and things like that. We had more than 100 people at each program. We try to run programs that tie into our collection in some way (and our *Star Wars* collection is truly an impressive thing to behold), and we've had a lot of success with that." —Adrienne Furness, Children's and Family Services Librarian, Webster (NY) Public Library

"*Whose Line Is It Anyway?* It was led by two high school students (from the Teen Advisory Board) who led all the audience members in improv games. The participants loved it and got very involved. We are having the two teens who led it perform here in September with their own nationally known improv group because they were so terrific!" —Anonymous Public Librarian

"For Teen Read Week (ALA), I try to have a local graphic artist come in to work with students after school, and I look for donations of graphic novels from the local bookstore to use for door prizes/raffles. For World Language Celebration, I offer a Top Ten of the Week list written in Latin, French, and Spanish, which the students have to translate into the English titles and tell what language they are written in. The contest is entitled 'World Languages Rock,' and I encourage research to the websites I used (iTunes, radio stations) to enable the students to figure out the song titles." —Anonymous School Media Specialist

"Teaching sock knitting in a three week program. Have done this several times over the last four years. Local knitters now meet monthly at the library! Asked to do other classes (mittens and simple lace scarf)." —Anonymous Public Librarian

"Family Jam has been the most successful. It is 25 minutes of music and movement to recorded songs once a week during summer library club, in place of traditional storytimes, which stop during the club. It is for 1- to 5-year-olds and their caregivers. Each week is a different genre (rock and roll, jazz, country, traditional, folk, tropical). We do flannel boards to songs, bubbles, beach balls, shakers, clappers, scarves, movement. We give it a storytime format, beginning with 'If You're Happy and You Know It' and ending with a different version of the Hokey Pokey each week. Everything from the Beatles to Joanie Bartels. We allow 60 people in a session for crowd control and safety, but we always turn people away (we're working on that for next year.) My favorite has been Weird Science, usually fourth to eighth grade boys, where we do weird at-home type science projects. I do it before Halloween, have stations, get messy, play old black-and-white sci-fi films in the background, make goop and rock candy, and plastic, and stack liquids and all that stuff you can find on the Internet. I had a 'guess the monster's body parts' with peeled tomatoes and grapes and cold noodles and gross stuff to touch while blindfolded. Boys just love to mess around, and it is a fun mad scientist thing to do before Halloween."
—Anonymous Public Librarian

"I did a presentation two months ago for the Tucson Computer Society, in which I showed the library's web site and some of our databases for research. There were nearly 100 people present, and several contacted me afterwards to arrange presentations for other organizations of which they are part. This was a good outreach opportunity, and made me some good contacts." —Anonymous Public Librarian

"Genealogy program sponsored by the library, DAR, local genealogy society and local museum." —Anonymous Public Librarian

"My teens most enjoy our Silent Scavenger Hunt—it is just that: They have to locate bits of information and objects around the library but they may not speak. They are given a notebook and pen to write down their questions." —Kimberly Paone, Supervisor, Adult/Teen Services, Elizabeth (NJ) Public Library

"On August 3 we had our first murder mystery dinner ... and the teens planned it totally by themselves. It was improv style (à la *Tony n' Tina's Wedding* ... interactive with audience participation and no assigned lines, just cues) and it was lots of fun. The teens were so excited to execute a program start to finish, and the fact that the audience enjoyed it was icing on the cake!" —Saleena Davidson, YA/Reference Librarian, South Brunswick Public Library, Monmouth Junction, NJ

"The 4th Annual Literary Luncheon! We selected 40 volunteer sixth graders to read *Lizzie Bright and the Buckminster Boy* and gave copies of the book to the senior citizens in town as well. In June when all were done reading, our library hosted a luncheon at which we discussed the book and the importance of reading it. We dined together on treats the parents and PTO provided in the decorated library filled with flowers and table cloths." —Anonymous School Media Specialist

"Fashion Fabuloso generated a great response from the teens. They brought their own T-shirts to cut, tear, etc., and had a blast. Afterward we took pictures of them posing à la *Fame*. It was fabulous." —Anonymous Public Librarian

"During the Teen Summer Reading program this year, we held a Mystery Game Night called 'Panic at the Prom.' Ten teens each took a character and made it their own. They dressed up in prom costumes, and several of the girls played boys, which made it extra funny. They decorated the room in streamers, balloons, and party favors to make it look like a high school prom, and played up their roles as much as possible. The Teen Library Council said this was their favorite summer program. They even liked it more than the Anime Festival, which was also extremely popular." —Anonymous Public Librarian

"We did a Pirate Ball in celebration of last year's 'International Talk Like a Pirate Day,' which I thought was fantastic." —Anonymous Public Librarian

POP PROGRAMMING YEAR-ROUND:
POP GOES THE YEAR

With programming, we're giving you license to be bold, to exercise your creativity, and to have fun! Since this is not strictly a programming book, and since each month can yield up to 31 days of unique programs, please regard the programs we describe here as just a beginning—an apéritif, if you will, to whet your appetite for the smorgasbord of programming possibilities represented by the full holiday and special event calendar in Appendix B.

Similarly, we don't want you to feel hemmed in by the calendar we provide—you need to keep your programming current, so give yourself and your staff the permission and mental space necessary to create additional programs nimbly, or even on the spur of the moment. The death of a noted author, entertainer, or politician might be the impetus for a book discussion, a film festival, or a panel discussion about the deceased's cultural contributions during the following week. On a happier note, when your local university goes to the national playoffs for the first time ever, you can celebrate with displays on the sport and the school, a TV tuned in to the big game, and a visit from one of the team's coaches or players. You will find additional ideas in various "Voices from the Field" sections throughout the chapter, hearing from library staff—from directors to librarians to paraprofessionals—who have shared their programming ideas with us.

January

Super Bowl

Held in late January or early February, the Super Bowl is one of the most-watched sports events of the year in the U.S. It's not just fanatical football fans who empty supermarket shelves of chips, salsa, bite-sized candies, beer, and soda, though. Thanks to the flashy halftime show and the creative, funny ads that run throughout the game, the Super Bowl attracts a broad cross-section of the viewing public. Capitalize on this phenomenon by holding your own Super Bowl party! To hold public viewings of shows on television, you must arrange for a business account with the local cable company of your choice. Public libraries fall under government accounts, the terms of which are not terribly pricey.

Before moving forward with a Super Bowl screening, consider your contract with your cable provider, your TV's screen size (potentially limited for public showings), whether you'll be charging admission, and how (and if) the event will be advertised. We cannot give you all the answers, and it's entirely possible that you should also ask yourself additional questions. We encourage you in the strongest possible terms to check on all of these issues before proceeding, because they are just as important as having a license to show movies in the library. Check with your cable provider; read the fine print.

Ramp up the excitement in the weeks leading up to the Super Bowl by hosting a football film festival. Screening films such as *Any*

Given Sunday, Friday Night Lights, Rudy, Remember the Titans, The Longest Yard, The Waterboy, and *Bring it On* during the two weeks prior to the Super Bowl will provide excellent word of mouth for the *pièce de résistance.* Organize the party however you want, but we suggest a potluck. Keep the library open on a Sunday night (yes, a Sunday night!) and ask for (paid!) staff volunteers to host the party. You'll want people who are sociable, organized, willing to refill the chip bowl, and who can work the circulation desk. Keep the circulation desk open, because there will be lulls in the game, and the people who come for the halftime show or the commercials will want to be able to browse and check out items. Remember: This is an open house, not a lock-in, so you'll want to keep the doors open and the atmosphere welcoming.

Do staffing issues and/or building constraints make it impossible for you to stay open on a Sunday night? Show your team pride, and let your community know you are jazzed about the upcoming game (yes, librarians watch sports!) by having a Team Jersey Day right before the Big Game. Staff members who wear a sports jersey from their favorite team (yes, their godchild's soccer team counts) advertise their love for sports just by the clothes they wear. Advertise the day ahead of time, with an added incentive: Fines will be waived for any patron who comes in that day wearing a team shirt! The basics of this program can be applied to any important sports event (including those that aren't scheduled for Sunday nights).

Related Links

Amazon.com list of films available on DVD, searched by keyword "American Football," www.amazon.com/s/ref=nb_ss_d?url= search-alias%3Ddvd&field-keywords=american+football

Motion Picture Licensing Company, www.mplc.com

Official Site of the Super Bowl, www.superbowl.com

Super Bowl Ads Information Clearinghouse, www.superbowl-ads.com

Voices from the Field

Sports-related programming highlights and comments included:

"I have included Olympic or Super Bowl programming to motivate students. For example, we may research a particular city or sport when the Olympics are going on." —Anonymous School Media Specialist

"Local sports including high school displays (community). We try to tap into community interest and also invite those with the interest to present the program." —Anonymous Public Librarian

"Our teen programming (for grades 7–12) is very pop-culture oriented. ... [W]e also try to offer activities for all kinds of teens, so we do fantasy baseball for the sports enthusiasts." —Anonymous Public Librarian

"I just 'launched' the fantasy sports program since they are so huge these days. We try to do anything that is timely." —Anonymous Public Librarian

"Our most popular summer program was the Wii Sports tournament." —Anonymous Public Librarian

"Watch NCAA basketball tournament, World Cup soccer, and other major events in the library, including hosting bracket updates." —Anonymous Teacher-Librarian

"The Eurocup (soccer) is in June 2008, so I will probably tie in with that." —Anonymous School Media Specialist

"We often try and tailor these game nights to reflect some current happenings in the world of Pop Culture. For instance last year sometime around the World Series we hosted a Mario Baseball tournament." —Anonymous Public Librarian

ALA Youth Book Awards

Announced with great fanfare each January at the close of ALA's Midwinter Meeting, the youth book awards given by the Association for Library Service to Children (ALSC) and the Young Adult Library Services Association (YALSA)—particularly the

Coretta Scott King Award, Ralph Caldecott Medal, the Newbery Award, and the Michael L. Printz Award—are the most prestigious awards in literature for children and young adults.

Both school and public libraries can celebrate these awards and claim some ownership over them by holding mock Printz, Caldecott, Newbery, and Coretta Scott King Awards. This is a wonderful opportunity to get children and teens involved in the library, and to give them a stake in something that feels real and relevant to them. It's easy for adults to forget that much of children's and teens' reading is prescribed by school and—particularly in the case of very young children—by parents. Here is an opportunity for children and teens to articulate to the adults in their community what they like and why, and to give those adults reading suggestions of their own.

Mock award discussions can be as simple, or complex, as you want. Consult with your youth services and teen librarians to create a reading list of eligible titles. Publicize and promote this list, and then make sure you have plenty of copies of each title, both for discussion purposes and for other interested patrons. Schedule a date for discussion, have copies of the relevant award rules ready, and let the discussion begin! Highly motivated libraries should consider holding a press conference to announce the awards, featuring the young chairs of the mock award committees as speakers.

For younger kids, turn your fall storytimes into a season-long mock award for both the Caldecott and Coretta Scott King awards. Parents and children are often familiar with older, classic titles; use your storytimes to expose kids and adults to exciting new books and illustrators. While patrons may be familiar with older titles, they may not be aware of who won an award or why. So during the fall storytimes, read as many of the Caldecott winners and honor books as possible with school-aged children. Invite local art teachers and artists to participate in discussions of what made a book worthy of the award.

Once the official and mock awards are announced, trumpet both the winners and the participants in the process by printing out press releases about the awards. Enlarge the releases and display them prominently at the entrances to your children's and young adult departments. These awards are the Oscars of our field, so let's treat them that way! This program could be duplicated for other book awards, as well—consider holding mock Pulitzer, Man/Booker, National Book Awards, PEN Awards, and so on.

Related Links

ALSC Literary Awards, www.ala.org/ala/alsc/awardsscholarships/
literaryawds/literaryrelated.htm
Canadian Library Association Book Awards, www.cla.ca/
awards/bookaw.htm
Children's Book Council of Australia Awards, www.cbc.org.
au/awards.htm
The CILIP Carnegie and Kate Greenaway Children's Book
Awards, www.carnegiegreenaway.org.uk
Costa Book Awards (formerly Whitbread Book Awards),
www.costa bookawards.com
The Man Booker Prize, www.themanbookerprize.com
National Book Awards, www.nationalbook.org/nba.html
Nestle/Smarties Prize, www.booktrustchildrensbooks.org.uk/Home
PEN/Faulkner Award, www.penfaulkner.org
The Pulitzer Prizes, www.pulitzer.org
Sydney Taylor Book Award, www.jewishlibraries.org/ajlweb/
awards/st_books.htm
YALSA Booklists and Book Awards, www.ala.org/yalsa/booklists

Voices from the Field

Book-related programming highlights from our survey participants included:

"Video conferences with Dan Gutman and Judy Schachner." —Anonymous School Media Specialist

"Book Hooks—Classroom activity in library: approximately five to six people per table and two to three books per participant (randomly chosen off of the shelves by the participants or purposely chosen by the librarian, depending on objective of a particular book hook activity). Students have three minutes to peruse each book—covers, flaps, TOC, index, read a chapter, read the end, whatever—they then report to the others on four things: (1) genre of book; (2) types of characters in book; (3) basic plot, story line, episode or theme; (4) if they would read the book and why or why not. Any students who want to participate can; repeat process as time allows." —Anonymous School Media Specialist

"Grade 2 Caldecott Battle of the Books. Students each read 25 Caldecott books and three classes compete with each other by answering questions about the books. Winning class receives stuffed animals from *Where the Wild Things Are* to display in classroom until the next year's battle." —Anonymous Public Library Associate

"Teacher book club. Monthly meetings—each month we all read a different book and discuss. Helps them keep up with trends and what the students are reading." —Anonymous School Media Specialist

"I run a series of reading incentive contests for students that are really well received. They change monthly and are open to any student who wishes to participate. They range from a 'world series' read—where kids join a team and read books from a specific series—to a 'prize' nominating committee that picks a book akin to the AASL prizes." —Judi Paradis, Library Teacher, Plympton School Library, Waltham MA

Chinese New Year

Celebrated over a seven-day period beginning on the day after the second new moon after the winter solstice, Chinese New Year (*nongli xinnian*), also known as Spring Festival (*chunjie*), is the most important of China's major traditional holidays (which also include the Lantern Festival and the Dragon Boat Festival). If your community has a large Chinese population, here is a perfect opportunity to attract members of that community into your library, while educating non-Chinese community members about this important cultural event.

Many people are familiar with the firecrackers, dragon dancers, and red envelopes (called *laisee* in Cantonese and *hongbao* in Mandarin, the two major Chinese dialects) associated with Chinese New Year. Other lesser-known accoutrements of the holiday include displays of tangerines and oranges, which signify luck and wealth, special foods such as mooncakes, and the fact that the Chinese New Year is considered everyone's birthday. Everyone in China adds a year to their age at the New Year, rather than on their actual birthday.

Programming ideas for this holiday abound; here are just a few highlights to get you started. Chinese New Year lends itself beautifully to crafts of all kinds. Take a page from the storefronts of Chinese businesses and festoon your library with patron-made red decorations, which can be as simple as paper chains. These will brighten up your library's decor, and will alert your Chinese patrons that you are honoring their holiday. Host a performance of dragon dancers, either inside or (if weather permits) outside your library. Make it an all-ages program, and invite children to dance along behind the dragon and its attendant musicians.

Reach out to leaders in your Chinese community to find a calligrapher who is willing and able to lead a workshop on Chinese calligraphy. Attendees—as young as eight and as old as they're willing to admit—could create traditional banners of Spring Couplets. According to the Chinese Culture Center of San Francisco, "spring couplets are traditionally written with black ink on red paper. They are hung in storefronts in the month before the New Year's Day, and often stay up for two months. They express best wishes and fortune for the coming year. There is a great variety in the writing of these poetic couplets to fit the situation. A store would generally use couplets that make references to their line of trade. Couplets that say 'Happy New Year' and 'Continuing Advancement in Education' are appropriate for a school" (www.c-c-c.org/chineseculture/festival/ newyear/newyear.html). All-ages programs like these are wonderful community-builders, opening a space for reciprocal teaching across generations.

Since the New Year is also considered everyone's birthday in China, you might consider holding an Everyone's Birthday Party at your library. This program would be particularly effective as a school-wide celebration. Order a cake large enough to feed everyone, and decorate the library with symbols of the 12-year Chinese Zodiac cycle.

Libraries looking for fundraising opportunities could consider raffling off several fruit baskets full of tangerines, oranges, and pomelos, with the funds received dedicated to improving multicultural collections in all departments.

Related Links

Chinese Cultural Center of San Francisco, Celebration of the Chinese New Year, www.c-c-c.org/chineseculture/festival/new year/newyear.html

Information on the Chinese New Year, Government Information Office, Republic of China (Taiwan), www.gio.gov.tw/info/ festival_c/spring_e/spring.htm

Sundance Film Festival

The Sundance Film Festival, held each year in Park City, Utah, is the annual crowning event hosted by the Sundance Institute. Sundance, according to its website, "seeks to discover, support, and inspire independent film and theater artists from the United States and around the world, and to introduce audiences to their new work." As covered by *Variety*, *Entertainment Weekly*, and a host of other film industry periodicals, the festival is also the scene of some spectacularly expensive backroom negotiations for new films that just the week before had no distributors. It's an impressive blend of art and commerce, and libraries can mine both experiences for programming ideas.

Choose a weekend and hold a film festival of your own. This can either be a festival of movies your library owns on DVD (make sure you have your license to show these—get permission directly from the filmmakers or see the Related Links section for licensing companies) or a festival of films made by local auteurs. To assemble your jury, invite film critics from local newspapers and one or two members of the local high school's film club, and raffle off a place on the jury to a lucky member of the public. A three- or five-person jury will prevent deadlocks, and a range of age groups ensures a diversity of opinions about the films. Your library can offer prizes modeled on those given out at Sundance, or you can create your own categories that reference aspects of your community.

If your local film critics have ever attended a major film festival, invite them to come speak about those experiences and give their behind-the-scenes view of what really goes on at Cannes, South by Southwest, Sundance, or Toronto. In our experience, humorous anecdotes involving celebrity behavior are always a winner. Consider, too, the possibility of hosting a mock bidding session for films submitted by local talent. As always, displays are a wonderful way to cross-promote your collections and related programming. Artfully arrange copies of Sundance winners from years past, and also include books about the movie industry in general.

Related Links

ALA Fact Sheet Number 7, Video and Copyright, www.ala.org/ala/alalibrary/libraryfactsheet/alalibraryfactsheet7.htm
IMDb Movie Festivals and Events Worldwide, www.imdb.com/festivals
Motion Picture Licensing Corporation Umbrella License, www.mplc.com/umbrella.php

Movie Licensing USA—Public Libraries, www.movlic.com/
library/index.html

Sundance Institute, www2.sundance.org

Voices from the Field

Film-related highlights from our survey included:

"This fall, we're participating in a Big Read using the *Maltese Falcon*, which is a fine excuse for running film noir programs." —Anonymous Public Library Administrator

"'Looking at Jazz: America's Art Form' film and lecture series (www.nvr.org/lookingatjazz) succeeded in building a healthy audience over the six-week series, the first use of our new theater space." —Anonymous Public Librarian

"We have monthly independent films through Film Movement (www.film-movement.com)." —Anonymous Public Librarian *(Authors' Note: Thank you so much for bringing Film Movement to everyone's attention! What a great way to show foreign and independent films at the library.)*

"Student film festival." —Anonymous Public Librarian

"We also try to do adult programs featuring popular topics when there is a presenter or tie in available, as in the case of a *Da Vinci Code* panel discussion from our local university." —Anonymous Public Librarian

February

Black History Month

Black History Month celebrates the contributions of African Americans, but we believe that diversity shouldn't be a one-month-only event. While these programs are listed in February, we encourage libraries to use them year-round.

Music programs are often the best-attended library events. Plan your programs based on your knowledge of the music interests of your customers: Would they prefer a program on the history of jazz? A hip-hop performance? You don't need a lot of money—contact local groups, such as schools and churches, to see if they have a choral group or choir interested in singing in the library. Throw a party with all Motown karaoke! While music and dance can be attention grabbing, also don't forget art and sculpture. Invite an art professor from a local college to speak about contributions of African-American artists, and plan corresponding children's crafts.

Voices from the Field

Programming highlights and comments appropriate for Black History Month included:

"YES! My teens are very pop culture oriented and I try to make my programs reflect that. I had a Southfield Idol Singing Competition and also an African American Pop Culture Trivia Game Show. Both were very well attended and the teens had tons of fun." —Shari Fesko, Teen Librarian, Southfield (MI) Public Library

"My library serves a largely African American population, so we try and craft programs that appeal to our community's interests. We've had Hip Hop month, Kwanzaa programs, black author talks, etc." —Anonymous Public Librarian

"Yes I do! … African-American programming is popular—we have an African-American Museum upstairs (separately run) which also helps and we sometimes offer joint programs." —Anonymous Public Librarian

"African drumming." —Anonymous Public Library Manager

"Authors from *Chicken Soup for the African American Woman's Soul*." —Anonymous Public Library Administrator

"My community is largely African-American, so I am putting together a Zane book club where the African-American ladies can come by and talk about the works of one of their favorite authors." —Anonymous Public Librarian

"Hip Hop Beat Making demonstration/performance with local teen Hip Hop artists. They brought their mix equipment and showed teens how to use it, and then performed. They talked about online programs like Fruity Loops (now FL Studio, www.flstudio.com) for mixing beats. Excellently received." —Anonymous Public Librarian

"Building off the community-wide one book read, we built a museum of the Harlem Renaissance and the 1920s in the library. The exhibit was set up in interactive stations (music, toys, poetry, art of the time period were some of the things included) and groups of students were asked to respond to each station in some way. All 975 students in the school were able to participate and the feedback received was overall very positive." —Anonymous School Media Specialist

"Hip Hop Café: a teen and family program that starred performances by a local rapper;, a visit, speech, and autograph signing from a well-known and popular WWE super-star; performances by Hip Hop dance groups; an airbrush artist painting on people's clothing; a fitness program from Bally's; video games; manga give-aways; and of course, free food (which we kept healthy—Sun Chips, baked Lays, fruit and yogurt parfaits). All of this was done on an inner-city library's property." —Anonymous Public Librarian

"My favorite program … was a performance given by a local cultural society on the dialect poetry of Paul Laurence Dunbar. Four actors performed selected poems (often with audience participation), some set to music, using a fiddle, guitar, and washboard. At one point, an 18-month-old ran into the middle of the aisle and started dancing." —Anonymous Public Library Director

Clutter, Be Gone!

Any time of year is a good time to declutter and organize. Why not highlight decluttering and organizing in February, just as many people are beginning to think of "spring cleaning"? This may be just the thing to energize patrons and staff in an otherwise dreary month! People love challenges and before-and-after photos. Start a *Clutter, Be Gone! Challenge*, and encourage both patrons and staff to sign up. Ask participants to bring in a photo of the space or room that is the focus of their personal challenge: a messy desk, overcrowded bookcase, or full garage, and display the photos (anonymously, of course!).

Support your participants by having workshops on decluttering or organizing. Facilitate the process of clearing out good but unwanted (or unneeded) objects by holding an "indoor garage sale" in your meeting room. At the end of the challenge, have participants share their "after" photos. Hopefully, this time they'll be proud to put their name by the photograph of the clean desk, attractive bookshelf, or garage with actual space for a car!

Voices from the Field

One of our "Voices from the Field" had this great advice:

> "Somehow, 'Clutter Control,' a program I did in January, was an unexpected hit! Thirty-some-odd people turned out for it. A woman came in and talked about how to go about de-junking your home. She gave [the participants] handouts and very useful tips. She was warm and personable, and the audience responded so well to her that they even chimed in with tips of their own. It was a lot more fun than I'd thought it would be."
> —Anonymous Public Librarian

March
Academy Awards

Every year, when the Academy Award nominations are announced, we wonder: How many libraries are hosting Oscar parties? It would be so much fun to roll out a cheap red carpet and invite your patrons to come dressed in all their finery for an evening of sparkling cider and cheese crackers, complete with catty remarks about the celebrity fashion missteps and a running commentary on the winners. Cash-strapped libraries could approach local carpet store owners to ask for donations of remnants or even regularly priced lengths of carpet in return for the opportunity to sponsor the "Community

Name Public Library" Oscar Party. Red is preferable, but the color doesn't really matter—just choose something festive and bright. The ambitious library could go one better by hosting a mock Oscars event, encouraging library users to vote both in the traditional categories as well as in humorous categories like *Most Expressive Hands, Most Annoying Fake Accent,* or *Best Method Facial Hair.*

People assume that libraries will have book discussion groups—so why not movie, TV, or even music discussion groups? The winter-long awards season—which encompasses the Golden Globes, Independent Spirit Awards, Oscars, and so on—is a wonderful time to kick off awards-related programming. For example, organize a Film Awards series, with programs organized around the categories Best Drama, Best Comedy or Musical, Best Foreign Film, Best Supporting Actor, etc. Don't forget similar programming opportunities to highlight the music awards: Grammys, Country Music Awards, Latin Grammys, and so on. What better time to have your own Performer's Showcase, with local singers sharing their talent? Tap into teens' love of music with a Battle of the Bands.

Related Links

Academy of Motion Pictures Arts and Sciences, Academy Awards,
www.oscars.org
Go Fug Yourself, gofugyourself.typepad.com
Infoplease.com's Movie Awards list, www.infoplease.com/ipa/
A0777584.html
Infoplease.com's Music Awards list, www.infoplease.com/ipa/
A0777597.html

Voices from the Field

In reading (and raving) about all the interesting programming ideas from survey respondents, we noticed that music (followed by food) was a sure-fire favorite. So, in addition to celebrating the music awards, why not check out one of these music-related programs?

"The majority of our pop culture programming is geared towards teens. ... We've done music programs—Name that Tune and Music Discussions." —Anonymous Public Librarian

"In collaboration with the music teacher, I designed an assignment for ninth graders. They chose the title of a piece of classical music out of a hat, styles and genres from the Renaissance through today, and we helped them use both print and online resources to research their composer, style, and time period. Culmination was an oral presentation to the class. It was a great way of exposing them to a variety of styles of music." —Anonymous School Media Specialist

"[Our Town] Teen Idol, which began at my branch but turned into a system-wide contest due to the diligent efforts of my teen librarian. Each branch held a local contest, and the winners at each branch competed in a final event downtown. We won a YALSA Excellence Award for it." —Anonymous Public Librarian

"We also offer things like 'New Music Tuesday,' where we burn CDs of the new stuff that's being released on iTunes, have Guitar Hero and DDR and the like, and try to bring in authors that the kids like." —Anonymous Public Librarian

"Most of our musical programs would qualify as 'pop culture,' that is, if you're age 50 and over. I do have trouble getting outside funding, though, for these programs, because they're considered 'entertainment' rather than 'art.' My programs are aimed at community interests and tastes, e.g., for a number of years I would have a Frank Sinatra-themed program in December to celebrate 'Ol' Blue Eyes' birthday. I used to get a lot of people for those, but the audience has died out (almost literally!), so I don't do them anymore." —Anonymous Public Reference Librarian

Women's History Month

Established in 1987, Women's History Month celebrates the achievements and contributions of women throughout history. Many organizations contribute to the observances of this month-long celebration, but the *capo di tutti capi* is the National Women's History Project, based in Santa Rosa, California.

When your library decides to celebrate women's contributions, think locally as well as globally and nationally. Sure, you should display biographies of notable women throughout the ages, but dig deeper! Your area is probably home to unsung heroines who would love to share their stories with younger generations, and even with their peers, who may not know of their achievements. Look to your local colleges and universities and invite professors in the history or women's studies departments to speak on local women's history. Ask the director of your local historical society for permission to display selected original documents at your library, and invite him or her to be a speaker at a Women's History Month function held at your library. Invite your patrons to make women's history of their own by holding an open-mic night, inviting women of all ages to come tell stories about themselves, about women who have inspired them, and about the women they hope to be.

Schools often assign students to interview family members as part of history assignments. The StoryCorps project has taken this idea several steps further, by building permanent story collection booths at two locations in New York City, and by sending two RVs on tour throughout the U.S. If your town isn't on the StoryCorps Mobile's itinerary, you can use the comprehensive do-it-yourself guide on the project's website (www.storycorps.net/record-your-story/cant-come-to-us/diy-guide) to replicate the experience of a StoryCorps booth locally.

School and public libraries should also consider holding women's history quiz bowl events, with teams for all age groups. Be sure to offer prizes!

Related Links

Gale Free Resources on Women's History, www.gale.com/free_resources/whm

Girlstart: Empowering Girls in Math, Science, and Technology,
www.girlstart.org

National Women's History Museum Educational Resources,
www.nwhm.org/Education/education_index.html

National Women's History Project, www.nwhp.org

StoryCorps, www.storycorps.net

Time for Kids—Women's History Month, www.timeforkids.com/
TFK/specials/whm/0,8805,101044,00.html

Wikipedia—Quizbowl, en.wikipedia.org/wiki/Quiz_bowl

The Women's Museum: An Institute for the Future, www.thewom-
ensmuseum.org

Teen Tech Week

YALSA launched Teen Tech Week in March 2007 as a celebration of teens' tech savvy. Tech literacy is on equal footing with traditional literacy, and libraries can do many things to join in the serious fun.

YALSA's participation guide, available for purchase through the ALA Store, is your main reference tool for launching your activities. Collaborate with your local high school's computer club adviser and members to plan some fun activities. These can include recording podcasts by teens, opening up your library's blog to teen contributors for the week (or longer, if the week-long experiment goes well), and hosting a LAN party. Let the principle of youth participation be your guide: Encourage the teens to generate more ideas and vote on them. You can do this in the formal setting of a Teen Advisory Board or Computer Club meeting, via a survey (online or paper-based), or via a discussion carried out in the comments on your library's teen blog. Giving teens a say in the subjects and organization of the programs will increase the likelihood of teens attending those programs. The most popular ideas (provided, of course, that they're feasible) are the ones you want to schedule.

Technology and teens can be a scary combination for many people. Everyone has heard the horror stories of online predators or teens and college students not realizing that "private" isn't always "private." Teen Tech Week can be the perfect time to educate your community, old and young, about online safety and Internet myths. Contact the local prosecutor's office for help in setting up a workshop.

Teens love to volunteer, to give something back to the community. They have grown up with technology, so what better way to support Teen Tech Week than to have teens share their tech expertise with others? Arrange to have teen volunteers available after school or on weekends to offer one-on-one computer help with tasks such as scanning pictures, using Google, or setting up a MySpace account.

Related Links

ALA Store, www.alastore.ala.org

LANParty.com's Small LANParty Network Setup, www.lanparty.com/theguide/network.shtm

LANParty.com's So You Wanna Host a LANParty?, www.lanparty.com/theguide/hostingaparty.shtm

Roger Hart's Ladder of Young People's Participation, www.freechild.org/ladder.htm

YALSA'S Teen Tech Week, www.ala.org/ala/yalsa/teentechweek

Voices from the Field

Even though Teen Tech Week was only one year old when we conducted our survey, our respondents had great ideas:

"Fave program was an all day tech event for Teen Tech Week. A first year college student presented a 1-hour workshop on how to make music using GarageBand, then a group of teens and I showcased the best of podcasts, and ended with a Pimp Your iPod craft. Recently we had a *Harry Potter*

lock-in overnight where 15 teens read until 7 AM. It was way cool!"
—Anonymous Public Librarian

"eBay for Beginners: a lecture-style presentation on the ins and outs of
buying and selling on eBay." —Anonymous Public Librarian

"With the help of the Library's Teen Advisory Board and Friends
Foundation, during Teen Tech Week 2007 the library debuted teen game
night, featuring pizza (of course), Nintendo Wii, DDR, Guitar Hero, old
school video games, and tons of board games. Because of the success of
the first program, which brought in 25 teens, we decided to make teen
game night a monthly event, drawing in 12–30 teens for each program.
This has by far been the most successful long running teen program in the
history of our library." —Anonymous Public Librarian

April
Taxes

Death and taxes: Which inevitably strikes more dread into the heart
of public library employees? We think most library staff in the U.S.
consider the annual tax season a fate worse than death. Displaying,
restocking, finding, and printing forms is time-consuming.
Explaining repeatedly that staff cannot offer tax advice is a
Sisyphean exercise in frustration: As soon as you've explained it to
one patron, along comes another asking the same question. Tax season is mind-numbing and demoralizing. Let's turn it on its head and
use this often-confusing time to our advantage, shall we?

Obviously, you have to display the forms. If you live in a state that
requires residents to file state tax returns, you're hit with a double-
whammy. Happily, the IRS and most state governments have made
tremendous progress with regard to making virtually every form and
accompanying set of instructions available online in PDF format.
This means you can display fewer forms—this is good! It also
means that you will spend some extra time holding on-the-fly training sessions showing patrons how to download the online forms—

this is, potentially, bad. Our advice? Offer daily tax form open houses, when one or two members of staff make themselves available to demonstrate and walk patrons through the process of searching for, downloading, and printing out the forms they need. Some forms can be filled out online and either saved or printed once complete, so be ready to provide instruction on how to do this, as well.

Hold the open houses at different, regular times on alternating days—for example, 10–11:30 AM on Mondays, Wednesdays, and Fridays, and 7:30–9 PM on Tuesdays and Thursdays, with two-hour open houses on weekend afternoons. By offering the open houses at different times on different days, you will be able to meet the needs of both retirees and working people.

If your library does not offer AARP tax assistance for senior citizens, find out if this service is offered instead by a community center, senior center, or other local agency by searching for your ZIP code on the AARP site (locator.aarp.org/vmis/sites/tax_aide_locator. jsp). If another agency offers this program, make sure you point your senior citizens to it; and if no other local agency offers it, contact AARP to offer your library as a potential location for this valuable program. AARP also offers year-round online tax assistance, including an FAQ and personalized answers to specific questions (www.aarp.org/money/taxaide/taxcounseling/ask_tax_question. html). Prepare a list of local community tax assistance sites and make it available to patrons.

Invite local CPAs or even a local IRS agent to give a talk on the dangers and pitfalls of letting one of the many heavily advertised "refund upfront" places complete your taxes, as these businesses prey on the poor and elderly. (Ideally, this event would take place in February or March.)

On April 16, throw a "Tax Season Is OVER!" party. Give out boxes of tacks as party favors. (Get it? "Tacks" rhymes with "tax"! We cannot resist a good pun. Nor should you.) Make paper chains and rosettes out of the now-outdated forms. Give out prizes for the best "I filed early" and "I filed on time (but just barely)" stories. Suitable prizes include fine amnesty, library mugs, and "I got tax help @ my library" T-shirts.

Related Links

AARP.org Tax-Aide, www.aarp.org/money/taxaide
American Institute of Certified Public Accountants, www.aicpa.org
CafePress.com, www.cafepress.com
Internal Revenue Service (IRS), www.irs.gov

Yom HaShoah/Holocaust Remembrance Day

Events commemorating the near extermination of European Jewry may not be as festive as other celebrations, but they should certainly be life-affirming and uplifting. Yom HaShoah is the Hebrew term for Holocaust Remembrance Day. Many Jews prefer Yom HaShoah because the term "holocaust" refers to a willing religious sacrifice, while the biblical term "shoah" means calamity.

Yom HaShoah is an appropriate time to display materials relating to the Nazi genocide of Jews and other ethnic groups during World War II, but you can also display materials related to other previous and subsequent genocides and mass exterminations. Examples include the decimation of Cambodia's population under the Khmer Rouge; the early 1990s genocide in Rwanda; the slaughter of Armenians in Turkey in the early 1900s; the Kurdish genocide perpetrated by Saddam Hussein's regime in the 1980s; the systematic annihilation of ethnic Albanians in Serbia in the 1990s; and the present crisis in the Darfur region of the Sudan.

Yom HaShoah is a perfect opportunity to host a One Book, One Community event with a genocide-themed title. Choose a crossover book—that is, a title with appeal for both teens and adults—and host a series of discussion groups. (A list of recommended titles for a One Book, One Community event is included at the end of this section.)

Look outside the library, too, and coordinate with schools and synagogues to co-sponsor events with survivors. You may also want to seek out survivors of other genocides, and invite them to tell their stories.

Related Links

United States Memorial Holocaust Museum: Organizing a Holocaust Remembrance Day, www.ushmm.org/remembrance/dor/organize

Yad Vashem: The Holocaust Martyrs' and Heroes' Remembrance Authority, www.yadvashem.org

Yom HaShoah (Holocaust Remembrance Day), Torah.org, www.torah.org/learning/yomtov/holocaust

Recommended Titles for One Book, One Community Events

Bagdasarian, Adam. *The Forgotten Fire*. New York: Laurel-Leaf Books, 2002.

Balakian, Peter. *The Burning Tigris: The Armenian Genocide and America's Response*. New York: HarperCollins, 2003.

Deng, Alephonsion, Benson Deng, Benjamin Ajak, and Judy Bernstein. *They Poured Fire on Us from the Sky: The True Story of Three Lost Boys From Sudan*. New York: Public Affairs, 2005.

Filipoviç, Zlata. *Zlata's Diary: A Child's Life in Sarajevo*. New York: Viking, 1994.

Frank, Anne. *Anne Frank: Diary of a Young Girl*. New York: Pocket Books, 1958.

Glatshteyn, Yankev. *Emil and Karl*. New Milford, CT: Roaring Brook Press, 2006.

Ilibagiza, Immaculée and Steve Erwin. *Left to Tell: Discovering God Amidst the Rwandan Holocaust*. Carlsbad, CA: Hay House, 2006.

Jansen, Hanna. *Over a Thousand Hills I Walk with You.* Minneapolis, MN: Carolrhoda Books, 2006.

Jungersen, Christian. *The Exception.* London: Wiedenfeld and Nicolson, 2006.

Kubert, Joe. *Fax From Sarajevo: A Story of Survival.* Milwaukie, OR: Dark Horse Comics, 1996.

Lowry, Lois. *Number the Stars.* Boston: Houghton Mifflin, 1989.

Menchú, Rigoberta and Elisabeth Burgos-Debray. *I, Rigoberta Menchú: An Indian Woman in Guatemala.* London: Verso, 1984.

Mikaelsen, Ben. *Red Midnight.* New York: HarperCollins, 2002.

Opdyk, Irene Gut and Jennifer Armstrong. *In My Hands: Memories of a Holocaust Rescuer.* New York: Knopf: Distributed by Random House, 1999.

Pausewang, Gudrun. *The Final Journey.* New York: Viking, 1996.

Rusesabagina, Paul and Tom Zoellner. *An Ordinary Man: An Autobiography.* New York: Viking, 2006.

Sacco, Joe. *Safe Area Gorazde.* Seattle: Fantagraphics, 2000.

Spiegelman, Art. *Maus: A Survivor's Tale.* New York: Pantheon, 1986.

Spiegelman, Art. *Maus II: A Survivor's Tale: And Here My Troubles Began.* New York: Pantheon, 1991.

Spinelli, Jerry. *Milkweed: A Novel.* New York: Alfred A. Knopf, 2003.

Stassen, Jean-Philippe. *Deogratias: A Tale of Rwanda.* New York: First Second, 2006.

Ung, Loung. *First They Killed My Father: A Daughter of Cambodia Remembers.* New York: HarperCollins, 2000.

Ung, Loung. *Lucky Child: A Daughter of Cambodia Reunites with the Sister She Left Behind.* New York: HarperCollins, 2005.

Zusak, Markus. *The Book Thief.* New York: Alfred A. Knopf, 2006.

May

Cinco de Mayo

Celebrated every May 5 in Mexico, Cinco de Mayo commemorates the victory of the Mexican Militia over the French Army at the Battle of Puebla in 1862. Although it is primarily a regional holiday in Mexico (where it is celebrated to varying degrees nationwide, but most enthusiastically in Puebla), it is often celebrated as a Mexican heritage festival in areas of the U.S. with large Mexican and Mexican-American populations.

We love the idea of a library-wide celebration of Mexican culture and heritage. Encourage staff to dress in the colors of the Mexican flag—red, green, and white—and post bilingual signage throughout the library. Display your Spanish-language materials, including films by noted Mexican directors Guillermo del Toro and Alfonso Cuarón, telenovelas (soap operas) on DVD, books, dictionaries, periodicals such as *People en Español*, and CDs by noted Mexican artists. Offer holiday-specific crafts and snacks throughout the day, and make sure to enlist your children's librarians in creating a story-time that features Mexican folk tales.

Related Links

Cinco de Mayo, holidays.kaboose.com/cinco-de-mayo

Martha Stewart—Cinco de Mayo, www.marthastewart.com/cinco-de-mayo?lnc=f97c442d8f35f010VgnVCM1000003d370a0aRCRD&rsc=leftnav_holiday_other-holidays

U.S. Census Bureau Fact Sheet on Cinco de Mayo, www.census.gov/Press-Release/www/releases/archives/facts_for_features_special_editions/009726.html

Gardening

Gardening is hot! Apart from the host of nonfiction titles available on gardening in different zones, written for gardeners of varying degrees of expertise, many patrons also enjoy botanical mysteries by such authors as Susan Wittig Albert, Rebecca Rothenberg and Taffy Cannon, Mary Freeman, Janis Harrison, and Ann Ripley, among others. Whether your patrons nurture seeds in egg containers or let their wildflowers run riot, many of them are spending a few hours a week planting, weeding, and watering. In Chapter 2, we discussed the benefits of inviting expert groups to provide your materials selectors with collection development ideas. A local garden club is a fine candidate for such active patron participation.

Sophie's hometown library always pairs its annual book and bake sale with a plant and produce sale hosted by the local garden club. What a wonderful idea! Pairing events that draw similar audiences is a great way to show the library's investment in the community while raising money for worthwhile causes. As an added bonus, attendees leave everything they want: books, pies, and plants. What could be better?

Other botanically minded programs could include plant identification programs for children, a grow-your-own contest, an organized bus trip to the annual Flower Show hosted by a nearby city's Horticultural Society, or the planting of a butterfly garden. Invite local garden club members to share "How does your garden grow?" Display monthly photos of the same gardens, so patrons can admire and be inspired by the various changing landscapes designed by local "green thumbs." Build on the garden club members' knowledge by inviting them to share tips and suggestions; ask them to look at your Gardening subject guide and help update it.

Christine Herz, Reference Librarian, Gloucester County College, Sewell, NJ, suggested the many gardening resources that follow.

Related Links

GardenWeb, www.gardenweb.com

National Gardening Association, www.garden.org

You Grow Girl, www.yougrowgirl.com

Plant Databases

National Invasive Species Information Center (National Agricultural Library, U.S. Department of Agriculture), www.invasivespeciesinfo.gov/plants/databases.shtml – Describes online databases related to invasive plant species.

PLANTS Database (Natural Resources Conservation Service, U.S. Department of Agriculture), plants.usda.gov – Provides standardized information about the vascular plants, mosses, liverworts, hornworts, and lichens of the U.S. and its territories. Some suggested programs are listed in the links on the right, including: plants in my state, wetland plants in my region, endangered plants of the U.S., invasive plants, etc.

UI Plants (University of Illinois at Urbana-Champaign), woodyplants.nres.uiuc.edu – A database on woody landscape plant identification, culture, and usage, including native and introduced species and their major varieties and cultivars. While geared primarily for the Midwest, it includes cultivars that will do well in any geographic area. Numerous photographs accompany the listings.

Online Gardening Publications

Brooklyn Botanic Garden All-Region Guides, www.bbg.org/gar2/handbooks – Published three times a year, the expert voice on gardening for plant lovers in all 50 states and Canada.

Fine Gardening, www.taunton.com/finegardening – Provides highlights from the current issue of the magazine, full-text of selected articles, an email newsletter, gardening basics, and ideas for garden plans and projects.

Horticulture Magazine, www.hortmag.com – The authoritative voice on gardening, providing inspiration, instruction, and entertainment for passionate gardeners. Selected articles, list of books, and a free email newsletter are available from the website.

General Gardening Web Sites

The Garden Conservancy, www.gardenconservancy.org – A national, nonprofit organization founded in 1989 to preserve exceptional American gardens for the public's education and enjoyment. The Open Days Program allows the public occasional access to gardens that are not generally open (www.garden conservancy.org/opendays).

National Gardening Association, www.garden.org/home – Includes sections on Home Gardening, Kids Gardening, and Garden Research.

Butterfly Gardening

North American Butterfly Association (NABA), www.naba.org – Includes Garden & Habitat Publications and information on its publication *Butterfly Gardener.*

Raising Butterflies from Your Garden, NABA, NJ Chapter, www.naba.org/chapters/nabanj/bgarden.html – Includes suggested classroom activities.

TV Program

PBS: *The Victory Garden*, www.pbs.org/wgbh/victorygarden – Companion site to the PBS series includes video podcasts, recipes, and show descriptions.

Victoria Day

Victoria Day, commemorating the birth of Queen Victoria, is celebrated in Canada each year on the Monday on or before May 24.

England no longer celebrates the birthday of its longest-reigning monarch; instead, the official birthday of the current Queen (or King, when appropriate) is celebrated on the first or second (or sometimes third) Saturday in June. We focus here on Victoria Day because we think the nostalgia factor of celebrating the woman who coined the phrase "we are not amused" is far more, well, amusing than celebrating the U.K.'s esteemed current monarch.

Canadian celebrations of Victoria Day often involve displays of fireworks. Obviously, this is not possible in a library setting. We recommend instead that you schedule some activities that capture the flavor of Victorian times. Introduce the children of your town to the pleasures of croquet. If your library lacks green space around it, you can play indoors, affixing the wickets to the floor with duct tape. Older children and adults can enjoy a fancy tea party, followed by a lecture on Victorian tea customs for the adults and a screening of *Alice in Wonderland* for the children.

Larger-scale celebrations could include a display of historic garments (either from your local historic society or from community members' attics), a walking tour of your community's historic neighborhoods, or a performance of songs from the light operas of W. S. Gilbert and Arthur Sullivan.

Related Links

Canadian Heritage—Victoria Day, www.canadianheritage.gc.ca/
    progs/cpsc-ccsp/jfa-ha/victoria_e.cfm
The Gilbert and Sullivan Archive, diamond.boisestate.edu/gas
United States Croquet Association, www.croquetamerica.com

June

End of School

Quoth the freedom-drunk school child on the last day of school: "No more homework, no more books, no more teacher's dirty looks!" Quoth Alice Cooper: "School's out! For summer! Schools out! Forever!" They're both right—until next year, that is.

Whether your local school gets out in May or June (or even if it's in session year-round) find a way to join in the "hip hip, hooray!" Our colleague Kimberly Paone of the Elizabeth (NJ) Public Library hosts an annual silent scavenger hunt for teens. This is a wonderful way to get teens in the library in droves, and to involve your library's staff in the fun, in a way that encourages the teens to have a wonderful time while preventing your colleagues and patrons from getting up in arms about the noise level.

Create a list of factoids, including both things you wouldn't expect to find in a library (but can find in a dollar store) and some items you would expect to find in a library. Make sure all facts are findable using materials in the library, but make using the Internet a no-no. Plant the dollar store items at service desks around your library (or, if you work in a small library, hide them in plain sight around the building). Establish your rules: No speaking out loud during the course of the hunt, no use of the Internet, and no roughhousing. Hand out the lists of items to your contestants, set the timer, and go!

TV Series Finales

While some networks have moved away from the traditional TV season, most stick to it—which means that, as the days get longer, your favorite TV show broadcasts its final episode of the season. (And, if it's a really sad year, it's the series finale!)

What to do? Embrace the end!

If you have TV shows on DVD in the library, have a season (or series) finale show day! For example, watch every season finale episode of *Buffy the Vampire Slayer.* For the month leading up to your "Series Finale: Saying Good-bye" night, conduct a poll. List some of the best, or most controversial, season endings: *MASH, Seinfeld, St. Elsewhere.* Have people vote on their favorites and show the winners. *(Authors' Note: At the time of this writing, we could not find a single clearinghouse that handles licensing to screen television shows on DVD the way that the MPLC and other entities do for movies. You will need to apply to the studios that produced the shows you wish to screen.)*

"Programming" can include silent programming, drop-in programming, or a kick-ass display. "Whatever Gets You Through the Summer" can be either a booklist or a display of "watch-alikes." If you're watching *Supernatural,* and are in withdrawal from no new episodes over the summer, then try movies like *Frailty* or TV shows like *Buffy the Vampire Slayer.* Try to get as much patron involvement as possible—list your watch-alikes on a library blog and encourage comment by patrons; include watch-alike suggestion slips in DVDs, asking patrons what they would recommend to people who liked that movie or TV show; put up a huge, mostly blank poster, supply plenty of pens, and invite your patrons to add their watching recommendations. Pick a popular show and build a booklist around it. *Lost* can inspire displays such as "Books to Have on a Desert Island" or "What Would Sawyer Read?"

Related Links

The Futon Critic, www.thefutoncritic.com
Internet Movie Database (IMDb), www.imdb.com
Television Without Pity, www.televisionwithoutpity.com
TV.com, www.tv.com

Gay Pride Month

While not every community is open-minded enough to let its library celebrate Gay Pride Month without furor, nearly every city or town is home to members of the gay, lesbian, bisexual, transgendered, and intersex (GLBTI) community. GLBTI people, their families, and their friends have unique informational needs that public and school libraries must meet. This is not a blue state vs. red state issue; this is about serving our constituents well.

Simple gay-friendly steps you can take to let your GLBTI customers know you are proud to serve them include displays of books by gay authors, films by gay directors, and music by gay artists. NPR contributor Mark Mobley provides a partial list of seminal gay artists (www.npr.org/templates/story/story.php?storyId=1306240).

Consider hosting a display highlighting the history of the gay rights struggle. Although gay-bashing is still a serious problem, many modern gay youth are unaware of how dangerous it was to be gay just 10 or 15 years ago. Today, students as young as 12 come out at school. In developed countries, AIDS is no longer the death sentence it once was. Gay marriage is legal throughout Canada and (as of this writing, at least) in Massachusetts.

Invite representatives from your local chapter of PFLAG: Parents, Families and Friends of Lesbians and Gays (www. pflag.org) and GLSEN: The Gay, Lesbian and Straight Education Network (www.glsen.org) to hold a Q&A session at your library. If you cannot gain director approval for such an event, display PFLAG and GLSEN brochures at your library.

This is also a good time to investigate how your library's blocking software handles gay content websites, especially those that serve teens. We're not talking about potentially salacious chatrooms, but about legitimate information resources covering sexual health, sexual identity, and gay community news.

Many large metropolitan areas hold Gay Pride parades during June—find out if the library can enter a float in the parade! Failing that, at least get a booth at the parade and hand out GLBTI booklists.

Related Links

COLAGE: Children of Lesbians and Gays Everywhere, www. colage.org

Gay Financial Network, www.gfn.com

GLSEN: The Gay, Lesbian and Straight Education Network, www. glsen.org

Lesbian and Gay Aging Issues Network, www.asaging.org/networks/LGAIN/about.cfm

National Women's History Project: History of Gay and Lesbian Pride Month, www.nwhp.org/news/gayandlesbian_month.php

PFLAG: Parents, Families and Friends of Lesbians and Gays, www.pflag.org

July

Canada Day

Held on July 1, Canada Day is Canada's national holiday, celebrating the joining of the Province of Canada (today's Ontario and Québec), New Brunswick, and Nova Scotia into the federation of Canada in 1867. (The rest of the provinces joined the federation at later points in Canada's history. The Dominion of Newfoundland and Labrador did not become a province until 1949.) Patriotic celebrations feature fireworks, displays of flags, and pancake breakfasts.

Although all Canadian libraries are closed on Canada Day, the week prior to the holiday is an excellent opportunity for libraries within and close to Canada to hold parallel celebrations. Since U.S. Independence Day and Canada Day celebrations bear so many similarities and are held so close together, it makes sense to combine the celebrations, while maintaining the distinct flavors of each.

Fourth of July/Independence Day

Libraries traditionally celebrate the Fourth of July by decorating with red, white, and blue, and plenty of American flags. Libraries, though, can celebrate many different aspects of the birthday of the U.S. An Independence Day film festival might include anything from musicals (*1776*) to Abbott and Costello (*The Time of Their Lives*), Disney classics (*Johnny Tremain*) to Al Pacino (*Revolution*), action adventure (*The Patriot*) to escapist fun (*National Treasure*). Don't neglect documentaries! The History Channel is popular because people like to know "the real story," and PBS supports its documentaries with a wealth of online resources. While sometimes it's a bit tricky to secure performance rights, it's well worth it.

The Declaration of Independence is one of the most important documents in U.S. history. Many government websites, such as the National Archives (www.archives.gov) and the Library of Congress (www.loc.gov), include its full text, images, and other information. (The signing of the Declaration of Independence marks the birthday of the U.S.; the Constitution, with its Bill of Rights and Amendments, is the document that is the law of the land.) Celebrate the Bill of Rights and highlight your legal collection, including books and films on landmark legal decisions. Display photos of the current Supreme Court Justices, and see how many patrons can "name that justice."

Kids and teens love drama, so why not include mock trials as a summer activity? Kids and teens can be lawyers, judges, and witnesses; invite your Friends group to serve as a jury. Does your community have a parade to celebrate Independence Day? Is the library part of it? Whether you're walking in the parade, riding on a library float, or showcasing your library drill cart team, this is a great way to be a member of your community.

Related Links

American Bar Association: Putting on Mock Trials, www.abanet.
org/publiced/mocktrialguide.pdf

History.com, www.history.com

IMDb list of films by keyword "American Revolution,"
www.imdb. com/keyword/american-revolution

Library of Congress—Declaration of Independence, www.loc.gov/
rr/program/bib/ourdocs/DeclarInd.html

Mock Trial Scripts, www.classbrain.com/artteensm/publish/cat_
index_11.shtml

The National Archives Experience—The Charters of Freedom,
www.archives.gov/national-archives-experience/charters/
declaration.html

New Jersey State Bar Foundation—Mock Trial Videotapes,
www.njsbf.org/njsbf/programs/videos/mock.cfm

PBS: *Liberty! The American Revolution*, www.pbs.org/ktca/liberty

Supreme Court of the United States, www.supremecourtus.gov

Bastille Day

Bastille Day is held on July 14 and referred to as *14 juillet* (though its official name is *Fête Nationale*). As we looked at Bastille Day, we wondered a little punchily, what one would do to mark Bastille Day? Show old episodes of *Prison Break*? Then we remembered our own advice: Sometimes you need to look outside the library to get ideas.

Take the lead from a Philadelphia restaurant, the White Dog Café, and have a Block Party celebrating all things French: French film, French food, French music. Contact your local school and enlist the help of the French teacher: Would the teacher or some students be willing to do a bilingual storytime or puppet show? (Of course, this call is best made well before the school year ends!)

Related Links

French Culture: Official Website of the Cultural Services of the
French Embassy, www.frenchculture.org
White Dog Café's Bastille Day Street Party, www.whitedog.
com/bastille.html

Comic-Con

Every year comic lovers gather in San Diego, California, for Comic-Con International, a four-day convention that in 2006 had more than 100,000 attendees. Comic-Con showcases comic books, but has expanded to include science fiction and fantasy, games, anime and manga, and collectibles, and in part because of San Diego's relative proximity to Los Angeles, it also includes television and film. It wouldn't be wrong to say this is *the* pop culture convention of the year.

Not everyone can make it to San Diego, so why not have your own mini comic-con? Display your graphic novels and comic books, your science fiction, fantasy, and horror books, and your films and TV series on DVD. Find out who the special guests are for that particular year (past guests have ranged from Neil Gaiman to Samuel L. Jackson) and have your own "screenings" of films and TV shows highlighting those guests. (*Snakes on a Plane*, anyone?) Or, since Comic-Con highlights new and upcoming projects, you could hold a short film contest for local film makers.

Comic-Con also hosts an artist's alley; create your own by inviting local artists to display their work. Ask the artists if they would be willing to conduct a drawing workshop. Costumes are big at Comic-Con; anime lovers call it cosplay. Comic-Con's costume contest is called The Masquerade, and the premise is fairly simple: Dress up as your favorite character. All you need for a library cosplay is your meeting room. You can be the MC; play some music, and set up a "stage" where people can highlight their costumes. Of course, it's always more fun when there are prizes—most original costume, best group costume.

The community element can be one of the best things about organizing your own Comic-Con: work with local comic book shops, anime clubs, and film teachers to ensure a wide level of participation (and maybe some donations from the comic shop). You can pick and choose how much you want to do. (Do you know someone who has gone to Comic-Con? Ask them to come speak at the library, and hope they bring some of the swag to show off!)

While San Diego is "the" Comic-Con, there are other, smaller cons held during the year throughout the country. You can schedule your Comic-Con events to coincide with a local convention.

Voices from the Field

One anonymous public librarian shares this story of starting a creating a local Comic-Con:

"Our finale program for this year's Summer Reading Program was a blast. My Teen Advisory Group and I wanted to do something like an Anime/Gaming convention … Thus, BellCon was born. We had video games (Smash Brothers and Guitar Hero), a screening of *Princess Mononoke*, inflatable sumo suits, a Graffiti wall, and much more. We had about 140 people attend, which is a phenomenal number for teen programs in my city."
—Anonymous Public Librarian

Related Links

Comic-Con International, San Diego, www.comic-con.org
ComicBookConventions.com's Conventions Calendar,
www.comicbookconventions.com/conventions.htm

August
Back to School

To borrow from a recent office supply store commercial (and with apologies to Christmas carolers everywhere), for many a harried parent, back-to-school truly is the most wonderful time of the year. Getting the kids back to school represents a return to blissfully scheduled order for the next nine months. For parents, it also presents the possibility of epic struggles over back-to-school expenses, and for students, anxiety over starting a new grade or a new school, for those making the transition from elementary, junior, or senior high school to the next level of schooling. How can libraries both celebrate and ease the transition for both parents and students?

Back-to-school picture book displays and storytimes are common for the youngest students. Expand this notion to encompass students up to college age. Programming for older students and their parents can include events on personal organization, how to get homework help at school and at the library, and how to handle the new freedoms (and, sometimes, separation anxiety) experienced by college freshmen away from home for the first time. Ease the transition for students of all ages with a series of prize drawings throughout the month, with winners receiving great school supplies like fancy Post-its, scented markers, bouquets of freshly sharpened pencils (idea stolen from the Tom Hanks and Meg Ryan romantic comedy *You've Got Mail*), snazzy pens, locker organizers and mirrors, and so on. This is an area ripe for collaborative programs with local schools and colleges—reach out to your colleagues at these institutions earlier in the year to set up at least a loose structure for making these programs work best.

Public and school librarians can, and should, collaborate on in-service programs for local teachers. Many teachers are aware of what their school libraries and librarians can offer them in terms of curriculum support, but how many view the local public library the same way? If you offer curriculum-related materials at your public library, make sure your local teachers know it, both for their own use and for their students' use.

Homeschooling is an increasingly popular choice for a wide variety of households. Though homeschoolers may not offer their children the classic 10-week summer vacation enjoyed by public and private schools students, August (or, in some states, September) probably feels like back-to-school to them as well. Reach out to homeschoolers and unschoolers with programming designed for them. Schedule a Back-to-Homeschool open house for homeschooling parents. Offer a tour of your library's fiction and nonfiction sections for their children, circulate a Wish List sheet for them to offer suggested purchases, and introduce them to your reference and reader's advisory services in a way that's targeted to their needs. Survey your homeschoolers to find out how many homeschool for religious reasons, and how many do it out of a desire to offer a more creative curriculum for their children. Educate yourself on the subject of homeschooling and unschooling; find useful online resources in the following related links section.

Related Links

American Academy of Pediatrics—Back to School Tips (also available in Spanish), www.aap.org/advocacy/releases/augschool.htm

KidsHealth—Going Back to School, kidshealth.org/kid/feeling/school/back_to_school.html

Learn in Freedom!, learninfreedom.org

National Center for Education Statistics—Homeschooling in the United States: 2003, nces.ed.gov/pubsearch/pubsinfo.asp?pubid=2006042

National Home Education Network, www.nhen.org

U.S. Department of Education—Getting Ready for College Early, www.ed.gov/pubs/GettingReadyCollegeEarly/index.html

Voices from the Field

Both school and public libraries shared creative back-to-school program ideas for you to adopt or adapt to suit your community's needs.

> "*Amazing Race* library orientation for new students to our school."
> —Anonymous School Media Specialist *(Authors' Note: We really like the idea of dressing up the "same old, same old" [library orientation] in a pop culture guise that makes the activity a lot more appealing to kids.)*

> "I do two back-to-school programs that are successful. One is Notebook Decorating, and the other is Make Your Own Magnets. ... I usually have at least 10 teens at each one." —Anonymous Public Librarian

> "I had sixth grade students write an Amazon type of review that I entered into the OPAC for others to see." —Patti Keller, Library Media Specialist, Grafton (MA) Middle School

Rakhi

Rakhi is a Hindu festival that celebrates the relationship between a brother and sister. It falls on the full moon of the month of Shraavana; in 2007, that was August 28. A sister gives her brother a bracelet, or Rakhi, and he gives her a gift in return. The August 2005 issue of *Highlights for Children* includes directions on how to make a Rakhi—what better way to celebrate that we are all one family than with this all-ages craft?

Related Links

Rakhi: The Thread of Love, hinduism.about.com/library/weekly/aa080800a.htm

Wikipedia—Rakhi (Raksha Bhandan), en.wikipedia.org/wiki/Raksha_Bhandan

Magazine Resources

Colón, Connie. "Make A Rakhi for Your Brother Or Friend."
Highlights for Children, 60:8 (August 2005): 11.

September
TV Premieres

TV premiere season brings two types of excitement: the joy of returning favorites and the promise of finding great new shows. The previous seasons of current TV shows are now commonly released on DVD before the start of the new season, creating the opportunity for new viewers to discover a show. Put together a library display of the "top ten returning shows," and show the season finales of popular shows to remind patrons how their favorite shows ended last season. Have a whiteboard by your front door, updated weekly, to let patrons know what new TV shows start that week. (The Futon Critic is a handy website for start dates.)

What about all those new shows? If you get cable at your library, why not turn on the TV and invite patrons to come and watch the premieres of the most-hyped shows? Ask for people's predictions: Distribute a list of the new shows with choices such as "renewed," "cancelled," and "fewer than six episodes." Collect the ballots, seal them up, and open them the following May. Share the results with your community. How well did you predict the big hits—and the disappointments?

Related Links

The Futon Critic, www.thefutoncritic.com
TV.com, www.tv.com

Food and Cooking

As the scorching afternoons of summer are replaced by autumnal breezes, one's mind turns to the homey, indulgent pleasures of good food. Thanksgiving and Christmas are on the horizon, farmers' markets are full of fall produce, and a new season of cooking shows debuts on FoodTV. Celebrate food and cooking at your library!

Think about collection issues—if popular cooking shows such as *$40 a Day with Rachael Ray*, *Nigella Express*, and *Good Deal with Dave Lieberman* are available on DVD, make sure you have them at your library. Many popular TV chefs publish books to accompany their series; buy them, too. Take a look at your cookbook collection—does it reflect regional tastes and interests? How comprehensive is your international cooking section? How current are the cookbooks you have on the shelves? And don't forget your fiction section! The Waterboro (ME) Public Library has a great list of culinary mysteries (link at the end of this section). Finally, what cooking magazines do you carry? If you subscribe to *Gourmet* and *Bon Appetit*, but nothing else, you need to branch out. *Cook's Illustrated*, *Cooking Light*, *Everyday with Rachael Ray*, and Martha Stewart's *Everyday Food* are all good places to begin. For more ideas, check your local magazine stand—food magazines are a hot segment of the magazine publishing industry. Don't forget online resources. Is your website up-to-date, and does it link to recipe websites?

Now, think about programs. Has there been a resurgence of interest in your community in the traditional arts of canning and freezing food? If so, contact a local home economics teacher or faculty member from a local university's extension service to present a demonstration of the proper technique in the library. Do local supermarkets invite local restaurateurs to demonstrate new techniques on weekend afternoons? Follow their lead!

Cooking shows are extremely popular, and most shows have websites that feature not only their recipes, but also video demonstrations. Have a computer class called All About Recipes, that covers everything from finding recipes highlighted on *Rachael Ray* or the *Today Show* to looking up back issues of popular magazines in your subscription databases. A book discussion on culinary mysteries (and other fiction with recipes) can be billed as a "book café," with readers sharing their favorite authors and titles, and bringing in cookies, cakes, and other munchies inspired by their favorite fiction.

For a library fundraiser with a bit more flavor (sorry, we couldn't resist!) than the usual mass-mail appeal, host a series of recipe-sharing potluck dinners at the library, then self-publish a library cookbook, with recipes for salads, appetizers, main dishes, and desserts, to be sold throughout the community.

Related Links

CheapCooking.com, www.cheapcooking.com
Cooking for Engineers, www.cookingforengineers.com
Cooking Light, www.cookinglight.com
Cook's Illustrated, www.cooksillustrated.com
Epicurious, www.epicurious.com
Every Day with Rachael Ray, www.rachaelraymag.com
Food Network, www.foodnetwork.com
HistoryCooks.com, www.historycooks.com
Martha Stewart's Everyday Food, www.marthastewart.com/
    everyday-food
Waterboro (ME) Public Library—Culinary Mysteries Booklist,
    www.waterborolibrary.org/oldsite/bklistm.htm#mystcul

Voices from the Field

While many of these suggestions come from teen programs, everyone likes food, and these programs really can be all ages:

"My favorite in the last 12 months was our Second Annual Teen Food Fear Factor. It was quite labor/prep intensive for me, but it was certainly a lot of

fun for all!! Attendance was excellent, too, and what was great was all the parental support and encouragement to do this program again!"
—Anonymous Public Librarian

"My favorite program was the Edible Book Festival my assistant and I planned. We had more than 25 entries, which for our community is substantial. We were extremely successful—even making it into the *Boston Globe*'s pick of the week. The program was also very fun to participate in."
—Anonymous Public Librarian

"In collaboration with the YA department, in July 2007 the YA librarian and I put on an *Iron Chef* program and had paired teens up with children in grades two and up. We had 16 teams of two. We had three judges, which included our director. Each team was judged on taste, originality, and plating (just like on the real *Iron Chef* program). We had a secret ingredient (pancakes) and a table full of ingredients (both sweet and savory). The kids were given the list of ingredients, after the secret ingredient was revealed, and allowed to come up with a game plan as to what they would make with which ingredients using the secret ingredients. They then had 15 minutes to create an edible dish using pancakes and then had to present to the judges. The brave judges tasted 16 dishes, rated each, and the team with the highest overall score won the competition and two gift certificates for a free pizza pie from a local pizzeria. The kids and teens worked well together and took the competition seriously." —Meredith Minkoff, Children's Librarian, Mineola (NY) Memorial Library

"For teens, Chocoholics Unanimous was pretty popular. Teens created their own chocolate bar recipe, using recipes for familiar bars as a starting point, while pigging out on a chocolate fountain. For our third through fifth graders, our *Ripley's Believe It or Not* program was quite successful. Kids tried to break Ripley's/Guinness records such as the number of M&Ms eaten in three minutes with chopsticks, how far you can blow a marshmallow from your nose, or the longest jump. We gave kids goodie bags with supplies to test their friends/family's record breaking ability, too."
—Anonymous Public Librarian

"Fear Factor Food was a huge hit for summer reading; it got some of the best attendance of any program in the system over the past couple of years. We had five rounds of gross food combinations, with a pickled-pigs-feet tiebreaker. It's amazing what teens will eat for a T-shirt :) Here's our blog post with a photo: dplteenservices.blogspot.com/2007/07/35-brave-souls-showed-up-for-fear.html." —April Witteveen, Teen Services Librarian, Deschutes Public Library, Bend Branch, Bend, Oregon

"We have a strong teen program calendar. Our most successful ones tend to involve food. In July, we had a cake-decorating program that was extremely popular with more than 22 teens. We even had to cut off the waiting list! Teens brought their own un-iced (blank) cakes. A volunteer from our town brought in her cake decorating supplies and taught the teens some basic cake decorating tips. Then the teens decorated their own cakes." —Anonymous Public Librarian

Patriot Day (9/11)

As we noted with regard to Yom HaShoah, pop culture can also be serious and somber. Patriot Day is another example of a day you don't want to ignore, but which may be too painful to observe in certain ways. You must know your community and be sensitive to their wants, needs, and experiences. If community members lost loved ones on 9/11, they may feel forgotten if the library does nothing. Or, a teen may walk into the library, see a photo of the towers falling, and be looking at the instant his parent died.

As with all programming, use common sense and sensitivity. How Patriot's Day is commemorated will vary, based on whether your town lost several members and your school children remember watching the towers collapse, or whether you live in an area where no one was directly touched.

October
Oktoberfest

Oktoberfest is a two-week festival held in Munich each year from the last week of September through the first week of October. The celebrations involve the quaffing of vast quantities of beer, sausage, sauerkraut, käsespätzle (cheese noodles), and other Bavarian delicacies. Of course, we understand that most libraries cannot serve alcoholic beverages on their premises—and we aren't suggesting that you do so! There's nothing to stop you, though, from hosting an event on brewing beer. Visit any liquor store and you'll see row upon row of microbrews, each more obscure than the last, and shoppers choosing these microbrews right alongside more popular national brands.

Spread your series of events over a two-week period, just like the original Oktoberfest. Invite a polka band to play at your library, and find some dance instructors willing to donate an evening of their time to teaching would-be polka fanatics of all ages how to dance—it's simple enough that even children can do it, and provides an impressive aerobic workout.

Another fun, community-wide event is a macaroni-and-cheese bake-off. It's not exactly käsespätzle, but it's close. Children are the hands-down experts in the subtleties of appropriate flavor, consistency, and crunchiness of the topping, so make sure none of your judges are older than 12. A mac-and-cheese bake-off would provide a delicious potluck dinner event for all library users, and would also be the perfect venue to display your collection of cookbooks. Make sure to take the winner's picture to send to local press outlets and to showcase in the library alongside the winner's recipe.

Related Links

BrewingTechniques magazine archive, brewingtechniques.com/index.html

Epicurious—Macaroni and Cheese recipes, tinyurl.com/y4xz9w

Oktoberfest in Leavenworth, WA, www.leavenworthoktoberfest.com

The Oktoberfest Website, www.oktoberfest.de/en

Halloween

Who doesn't like to dress up for Halloween?! OK, well, Liz doesn't. Which is why we believe staff should be encouraged to dress up, but it shouldn't be required. It's just as fun to relax your dress code to allow both costumes and Halloween-themed T-shirts.

Some of the best staff costumes (and ones that induce even curmudgeons like Liz to dress up) are group costumes. Get inspired by popular books, movies and TV shows. For example, on Halloween have all staff show up wearing variations of slacks and striped shirts, some with hats and some with glasses and some with both. Designate just one of the dressed-up staff members as "Waldo," and let the patrons go crazy trying to guess which one is the real Waldo. Or why not be the *American Idol* library, with three judges spouting Simon, Paula, and Randy's famous lines as the rest of the staff sings during the day?

Kids chant "trick or treat" as they go door to door. What treats does your library hand out to encourage parents and kids to include the library and all its departments on their holiday route? Candy, bookmarks, erasers, pens, and other library swag can be handed out to any child, teen, or grownup who visits. But why wait for someone to knock on your door? Does your town have a parade? Join in! Staff members can create a float, exhibit their synchronized book cart skills, or keep it low-key by simply marching with clever signs advertising the library and handing out library-branded goodies.

What about a costume party at night for grown-ups, you ask? Fundraising opportunity, we say! Hold it at the high school gym or in a big meeting room. Sell tickets for $10 each and make sure people know their donation is going to go towards refurbishing the children's room, adding wireless service, or some other thing your community wants. Not sure what people want? Survey your community to find out before deciding what the costume party will help fund.

Voices from the Field

We suspected that Halloween, with its scary appeal, would bring out some interesting programming ideas, and we weren't disappointed:

> "The vampire prom (Prom with Bite) came about when we got an online Ask a Librarian question about how one could host an Eclipse Prom [inspired by the popular book by Stephenie Meyer], and we said, 'Hey, that's a good idea. WE should do that!'" —Laura J, Public Services & Children's Librarian, Davis Library, Plano (TX) Public Library System

> "One of the libraries in our system offered a *HP* party. It is easier to offer teen programs since we have a structure in place to adapt to a current hot topic like *Harry Potter* or Stephenie Meyer. This October we are having a Prom with Bite, with Cynthia Leitich Smith coming to speak and other vampire themes for the program." —Anonymous Public Librarian

> "For the Teen Summer Reading program I invited a local paranormal society to visit our historic library and teach the teens about paranormal investigations. Then, with the experts' help, we conducted our own ghost hunt in the library, using all sorts of neat gadgets and techniques." —Anonymous Public Librarian

> "Visit by local paranormal investigators. They talked about their experiences, what they do during an investigation, their tools, and shared some recordings and pictures they have collected during investigations." —Anonymous Public Librarian

> "ESP Evening—students came to learn if they were psychic. We taught them three different tests using Zenner cards and then had a giant cookie." —Anonymous Public Librarian

Ramadan

The holy month of Ramadan is a rather somber holiday that celebrates the revelation of the Qur'an by emphasizing charity, fasting, and personal accountability, so it would not be appropriate to hold a big, splashy program. However, it would be both savvy and welcoming to invite a group from a local mosque to host a potluck for one of the daily break-fasts after sundown, or in honor of Eid al-Fitr, the feast holiday that marks the close of Ramadan. Also consider creating and distributing a fact sheet on the holiday, and make it an occasion to improve your collection of materials about Islam.

Related Links

CBC News InDepth: Islam, www.cbc.ca/news/background/islam
Essentials of Ramadan, the Fasting Month, www.usc.edu/dept/
    MSA/fundamentals/pillars/fasting/tajuddin/fast_1.html
Ramadan Fast and Eid-ul-Fitr, www.msichicago.org/scrapbook/
    scrapbook_exhibits/catw2004/traditions/countries/ramadan.html
U.S Department of State—Muslim Life in America, usinfo.state.
    gov/products/pubs/muslimlife

November
El Día de los Muertos

Due to religious objections from observant Christians and Jews alike, it can be problematic for public libraries to celebrate Halloween. Mounting concern regarding the nutritional value (or lack thereof) of Halloween candy also complicate matters. If your library has eliminated Halloween programming for religious or nutrition-related reasons, we offer El Día de los Muertos, Mexico's Day of the Dead, as an alternative.

Many people believe that El Día de los Muertos is strictly a Roman Catholic holiday, the equivalent to All Saints' Day. Not so, says the *New York Times*: "The Day of the Dead is not Mexico's answer to Halloween, nor is it a Latin-American interpretation of All Saints' Day. Like Mexican food, itself a complex blend of indigenous and Spanish influences, the Day of the Dead is an inextricable mix of pre-Hispanic spiritualism and post-conquest Roman

Catholicism" (www.nytimes.com/2004/10/27/dining/27DEAD.
html). More than anything else, El Día de los Muertos is a time to
honor and celebrate family members and friends who have died. It
could provide a wonderful opportunity to reach out to a substantial
and frequently underserved immigrant population, and also to
embark upon a whole series of programs on the folk traditions of the
various ethnic groups served by your library.

The *Arizona Republic* provides a comprehensive online guide to
the holiday (www.azcentral.com/ent/dead). Of particular use to public and school librarians is the Teacher's Packet (www.azcentral.
com/ent/dead/teachers/teacherpacket_edited.pdf), which includes a
bibliography, coloring sheets, and instructions for making both a
calavera (skull) mask and a *papel picado*. (*Papel picado* is a technique of cutting paper so that it forms repeated images of domestic
life, faces, or general lacy patterns.) For the even more ambitious,
try making sugar skulls, using specially designed molds. Detailed
instructions are included.

Related Links

Sugar Skull Making Instructions, www.mexicansugarskull.com/
mexicansugarskull/recipe.htm
Sugar Skull Molds & Supplies, www.mexicansugarskull.com/
mexicansugarskull/sugarskullmolds.htm

Veterans Day/Remembrance Day

Whether you live in the U.S. and call it Veterans Day or live any-
where in the British Commonwealth and call it Remembrance Day,
November 11 commemorates the signing of the Armistice that
brought the First World War to a close in 1918.

Many public libraries and schools in the U.S. and Canada are
closed on November 11, so schedule Veterans Day events during the
week leading up to the holiday. This holiday holds great potential

for cross-generational programming. Contact your local Veterans of Foreign Wars (VFW) chapter to gauge the members' interest in being guests of honor at your library's events. These can be as simple as a flag-raising ceremony or as elaborate as a community-wide discussion on service-related topics. If your library has invested in podcasting software and hardware (see Chapter 6), invite local veterans to record reminiscences of their experiences during wartime— what motivated them to enlist (or submit to the draft), what their active duty was like, how they fared upon returning home. Consider, too, inviting those left behind on the home front to record their experiences. Encourage young students to serve as interviewers (and encourage the history faculty at your local schools to offer students extra credit for interviewing veterans).

On a smaller scale, your library could consider teaming up for a fundraiser with your local VFW chapter by distributing red paper poppies for a small donation, the proceeds of which would go to support a veterans-related charity. Red poppies have been significant reminders of veterans' contributions and sacrifices since the publication of Canadian Major (later Lieutenant Colonel) John McCrae's poem *In Flanders Fields*:

> In Flanders fields the poppies blow
> Between the crosses, row on row,
> That mark our place; and in the sky
> The larks, still bravely singing, fly
> Scarce heard amid the guns below

Related Links

BritainUSA—Remembrance Day, www.britainusa.com/sections/
   articles_show_nt1.asp?d=0&i=60062&L1=41013&L2=41013&
   a=45235
Canadian War Museum—Armistice Day, www.warmuseum.ca/
   cwm/remember/armisticeday_e.html

In Flanders Field by John McCrae (full text),
　　www.poets.org/viewmedia.php/prmMID/19464
Library of Congress on Flicker.com—1930s–40s in color photoset,
　　www.flicker.com/photos/library-of-congress/sets/
　　72157603671370361
U.S. Department of Veterans Affairs—Veterans Day,
　　www1.va.gov/ opa/vetsday
Veterans of Foreign Wars, www.vfw.org

December
Holiday Dilemma

Many interfaith families talk about the "December Dilemma" when it comes to celebrating holidays, citing arguments and hurt feelings about the religious and secular aspects of Christmas and Chanukah. If families don't know what to do, what should libraries do? Some patrons may get upset if "their" holiday is ignored by the library. Others may be bothered by what they see as a strictly religious holiday being treated as secular. Still others simply don't care. Some libraries opt out of the argument altogether by avoiding any decorations, displays, or programs associated with the December holidays, electing instead to have "winter" displays and snowflake crafts.

Our suggestion for December follows familiar lines: Know your local community. Know that your community is local, but is also part of a bigger community (the state, the country, the world). Be respectful, and be inventive. Decorate for all holidays, but make sure you know your dates—so that you don't put up the Chanukah decorations after Chanukah has ended. Use your patrons' response (or non-response) to plan events.

One trap to avoid: Be sure that Chanukah is not the only Jewish holiday ever celebrated at your library. Many non-Jews do not realize that Chanukah is actually a fairly minor holiday on the Jewish calendar, and they may not be familiar at all with equally festive holidays such as Sukkoth and Purim. The Torah Tots website has great craft ideas for these festivals.

Another option is to address the December dilemma head on by offering programs aimed at interfaith families. Look beyond the specifics of the holidays to see what the celebrations have in common: food and entertaining. What a great time to have computer classes on finding recipes online, scrapbooking workshops, and classes on digital cameras.

Related Links

Celebrating the Holidays in an Interfaith Family, www.baby center.com/0_celebrating-the-holidays-in-an-interfaith-family_ 9838.bc

Interfaith Calendar, www.interfaithcalendar.org

InterfaithFamily.com, www.interfaithfamily.com

Torah Tots, www.torahtots.com/home.htm

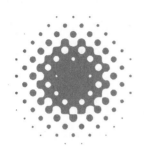

APPENDIX A: CORE POP CULTURE RESOURCES FOR LIBRARY PROFESSIONALS

We are inveterate list-makers, and now you can benefit from our passion for bullet points! What you'll find here are collected lists of online, print, and televised resources that will help you build collections, invent programming, and generally hone your pop cultural savvy. These lists are by no means exhaustive or comprehensive; however, they represent some of the most useful and reliable sources of information on pop culture materials available at publication. Balancing the use of books written for the library market with up-to-date periodicals, great websites, and TV shows is the best way to furnish your patrons with the right balance of quality and popular materials. As always, use your own interests to guide you—if you know anime is not your cup of tea but you love music, skip *PiQ*, *Shonen Jump*, and *Shojo Beat* in favor of trawling the reviews on Pitchfork or Stereogum—and have fun with this. These lists aren't homework; using them shouldn't feel like it. We'll continue to post core resources at www.popgoesthelibrary.com/popbook as we discover them.

Online Resources
Blogs and Websites

Ain't It Cool News, www.aintitcool.com
Get information, reviews, and gossip about everything related to the film, television, and comic book industries.

AllMovie.com, www.allmovie.com
This database is dedicated to movies, their directors, stars, and connections.

AllMusic.com, www.allmusic.com
This database and review site is related to, as the name would suggest, all types of music. Exhaustive and comprehensive.

Blog Carnival, blogcarnival.com/bc
This site gives a round-up of blog posts on a particular topic, usually done periodically. A great way to find up-to-date information, news, and posts on a particular topic.

The Book of Zines, www.zinebook.com
Find out everything you need to know about zines (self-published magazines).

Bookslut, www.bookslut.com
"Bookslut is a monthly web magazine and daily blog dedicated to those who love to read. We provide a constant supply of news, reviews, commentary, insight, and more than occasional opinions."

BuzzFeed, www.buzzfeed.com
This site combs the Web to track, compile, and promote what bloggers, journalists, and fans are discussing online right now. A great jumping-off point for trendspotters everywhere.

Chasing Ray, www.chasingray.com

Read this literary blog by Colleen Mondor, with interviews, blog tours, and reviews.

The Edge of the Forest, www.theedgeoftheforest.com

"A monthly online journal devoted to children's literature." (Disclosure: Liz is on the Editorial Board.)

The Elegant Variation, marksarvas.blogs.com/elegvar

Check out this literary blog by Mark Sarvas.

ESPN Sports, espn.go.com

This vast, comprehensive sports website incorporates text, podcasts, and video. Some coverage in Spanish.

The Futon Critic, www.thefutoncritic.com

This television resource has all the news about TV shows: what pilots are being shopped, what got picked up, what is a midseason replacement, information on past shows, reviews, and an A-to-Z guide to TV.

ICv2.com, www.icv2.com

"The top source for information on the business of pop culture products in five important categories:

- Anime and Manga
- Graphic Novels and Comics
- Games
- Movie/TV Licensed Products
- Toys"

While ICv2 is targeted at pop culture business-owners, its reports and interviews are very useful for librarians. Additionally, the magazines it publishes include reviews written by librarians.

IGN.com, www.ign.com

Find games and reviews of games, along with cheat codes and walkthroughs; a "broad and deep offering of videogame, entertainment and lifestyle content and resources with some of the largest message boards on the web."

Internet Movie Database, www.imdb.com

This site is more famous than AllMovie.com, but more basic than its competitor. Go here if all you need to know is who was the third point in the Demi Moore–Robert Redford love triangle in 1993's *Indecent Proposal*. (It was Woody Harrelson, by the way.)

Lifehacker, www.lifehacker.com

One of the 14 blogs under the umbrella of Gawker Media (this list includes New York gossip blog Gawker, Los Angeles gossip blog Defamer, science fiction blog io9, electronics and gadgetry blog Gizmodo, and car culture blog Jalopnik), Lifehacker is a wonderland of productivity tools and advice. All Gawker Media blogs feature solid, often witty writing and up-to-the-minute (these team-written blogs are updated upward of 10 times each day) tracking of what is going on in an impressively broad range of niche interests. Lifehacker won over Liz when she found the answer to fixing scratched DVDs: Pledge (www.lifehacker.com/software/macgyver/macgyver-tip—smooth-a-scratched-dvd-with-pledge-190634.php)!

LISNews: Library and Information Science News, lisnews.org

Get library news from around the world. Helps you keep on top of what is going on with libraries, both good and bad.

Newsarama.com, www.newsarama.com

"Daily comic book news, previews, reviews and commentary."

No Depression, www.nodepression.net

This bimonthly magazine focused on the alt-country music scene but went out of print in mid-2008. However, a fair amount of every back-issue's content is available to read (click "Browse Our Back Issues"), and every back issue going back to 1995 is available for purchase. The site also includes blogs written by co-editors Grant Alden and Peter Blackstock.

No Flying, No Tights (NFNT), www.noflyingnotights.com

Robin Brenner's masterful, comprehensive comics and graphic novels review site, written by and for collection development librarians, is notable not only for the quality of its reviews, but also for its division into three audience-specific subdomains: NFNT is for teens, the Lair is for teens and adults, and Sidekicks is for kids.

Pitchfork Media, www.pitchforkmedia.com

This is indie rock review central. Pitchfork's reviewers are hugely influential, and they know it. They're also occasionally a little bit off the wall—reviews sometimes take the form of stream-of-consciousness ramblings. If you want to read reviews of CDs on tiny labels like Jade Tree or SpinArt, as well as larger ones like Matador, this is where to go.

The PlanetEsme Plan: The Best New Children's Books from Esme's Shelf, planetesme.blogspot.com

This blog, written by Esmé Raji Codell (*How to Get Your Child to Love Reading*), reviews and promotes the best new books for children, combining this coverage with a retrospective look at similarly themed titles. Very useful for lesson plans, harried parents, and busy school librarians looking for the Next Big Thing from picture books to middle-grade fiction.

Pop Candy, blogs.usatoday.com/popcandy

Whitney Matheson unwraps pop culture's "hip and hidden treasures" for USAToday.com.

Pop Goes the Library, www.popgoesthelibrary.com

If using our own book to engage in a little blatant self-promotion is wrong, we don't want to be right.

Popjournalism Blog, popjournalism.ca/blog

Read about pop culture from a Canadian perspective.

PopWatch, popwatch.ew.com

EW.com trains its eagle eye on pop culture.

Premiere, www.premiere.com

Premiere Magazine ended its print run in April 2007 and is now strictly an online news source for movie news, including information about films in production and DVD reviews. If your customers are movie fans, and clamoring for DVDs, this is a must-read resource.

Rotten Tomatoes, www.rottentomatoes.com

"Created by movie-buff Senh Duong in 1998, Rotten Tomatoes has grown to become a premier destination for both casual moviegoers and film buffs alike ... Over 5.4 million readers each month use Rotten Tomatoes as a dependable, objective resource for coverage of movies and videos ... With more than 127,000 titles and 644,000 review links in its ever-growing database, Rotten Tomatoes offers a fun and informative way to discover the critical reaction on movies from the nation's top print and online film critics, neatly summarized via the Tomatometer."

Salon, www.salon.com

This site offers classic online reporting and commentary.

School Library Journal (SLJ), www.schoollibraryjournal.com

In addition to containing articles from its print edition, the SLJ website is a don't-miss if you're doing anything related to schools or children's and YA fiction. The blogs contain news, reviews, updates, and commentary. Also check out its affiliated blogs at www.schoollibraryjournal.com/blogs.html.

Slate, www.slate.com

Get political and cultural commentary, served up daily online. Slate also has a bit of a crossover deal going on with NPR's daily midday show, *Day to Day*.

So You'd Like To … Guides by Amazon.com Music Editors, www. amazon.com/gp/richpub/syltguides/byauthor/AJM38DLD0P3H8 /ref=cm_pdp_sylt_seeAll/002-9650225-7084037

Amazon.com's clever, appealing, and well-informed mix of commercialism and social networking—they let anyone create these recommendation lists—is part of what makes the site useful. It's a great model for what libraries could be doing with their OPACs using the SOPAC model discussed in Chapter 6. Liz has found these Amazon.com lists very helpful for figuring out things like the proper order to read the Civil War graphic novels, and Sophie uses them regularly to find sound- and read-alikes for her library's music and YA collections.

Technorati, www.technorati.com

Did we overlook your particular pop culture area of interest? Go to a blog search engine such as Technorati and find the blogs that will have the news and reviews you are looking for!

Totally Wired, www.ypulse.com/totallywired

From Anastasia Goodstein of Ypulse, "Totally Wired (the blog) is a resource for parents, aunts, uncles, teachers, librarians youth workers or any adult trying to decode what teens are doing online and with technology." Goodstein stopped updating this blog (which she created as a marketing device for her book of the same name) in late 2007, but the archives are excellent and well worth reading.

YALSA blog, yalsa.ala.org/blog

This is the blog of the Young Adult Library Services Association of the American Library Association.

Ypulse, www.ypulse.com

Anastasia Goodstein has her finger on the pulse of youth culture. If you only read one blog about Gen Y, read this one. "Ypulse is an independent blog for teen/youth media and marketing professionals providing news, commentary and resources on commercial teen media for teens (teen magazines, websites), entertainment for teens (movies, games, television, music), technology used by teens (cell phones, instant messaging, SMS), the news media's desire to attract teens (newspapers, cable news), marketing and advertising (targeting the teen market) and civic youth media (highlighting organizations' efforts at promoting youth voices in media)." If you don't have time to scan your RSS feeds or visit the blog itself, Goodstein delivers the content daily via an email newsletter.

Lists

Adbooks, www.adbooks.org

"Adbooks is an e-mail list created to discuss books written for adolescent readers. Our members love to read and to talk about good books."

Fiction_L, www.webrary.org/rs/flmenu.html

"Fiction_L is an electronic mailing list devoted to reader's advisory topics such as book discussions, booktalks, collection development issues, booklists and bibliographies, and a wide variety of other topics of interest to librarians, book discussion leaders, and others with an interest in reader's advisory."

GNLIB-L: Graphic Novels in Libraries, lists.topica.com/lists/ GNLIB-L

"Just for young adult/adult Librarians! Share reviews and resources for collection development of your graphic or comic novel section."

LibGaming, groups.google.com/group/LibGaming

"LibGaming is a forum for discussion of gaming in libraries, including

- Circulating video games for PC & consoles
- Game Collection Development
- Gaming Programs (LAN parties and tournaments)
- Role-playing (pencil and dice gaming) & Card Gaming (Magic)
- Online gaming
- Gaming reviews & resources
- News & Research"

LM_NET, www.eduref.org/lm_net

"LM_NET is a discussion group open to school library media specialists worldwide, and to people involved with the school library media field. It is not for general librarians or educators. We want to keep the activity and discussion focused on school library media."

PUBLIB, lists.webjunction.org/publib

"An electronic discussion list for public librarians and those interested in public libraries."

ya-music, lists.ala.org/wws/info/ya-music

"This list, started by YALSA's Teen Music Interest Group, will be used to discuss and develop recommended practices in collections, programming, and related topics in the field of music and media, including CDs, MP3s, and emerging technologies and services in music media for teens. This list is open to anyone interested in teen music and media."

yalsa-bk, lists.ala.org/wws/info/yalsa-bk

"This open list for book discussion invites subscribers to discuss specific titles, as well as other issues concerning young adult reading and young adult literature."

Survey Creation Websites

QuestionPro, www.questionpro.com
SurveyMonkey, www.surveymonkey.com
Zoomerang, info.zoomerang.com

Major Library Materials Wholesalers

Baker & Taylor, www.btol.com
BWI/Book Wholesalers, Inc., www.bwibooks.com
Follett Library Resources, www.titlewave.com
Ingram Book Company, www.ingrambook.com

Print Resources
Books

Barr, Catherine. *Best New Media, K–12: A Guide to Movies, Subscription Websites, and Educational Software and Games.* Westport, CT: Libraries Unlimited, 2008.

Bartel, Julie. *From A to Zine: Building a Winning Zine Collection in Your Library.* Chicago: ALA Editions, 2004.

Brenner, Robin E. *Understanding Manga and Anime.* Westport, CT: Libraries Unlimited, 2007.

Emmons, Mark. *Film and Television: A Guide to the Reference Literature.* Westport, CT: Libraries Unlimited, 2006.

Furness, Adrienne. *Helping Homeschoolers in the Library.* Chicago: ALA Editions, 2008.

Gallaway, Beth. *Game On!: Gaming At the Library.* New York: Neal-Schuman, 2007.

Goldsmith, Francisca. *Graphic Novels Now: Building, Managing, and Marketing a Dynamic Collection.* Chicago: ALA Editions, 2005.

Hutchison, David. *Playing to Learn: Video Games in the Library.* Westport, CT: Libraries Unlimited, 2007.

McCloud, Scott. *Making Comics: Storytelling Secrets of Comics, Manga and Graphic Novels.* New York: Harper, 2006.

Miller, Steve. *Developing and Promoting Graphic Novel Collections.* New York: Neal-Schuman, 2005.

Nichols, C. Allen, ed. *Thinking Outside the Book: Alternatives for Today's Teen Library Collections.* Westport, CT: Libraries Unlimited, 2004.

Pawuk, Michael. *Graphic Novels: A Genre Guide to Comic Books, Manga, and More.* Westport, CT: Libraries Unlimited, 2007.

Serchay, David. *A Librarian's Guide to Graphic Novels for Children and 'Tweens.* New York: Neal-Schuman, 2008.

Todd, Mark and Esther Pearl Watson. *Whatcha Mean, What's a Zine?* Boston: Graphia, 2006.

Magazines and Newspapers

The Christian Science Monitor, www.csmonitor.com

This is not a religious paper, but a paper owned by a church. There's a significant difference, and the *Monitor*'s fair, intelligent coverage of international and national (U.S.) topics is very well regarded.

Chronicle of Higher Education, chronicle.com

If you're in academia, you are already reading the *Chronicle*, but it's something to consider if you work within education at all, and particularly if you work with older teens.

The Comics Journal, www.tcj.com

Comics are a unique blend of words and art, which combine to create powerful, engrossing, and plain old entertaining stories. *The Comics Journal* takes an "arts-first perspective."

Entertainment Weekly, www.ew.com

With its weekly round-up of music, television, movies, books, and DVD releases, this is the one-stop shop for general pop coverage, and for tracking the Next Big Things.

Giant Robot, www.giantrobot.com

This guide to Asian-American culture started as a self-published zine, and even though it's graduated to a large, glossy format, it still retains that labor of love feel that makes it so appealing. Essential for communities serving large Asian-American populations, particularly for those patrons who may have outgrown *Shonen Jump* and *Shojo Beat*.

ICv2 Guide to Manga, Anime and Gaming, www.icv2.com

These guides take you "inside pop culture," aiming to provide you with a "one-stop resource on graphic novels, anime and manga, and games." Many graphic novel-loving librarians review for this journal.

J-14, www.j-14.hollywood.com

When thinking magazines for teens, don't start and stop with *Seventeen*. *J-14* is a pop culture magazine for and about teens, with gossip on the latest teen celebrities, horoscopes, and fashion.

Local Daily Newspapers and Local Weekly Alternative Newspapers

Nothing beats local news sources for community-based trendspotting and program idea-generating.

Magnet, www.magnetmagazine.com

This quarterly bills itself as a home for "real musical alternatives," and it lives splendidly up to that promise, covering musicians whose work is rarely covered by mainstream magazines like *Rolling Stone* or *SPIN*.

Metal Edge, www.metaledgemag.com

Do you have patrons who love heavy metal and hard rock? This is the magazine to get for them. (Or, to explain to all those *Supernatural* fans: This is Dean Winchester's music magazine of choice.)

Mojo, www.mojo4music.com

This British music magazine focuses on classic and roots rock; in their own words, "we like to think it's the music magazine you go to when you've grown out of all the others."

New York Times, www.nytimes.com

The *New York Times* is the national paper of record. You can disagree with its liberal bent, but you should still read it.

Newsweek, www.newsweek.com, and *Time,* www.time.com

These magazines are general knowledge and current events must-reads.

Oprah, www.oprah.com

Oprah's influence cannot be overstated; we all know that from the wild popularity of even the most obscure of her Book Club picks. Her magazine features those things Oprah is interested and believes her viewers are interested in, from friendships to family, worklife to makeup, and recipes to health issues.

People, www.people.com

People walks a fine line by featuring not only celebrity gossip (less pruriently than, say *Us* or *OK!*, but still …) but it also features regular folks who are in the news because they have adopted 20-plus children or started a food bank at age seven. This is the gossip magazine for people who don't want to admit they are reading gossip.

PiQ, www.piqmag.com

To be perfectly honest, we're not sure how essential this magazine is, or how long it will last—at publication, this replacement for *NewTypeUSA* was just two issues old. Unlike *NewType, PiQ* doesn't come with glossy posters or preview DVDs, and it doesn't seem to be for hardcore anime and manga fans anymore, either. However, it does have an excellent, frequently updated website, and the editors seem to be working hard to make the magazine what their readers are looking for. Keep an eye on this one.

Rolling Stone, www.rollingstone.com

Founded in 1967, this American classic inspired the Shel Silverstein song "The Cover of the Rolling Stone" (featured a capella in former *Rolling Stone* writer Cameron Crowe's film *Almost Famous*). Don't stop at the cover, though—over the years,

Rolling Stone has published in-depth articles on politics, the environment, and pop culture beyond the music business.

Shojo Beat, www.shojobeat.com

Shojo manga are drawn with a female audience in mind (shojo means "girl" in Japanese), and they focus primarily on humorous, romantic stories. *Shojo Beat* covers not only manga, but also trends in publishing, fashion, and culture for shojo readers.

Shonen Jump, www.shonenjump.com

Like its sister publication *Shojo Beat*, *Shonen Jump* is aimed at a specific audience: readers and fans of shonen, or "boy" manga. These stories are often more action-based than shojo manga. *Shonen Jump* serializes shonen manga, offers sneak peeks at different stories, and covers gaming as well.

SPIN, www.spin.com

SPIN covers pop music in every sense of the phrase—everything from Panic at the Disco to Jay-Z, Lupe Fiasco to Morrissey, and everything in between.

TV Guide, www.tvguide.com

This weekly guide to television viewing includes articles on TV stars and shows. Remember Frank Constanza's prized *TV Guide* collection on *Seinfeld*? With increased online competition in the weekly guide market, this title has been reinventing itself in both content and format, so it is once more (if you'll forgive the atrocious pun) one to watch. (Thank you! We'll be here all week! Tip your waitress!)

Us Weekly, www.usmagazine.com

For those who want dirtier celebrity news than *People*'s "keep it nice, keep it positive" approach affords, *Us Weekly* offers dishy tabloid news.

Variety, **www.variety.com**

For information on the entertainment industry, particularly the film industry, this daily has no peer.

VIBE, **www.vibe.com**

Founded by Quincy Jones in 1993, *VIBE* covers urban music and culture. The magazine's frequent "Best of" and "Essential" lists are terrific collection development resources.

Wall Street Journal, **online.wsj.com/public/us**

The *Wall Street Journal* is essential reading for those working with people who deal with money matters. In other words, for everyone.

Television Shows

Breakfast TV Shows, Daytime, and Late-Night Talk Shows (various networks)

An endless parade of celebrities, authors, and performers traipse through the studios of every major morning, daytime, and late-night talk show. You can get an idea of what and who is approaching hotness just by taking a look at these shows' schedules, available on their network websites. This category comprises everything from *Today* and *Good Morning America* to *The View* and *Oprah* and *The Tonight Show*.

The Colbert Report (Comedy Central)

The Colbert Report takes a satirical look at the day's news. Steven Colbert, as "Steven Colbert," casts a gimlet eye on the political news of the day. Considerably more outrageous than its brother program (see *The Daily Show*), Mr. Colbert has brought us such neologisms as "truthiness" and "wikiality."

The Daily Show (Comedy Central)

The Daily Show is Must-See TV for Generations X and Y, thanks to the snarky yet humane intelligence of host Jon Stewart. The pepper to *The Colbert Report*'s salt.

The O'Reilly Factor (Fox News)

This immensely popular daily commentary show, hosted by Bill O'Reilly, is always controversial. This show is a good way to keep a finger on the pulse of conservative thought. Fun pop fact: O'Reilly is the pundit whose style has most influenced the character "Steven Colbert" on *The Colbert Report*.

Saturday Night Live (NBC)

This workhorse sketch comedy show has its ups and downs, but when the cast is really good (or sometimes just the guest host—see Justin Timberlake's immortal, if unprintable, sketch-song from his December 2006 Christmas episode), you cannot beat *SNL*'s ability to generate catchphrases and future stars of comedy.

TRL (MTV) and *106th & Park* (BET)

On these live, daily call-in Top 10 music video countdown shows, viewers vote for their favorite videos of the day online and via text message. Both shows feature attractive, youthful hosts, screaming tween and teen audience members, lavishly produced videos, and a stream of next big thing guests. Essential viewing, because it's no longer enough (and really, it hasn't been enough since 1981, when MTV was founded) to know how a Top 40 song sounds. You need to know how it looks, too.

APPENDIX B:
POP PROGRAMMING
YEAR-ROUND CALENDAR

January

January 1 – New Year's Day

Third Monday – Martin Luther King Jr.'s Birthday (observed)

Third Monday – ALA Youth Book Awards

Last Sunday – Super Bowl (sometimes in February)

Chinese New Year

Golden Globe Awards

Sundance Film Festival

February

February 5 – Mexican Constitution Anniversary

February 14 – Valentine's Day

February 24 – Mexican Flag Day

Third Monday – President's Day (observed)

Black History Month

BAFTAs (British Academy of Film and Television Awards)

Grammy Awards

WWE Wrestlemania

Winter Olympics and Paralympics: Vancouver (2010)

New York Fashion Week

March

March 17 – St. Patrick's Day

March 20 or 21 – Vernal Equinox

March 21 – Benito Juàrez' birthday (Mexico)

Women's History Month

Mothering Sunday (U.K.)

Academy Awards

Soul Train Awards

Filmfare Awards (Bollywood Oscars)

March Madness

YALSA's Teen Tech Week

MLB Spring Training and Opening Day

Daylight Savings begins

April

April 15 – Tax Day!

April 23 – St. George's Day

April 25 – Yom HaShoah/Holocaust Remembrance Day

National Poetry Month

Passover (sometimes in March)

Easter (sometimes in March)

New York Comic Con

Juno Awards (Canadian music awards)

Genie Awards (Canadian film awards)

May

May 5 – Cinco de Mayo

First Saturday – Free Comic Book Day

First Saturday – Kentucky Derby

Second Sunday – Mother's Day

Monday before or on May 24 – Victoria Day (Canada)

Last Monday – Memorial Day

Asian Pacific Islander Heritage Month

PEN/Faulkner Awards

TV Finales

End of School

Stanley Cup Finals

June

June 14 – Flag Day

June 21 – Summer Solstice

June 23 and 24 – Fête Nationale du Québec (Saint Jean Baptiste Day)

First or Second Sunday – Queen's Birthday (U.K.)

Third Sunday – Father's Day

Gay Pride Month

Wimbledon

End of School

TV Finales

NBA Finals

Tony Awards

Daytime Emmy Awards

BET Awards

Bollywood Movie Awards (Long Island, NY)

All Wheeled Conveyance Safety

Summer Reading

July

July 1 – Canada Day

July 4 – Independence Day

July 14 – Bastille Day

San Diego Comic-Con

Summer Olympics and Paralympics: Beijing (2008), London (2012)

World Cup Soccer: Durban, South Africa (2010)

Commonwealth Games: Delhi, India (2010); Glasgow, Scotland (2014)

Summer Reading

August

Back to School

TV Premieres

Otakon

X Games

NFL Training Camp

September

September 11 – Patriot Day

September 15 through October 15 – Hispanic Heritage Month

September 16 – Independence Day (Mexico)

First Monday – Labor Day

Rosh Hashanah

Yom Kippur (sometimes in October)

Back to School

TV Premieres

New York Fashion Week

MTV Video Music Awards

Primetime Emmy Awards

October

October 12 – Día de la Raza (Mexico)

October 24 – UN Day

October 31 – Halloween

Second Monday – Columbus Day (observed)

Second Monday – Thanksgiving (Canada)

Third Saturday – Sweetest Day

Third Week – Teen Read Week

Oktoberfest

Ramadan/Eid al-Fitr

Sukkot (sometimes in September)

World Series

Gemini Awards (Canadian television awards)

November

November 1 – El Día de los Muertos (Mexico)

November 5 – Guy Fawkes Day/Bonfire Night (U.K.)

November 11 – Veterans Day (U.S.)/Remembrance Day (Canada)

November 20 – Mexican Revolution Anniversary

First Tuesday – Election Day

Fourth Thursday – Thanksgiving

End of Daylight Savings

National American Indian Heritage Month

Country Music Association Awards

Latin Grammy Awards

Bollywood Music and Fashion Awards

National Book Awards

Diwali (sometimes in October or December)

December

December 7 – Pearl Harbor Day

December 12 – Our Lady of Guadalupe (Mexico)

December 21 – Winter Solstice

December 25 – Christmas

December 26 – Boxing Day

December 26 to January 1 – Kwanzaa

December 31 – New Year's Eve

Chanukah (sometimes in November)

Appendix C:
Survey Questions

Quotes and comments throughout this book are drawn from responses to an online survey we conducted on our blog about how our readers view, consume, and apply pop culture knowledge at their libraries. We were bowled over by the response to the survey—we had more than 700 respondents (!) from public, school, and academic libraries—and we appreciate everyone's views on these questions. We have tried to incorporate as many points of view as were expressed in the responses, and believe us, they ran the gamut from dismissive to enthusiastic.

The following survey was posted online using SurveyMonkey.com in July 2007 and was publicized widely online through posts to lists, our respective blogs, Facebook, and Flickr.

> What kind of library do you work in? Please check all that apply. (Choices: public library, school library, college/university library, special library, other)

How would you describe your position? Please check all that apply. (Choices: Children's, YA/Teen, Youth Services, Reference, Acquisitions, Technical Services, Library Media Specialist, Administrator, Library Associate, Library Assistant, Other)

How would you describe your library's location? (Choices: urban, suburban, rural)

How large is your library? (Choices: single facility, 2–5 branches, 6–10 branches, 11 or more branches)

How involved are you with collection development and maintenance? Please describe your responsibilities below.

Are you involved in the planning and execution of library programming? (Y/N)

If you are involved in library programming, check all that apply. (Choices: computer/technology classes, literary programming, storytimes, other children's programming, teen programming, informational programming, other)

Please describe your favorite or most successful program of the last 12 months below:

How do you define pop culture? What do you include or exclude in your definition? How does your definition (and inclusions and exclusions) of pop culture change when you apply it to your work in libraries?

Please describe how, if at all, your definition of pop culture influences your collection development choices. What criteria do you use in selecting materials such as DVDs and music? Do you seek out Top 40 artists and blockbusters on DVD? Do you take a more educational or best-of-the-best approach? What is your pop culture collection development style?

What kind of pop culture programming do you offer at your library? For what age groups do you offer it? Do you offer programs tied to current events (for example, a *Harry Potter* book-launch party)? Do you create programs to match your collection and community interests as they arise?

How do you market your collections and services to your community? Have you had to defend or advocate for the inclusion of pop culture programs or materials to library staff, board members, customers, or others? What specific steps, if any, have you taken in so doing?

How do you track your patrons' pop culture interests? Do you use this information in the collection development process, and in the planning of programs and events at your library?

How do you keep abreast of new developments that could be useful to staff and patrons? How do you publicize your finds?

How do you incorporate trends in technology—for example, PDAs for roving reference, social networking sites like Flickr, MySpace, Facebook, IM reference—

into your library's services? If you do, what do you use, and why? If you don't, why not?

Thank you for your participation! You're nearly done, we promise. Are you willing to have your name associated with your responses to this survey? (Choose: I grant permission to attribute my responses to me by my name and my library. / I grant permission to use my responses anonymously.)

Please enter your name, position, library name, and location below. Thank you! (Name, Title, Library Name, Library Location)

May we contact you later if we have follow-up questions regarding your responses to this survey? If so, please enter your email address. If not, please leave blank.

APPENDIX D: WEBSITES

www.popgoesthelibrary.com/popbook

Websites are listed in the order in which they appear in each chapter. URLs are subject to change, and will be updated as available on the book's companion website: www.popgoesthelibrary.com/popbook.

Chapter 1: Defining and Using Pop Culture to Connect

MySpace, www.myspace.com
Facebook, www.facebook.com
Ypulse, www.ypulse.com
Trends & Tudes from Harris Interactive,
    www.harrisinteractive.com/news/newsletters_k12.asp

Chapter 2: Creating a Pop Niche for Yourself and Your Library

YALSA: TAGS, www.ala.org/ala/yalsa/tags/tagsresources/tags resources.cfm

YA-YAAC, lists.ala.org/wws/info/ya-yaac
BoingBoing, www.boingboing.net
Go Fug Yourself, gofugyourself.typepad.com

Chapter 3: Building a Collection That Really Pops

School Library Journal, www.schoollibraryjournal.com
The Horn Book Magazine, www.hbook.com/magazine
Bookslut, www.bookslut.com
The Edge of the Forest, www.theedgeoftheforest.com
Technorati, www.technorati.com
Google Blog Search, blogsearch.google.com
Blogger, www.blogger.com
WordPress, www.wordpress.org
Dewey Decimal Classification System, www.oclc.org/dewey
Library of Congress Classification, www.loc.gov/aba
Book Industry Study Group subject headings, www.bisg.org/
   standards/bisac_subject/major_subjects.html

Chapter 4: Advocacy, Marketing, Public Relations, and Outreach

American Library Association (ALA) Advocacy Resource Center,
   www.ala.org/pio/advocacy
Library Advocate's Handbook, 2nd ed. (ALA),
   www.ala.org/ala/advocacybucket/libraryadvocateshandbook.pdf
American Association of School Librarians (AASL) Advocacy
   Toolkit, www.ala.org/ala/aasl/aaslproftools/toolkits/aasl
   advocacy.htm
Highlands Regional Library Cooperative (HRLC), Valuing
   Libraries—Demonstrating the Contributions Libraries Make to
   Their Communities, www.hrlc.org/funding/valuinglibs.htm

Flickr, www.flickr.com

Library Marketing—Thinking Outside the Book, library marketing.blogspot.com

ALA's Office for Literacy and Outreach Services, www.ala.org/ala/olos/outreachresource/outreachtipsheets/ outreachtipsheets.htm

Chapter 5: Trendspotting

Oh, No They Didn't!, community.livejournal.com/ohnotheydidnt

PerezHilton.com, www.perezhilton.com

Advergirl.com, leighhouse.typepad.com/advergirl

Creative Think, www.creativethink.com

Seth Godin's Blog, sethgodin.typepad.com

Smart Mobs, www.smartmobs.com

PostSecret, postsecret.blogspot.com

Cute Overload, www.cuteoverload.com

Chapter 6: Information Technology Is Everyone's Job

Flickr, www.flickr.com

YouTube, www.youtube.com

iTunes, www.itunes.com

ListenNJ, www.listennj.com

OverDrive, www.overdrive.com

Sony Reader, www.sonystyle.com

Amazon Kindle, www.kindle.com

Sparta Public Library, www.spartalibrary.com

Playaway, store.playawaydigital.com

iMix Tutorial, www.apple.com/support/ilife/tutorials/itunes/ it6-2.html

Pop Goes the Library, www.popgoesthelibrary.com

A Chair, a Fireplace and a Tea Cozy, yzocaet.blogspot.com

Blogger, www.blogger.com

New York Times online, www.nytimes.com

del.icio.us, del.icio.us

Facebook, www.facebook.com

RSS2Java, www.rss2java.com

RSS to JavaScript, www.rss-to-javascript.com

Bloglines, www.bloglines.com

Google Reader, www.google.com/reader/view

Friends Page of LiveJournal,
   www.livejournal.com/support/faqbrowse.bml?faqid=219

Handouts and Resources from ... Community Building Through
   Your Web Site: Library Blogs and RSS (Michael Stephens),
   www.sjrlc.org/web20/handouts

Wikipedia, en.wikipedia.org

Library Success: A Best Practices Wiki, www.libsuccess.org

YALSA Wiki, wikis.ala.org/yalsa

The Children's Series Binder Wiki, seriesbinder.lishost.org

MediaWiki, www.mediawiki.org/wiki/MediaWiki

Google Sites, sites.google.com

PBWiki, pbwiki.com

Saint Joseph County Public Library (SJCPL) Blog,
   www.sjcpl.org/blogs/lifeline

SJCPL Subject Guides,
   www.sjcpl.lib.in.us/subjectguides/index.php/Main_Page

ZoomClouds, zoomclouds.com

New Blogger Tag Cloud, phy3blog.googlepages.com/Beta-
   Blogger-Label-Cloud.html

SnapShirts, www.snapshirts.com

Photobucket, www.photobucket.com

Picasa Web Albums, picasaweb.google.com

Allen County Public Library, Talk Like a Pirate Day 2007, www.flickr.com/photos/acplinfo/sets/72157602196843961

Georgia State University Library's Photos, www.flickr.com/photos/gsulibrary/sets

Flat Bobby, www.flickr.com/photos/tracylee/sets/1749585

Lewis Elementary School's Community Care Day 2007, www.flickr.com/photos/lewiselementary/sets/721576016555 49404

Osage Middle School's Bluebirds July 2007, www.flickr.com/photos/srussell/sets/72157600938116644

Hennepin County Library, Send a Photo of Yourself Reading *Harry Potter*, www.hclib.org/pub/bookspace/hpphotos.cfm

MOO, www.moo.com/flickr

Digg, digg.com

Cleveland (OH) Public Library, www.cpl.org

City of San Mateo (CA) Public Library, www.cityofsanmateo.org/dept/library

City of San Mateo Public Library's del.icio.us page, del.icio.us/SanMateoLibrary

Ocean County (NJ) Library's Summer Reading List, del.icio.us/srms_summer_reading_list

Library Success: A Best Practices Wiki—Gaming, www.libsuccess.org/index.php?title=Gaming

Ann Arbor (MI) District Library (AADL) Axis Teen Blog, www.aadl.org/axis

RuneScape, www.runescape.com

LibraryThing, www.librarything.com

LibraryThing for Libraries, www.librarything.com/forlibraries

Shelfari, www.shelfari.com

Goodreads, www.goodreads.com

AADL Catalog, www.aadl.org/catalog

Hennepin County Library, www.hclib.org/pub

PennTags, University of Pennsylvania, tags.library.upenn.edu

Podcast.net, www.podcast.net

Odeo, odeo.com

NPR Podcast Directory, www.npr.org/rss/podcast/podcast_
directory.php

Odeo Studio, studio.odeo.com/create/home

Audacity, audacity.sourceforge.net

PodOmatic, www.podomatic.com

AOL Instant Messenger (AIM), www.aim.com

Windows Live Messenger, get.live.com/messenger/overview

Yahoo! Messenger, messenger.yahoo.com

Google Talk, www.google.com/talk

Meebo, www.meebo.com

Trillian, www.ceruleanstudios.com

LISWiki—Chat Reference Libraries, liswiki.org/wiki/List_of_
libraries_providing_virtual_reference_services

Ning, www.ning.com

Chapter 7: Programming That Pops

PerezHilton.com, www.perezhilton.com

Monopoly Tournament Kit, www.hasbro.com/games/
kid-games/monopoly/default.cfm?page=News/tournament

Google calendar, www.google.com/calendar

Defamer, www.defamer.com

E!Online, www.eonline.com

FindLaw, www.findlaw.com

Free Comic Book Day, www.freecomicbookday.com

Mary Minow's Library Law Blog, blog.librarylaw.com

"Carrie on Copyright" column in *School Library Journal*,
www.schoollibraryjournal.com/community/Copyright/
47058.html

New Jersey Department of Banking and Insurance Office of Public
Affairs Education Section Consumer Awareness Programs,

www.state.nj.us/dobi/division_consumers/pdf/education
programs.pdf

Chapter 8: Pop Programming Year-Round: Pop Goes the Year

Amazon.com, list of films available on DVD, searched by keyword "American Football," www.amazon.com/s/ref=nb_ss_d?
url=search-alias%3Ddvd&field-keywords=american+football

Motion Picture Licensing Company, www.mplc.com

Official Super Bowl Website, www.superbowl.com

Super Bowl Ads Information Clearinghouse, www.superbowl-ads.com

Association for Library Services to Children (ALSC) Literary Awards,
www.ala.org/ala/alsc/awardsscholarships/literaryawds/literary related.htm

Canadian Library Association Book Awards,
www.cla.ca/awards/bookaw.htm

Children's Book Council of Australia Awards,
www.cbc.org.au/awards.htm

The CILIP Carnegie and Kate Greenaway Children's Book Awards, www.carnegiegreenaway.org.uk

Costa Book Awards (formerly Whitbread Book Awards),
www.costabookawards.com

The Man Booker Prize, www.themanbookerprize.com

National Book Awards, www.nationalbook.org/nba.html

Nestle/Smarties Prize, www.booktrusted.co.uk/nestle

PEN/Faulkner Award, www.penfaulkner.org

The Pulitzer Prizes, www.pulitzer.org

Sydney Taylor Book Award,
www.jewishlibraries.org/ajlweb/awards/st_books.htm

YALSA Booklists and Book Awards, www.ala.org/yalsa/booklists

Chinese Cultural Center of San Francisco, Celebration of the Chinese New Year, www.c-c-c.org/chineseculture/festival/new year/newyear.html

Information on the Chinese New Year, Government Information Office, Republic of China (Taiwan), www.gio.gov.tw/info/festival_c/spring_e/spring.htm

ALA Fact Sheet Number 7, Video and Copyright, www.ala.org/ala/alalibrary/libraryfactsheet/alalibrary factsheet7.htm

IMDb Movie Festivals and Events Worldwide, www.imdb.com/festivals

Motion Picture Licensing Corporation Umbrella License, www.mplc.com/umbrella.php

Movie Licensing USA—Public Libraries, www.movlic.com/library/index.html

Sundance Institute, www2.sundance.org

Renew Media, Looking At: Jazz, www.nvr.org/lookingatjazz

Film Movement, www.filmmovement.com

FL Studio (formerly Fruity Loops), www.flstudio.com

Academy of Motion Pictures Arts and Sciences, Academy Awards, www.oscars.org

Go Fug Yourself, gofugyourself.typepad.com

Infoplease.com's Movie Awards, www.infoplease.com/ipa/A0777584.html

Infoplease.com's Music Awards list, www.infoplease.com/ipa/A0777597.html

StoryCorps' DIY Guide, www.storycorps.net/record-your-story/cant-come-to-us/diy-guide

Gale Free Resources on Women's History, www.gale.com/free_resources/whm

Girlstart: Empowering Girls in Math, Science, and Technology, www.girlstart.org

National Women's History Museum, Educational Resources,
   www.nwhm.org/Education/education_index.html

National Women's History Project, www.nwhp.org

StoryCorps, www.storycorps.net

Time for Kids—Women's History Month, www.timeforkids.com/
   TFK/specials/whm/0,8805,101044,00.html

Wikipedia—Quizbowl, en.wikipedia.org/wiki/Quiz_bowl

The Women's Museum: An Institute for the Future, www.the
   womensmuseum.org

ALA Store, www.alastore.ala.org

LANParty.com's Small LANParty Network Setup,
   www.lanparty.com/theguide/network.shtm

LANParty.com's So You Wanna Host a LANParty?, www.
   lanparty.com/theguide/hostingaparty.shtm

Roger Hart's Ladder of Young People's Participation,
   www.freechild.org/ladder.htm

YALSA'S Teen Tech Week, www.ala.org/ala/yalsa/teentechweek

AARP.org Tax-Aide Locator,
   locator.aarp.org/vmis/sites/tax_aide_locator.jsp

AARP.org, Ask Your Federal Tax Questions, www.aarp.org/
   money/taxaide/taxcounseling/ask_tax_question.html

AARP.org Tax-Aide, www.aarp.org/money/taxaide

American Institute of Certified Public Accountants, www.aicpa.org

CafePress.com, www.cafepress.com

Internal Revenue Service (IRS), www.irs.gov

United States Memorial Holocaust Museum: Organizing a
   Holocaust Remembrance Day,
   www.ushmm.org/remembrance/dor/organize

Yad Vashem: The Holocaust Martyrs' and Heroes' Remembrance
   Authority, www.yadvashem.org

Yom HaShoah (Holocaust Remembrance Day), Torah.org,
   www.torah.org/learning/yomtov/holocaust

Cinco de Mayo, holidays.kaboose.com/cinco-de-mayo

Martha Stewart—Cinco de Mayo, www.marthastewart.com/
cinco-de-mayo?lnc=f97c442d8f35f010VgnVCM
1000003d370a0aRCRD&rsc=leftnav_holiday_other-holidays

U.S. Census Bureau Fact Sheet on Cinco de Mayo,
www.census.gov/Press-Release/www/releases/archives/
facts_for_features_special_editions/009726.html

GardenWeb, www.gardenweb.com

National Gardening Association, www.garden.org

You Grow Girl, www.yougrowgirl.com

National Invasive Species Information Center (National
Agricultural Library, U.S. Department of Agriculture),
www.invasivespeciesinfo.gov/plants/databases.shtml

PLANTS Database (Natural Resources Conservation Service, U.S.
Department of Agriculture), plants.usda.gov

UI Plants (University of Illinois at Urbana-Champaign), woody-
plants.nres.uiuc.edu

Brooklyn Botanic Garden All-Region Guides,
www.bbg.org/gar2/handbooks

Fine Gardening, www.taunton.com/finegardening

Horticulture Magazine, www.hortmag.com

The Garden Conservancy, www.gardenconservancy.org

The Garden Conservancy's Open Days Program, www.garden
conservancy.org/opendays

North American Butterfly Association (NABA), www.naba.org

Raising Butterflies from Your Garden, NABA, NJ Chapter,
www.naba.org/chapters/nabanj/bgarden.html

PBS: *The Victory Garden*, www.pbs.org/wgbh/victorygarden

Canadian Heritage—Victoria Day, www.canadianheritage.gc.
ca/progs/cpsc-ccsp/jfa-ha/victoria_e.cfm

The Gilbert and Sullivan Archive, diamond.boisestate.edu/gas

United States Croquet Association, www.croquetamerica.com

The Futon Critic, www.thefutoncritic.com

Internet Movie Database (IMDb), www.imdb.com

TV.com, www.tv.com

NPR: Gay Pop Music: Three Albums Reflect the Rise of Gay Civil Rights, www.npr.org/templates/story/story.php?storyId= 1306240

PFLAG: Parents, Families and Friends of Lesbians and Gays, www.pflag.org

GLSEN: The Gay, Lesbian and Straight Education Network, www.glsen.org

COLAGE: Children of Lesbians and Gays Everywhere, www.colage.org

Gay Financial Network, www.gfn.com

Lesbian and Gay Aging Issues Network, www.asaging.org/ networks/LGAIN/about.cfm

National Women's History Project: History of Gay and Lesbian Pride Month, www.nwhp.org/news/gayandlesbian_month.php

National Archives, www.archives.gov

Library of Congress, www.loc.gov

American Bar Association: Putting on Mock Trials, www.abanet.org/publiced/mocktrialguide.pdf

Library of Congress—Declaration of Independence, www.loc.gov/rr/program/bib/ourdocs/DeclarInd.html

Mock Trial Scripts, www.classbrain.com/artteensm/publish/cat_index_11.shtml

The National Archives Experience—The Charters of Freedom, www.archives.gov/national-archives-experience/charters/ declaration.html

New Jersey State Bar Foundation—Mock Trial Videotapes, www.njsbf.org/njsbf/programs/videos/mock.cfm

PBS: *Liberty! The American Revolution*, www.pbs.org/ktca/liberty

Supreme Court of the United States, www.supremecourtus.gov

French Culture: Official Website of the Cultural Services of the French Embassy, www.frenchculture.org

White Dog Café's Bastille Day Street Party, www.whitedog.
com/bastille.html

Comic-Con International, San Diego, www.comic-con.org

ComicBookConventions.com's Conventions Calendar,
www.comicbookconventions.com/conventions.htm

American Academy of Pediatrics—Back to School Tips (also
available in Spanish), www.aap.org/advocacy/releases/
augschool.htm

KidsHealth—Going Back to School,
kidshealth.org/kid/feeling/school/back_to_school.html

Learn in Freedom!, learninfreedom.org

National Center for Education Statistics—Homeschooling in the
United States: 2003, nces.ed.gov/pubsearch/pubsinfo.asp?
pubid=2006042

National Home Education Network, www.nhen.org

U.S. Department of Education—Getting Ready for College Early,
www.ed.gov/pubs/GettingReadyCollegeEarly/index.html

Rakhi: The Thread of Love,
hinduism.about.com/library/weekly/aa080800a.htm

Wikipedia—Rakhi (Raksha Bhandan), en.wikipedia.org/
wiki/Raksha_Bhandan

Defamer, www.defamer.com

E!Online, www.eonline.com

FindLaw, www.findlaw.com

CheapCooking.com, www.cheapcooking.com

Cooking for Engineers, www.cookingforengineers.com

Cooking Light, www.cookinglight.com

Epicurious, www.epicurious.com

Every Day with Rachael Ray, www.rachaelraymag.com

Food Network, www.foodnetwork.com

HistoryCooks.com, www.historycooks.com

Martha Stewart's Everyday Food, www.marthastewart.com/every-
day-food

Waterboro (ME) Public Library—Culinary Mysteries Booklist,
www.waterborolibrary.org/oldsite/bklistm.htm#mystcul

DPL Teen Service Blog—Fear Factor,
dplteenservices.blogspot.com/2007/07/35-brave-souls-showed-up-for-fear.html

Brewing Techniques, magazine archive,
brewingtechniques.com/index.html

Epicurious—Macaroni and Cheese recipes, tinyurl.com/y4xz9w

Oktoberfest in Leavenworth, WA, www.leavenworth
oktoberfest.com

The Oktoberfest Website, www.oktoberfest.de/en

CBC News InDepth: Islam, www.cbc.ca/news/background/islam

Essentials of Ramadan, the Fasting Month, www.usc.edu/dept/
MSA/fundamentals/pillars/fasting/tajuddin/fast_1.html

Ramadan Fast and Eid-ul-Fitr,
www.msichicago.org/scrapbook/scrapbook_exhibits/catw2004/tr
aditions/countries/ramadan.html

U.S Department of State—Muslim Life in America,
usinfo.state.gov/products/pubs/muslimlife

New York Times, "A Mexican Feast for Bodies and Souls,"
www.nytimes.com/2004/10/27/dining/27DEAD.html

Arizona Republic, Día de los Muertos (Day of the Dead),
www.azcentral.com/ent/dead

Arizona Republic, Día de los Muertos (Day of the Dead), Teacher
Packet, www.azcentral.com/ent/dead/teachers/teacherpacket_
edited.pdf

Sugar Skull Making Instructions,
www.mexicansugarskull.com/mexicansugarskull/recipe.htm

Sugar Skull Molds & Supplies, www.mexicansugarskull.com/
mexicansugarskull/sugarskullmolds.htm

BritainUSA—Remembrance Day, www.britainusa.com/sections/
articles_show_nt1.asp?d=0&i=60062&L1=41013&L2=41013&
a=45235

Canadian War Museum—Armistice Day, www.warmuseum.
ca/cwm/remember/armisticeday_e.html

In Flanders Field by John McCrae (full text),
www.poets.org/viewmedia.php/prmMID/19464

Library of Congress on Flickr—1930s–40s in color photoset,
www.flicker.com/photos/library-of-congress/sets/7215760367
1370361

U.S. Department of Veterans Affairs—Veterans Day, www1.va.
gov/opa/vetsday

Veterans of Foreign Wars, www.vfw.org

Celebrating the Holidays in an Interfaith Family, www.baby
center.com/0_celebrating-the-holidays-in-an-interfaith-
family_9838.bc

Interfaith Calendar, www.interfaithcalendar.org

InterfaithFamily.com, www.interfaithfamily.com

Torah Tots, www.torahtots.com

RESOURCES AND RECOMMENDED READING

Chapter 1: Defining and Using Pop Culture to Connect

Ashby, LeRoy. *With Amusement for All: A History of American Popular Culture Since 1830*. Lexington: The University Press of Kentucky, 2006.

DeRosa, Cathy, Joanne Cantrell, Diane Cellentani, Janet Hawk, Lillie Jenkins, and Alane Wilson. *Perceptions of Libraries and Information Resources*. Dublin, OH: OCLC Online Computer Library Center, Inc., 2005. www.oclc.org/reports/2005 perceptions.htm.

Genco, Barbara A., Eleanor K. MacDonald, and Betsy Hearne. "Juggling Popularity and Quality." *School Library Journal,* 37:3 (March 1991): 115–119.

Johnson, Steven. *Everything Bad Is Good for You: How Today's Popular Culture Is Actually Making Us Smarter*. New York: Riverhead, 2005.

Lazar, Allan, Dan Karlan, and Jeremy Salter. *The 101 Most Influential People Who Never Lived: How Characters of*

Fiction, Myth, Legends, Television, and Movies Have Shaped Our Society, Changed Our Behavior, and Set the Course of History. New York: HarperCollins, 2006.

Niedzviecki, Ned. *The Big Book of Pop Culture: A How-to Guide for Young Artists*. Toronto: Annick Press, 2007.

The Oxford American Dictionary of Current English. Oxford: Oxford University Press, 1999. www.oxfordreference.com.

Postman, Neil. *Amusing Ourselves to Death: Public Discourse in the Age of Show Business*. New York: Viking, 1986.

Schrum, Kelly. *Some Wore Bobby Sox: The Emergence of Teenage Girls' Culture, 1920–1945*. New York: Palgrave Macmillan, 2004.

Scott, John and Gordon Marshall. *A Dictionary of Sociology*. Oxford: Oxford University Press, 2005. s.v. "popular culture." www.oxfordreference.com/views/ENTRY.html?subview=Main& entry=t88.e1753.

Smith, Martin J. and Patrick J. Kiger. *Poplorica: A Popular History of the Fads, Mavericks, Inventions, and Lore that Shaped Modern America*. New York: HarperCollins, 2004.

Warren, Kay. *Dangerous Surrender*. Grand Rapids, MI: Zondervan, 2007.

Warren, Rick. *The Purpose-Driven Life*. Grand Rapids, MI: Zondervan, 2002.

Winkler, Allan M., Susan V. Spellman, and Gary B. Nash, eds. *Encyclopedia of American History: Postwar United States, 1946 to 1968*. New York: Facts on File, Inc. 2003. s.v. "popular culture, post—World War II" (by Sarah Brenner). www.fofweb. com/activelink2.asp?ItemID=WE52&iPin=EAHIX198&Single Record=True.

Woodward, John, ed. *Popular Culture: Opposing Viewpoints*. Detroit, MI: Thomson/Gale, 2005.

Wynter, Leon E. *American Skin: Pop Culture, Big Business and the End of White America*. New York: Crown Publishers, 2002.

Chapter 2: Creating a Pop Niche for Yourself and Your Library

McNamara, Carter. "Basics of Conducting Focus Groups." Free
Management Library. www.managementhelp.org/evaluatn/
focusgrp.htm.

Moore, Rebecca C. "All Shapes of Hunger: Teenagers and
Fanfiction." *Voice of Youth Advocates* (April 2005): 15–19.
pdfs.voya.com/VO/YA2/VOYA200504Fanfiction.pdf.

Silverman, George. "The Focus Group Center." Market
Navigation, Inc. www.mnav.com/qualitative_research.htm.

Toledano, Yann. "Use Online Surveys to Get the Feedback You
Need." TechSoup. June 10, 2005. www.techsoup.org/learning
center/internet/page5048.cfm.

Tuccillo, Diane P. "Successful Teen Advisory Groups: Teen Driven
… with Guidance and a Helping Hand." *Voice of Youth
Advocates*. December 2005. pdfs.voya.com/VO/YA2/VOYA
200512SuccessfulTeens.pdf.

Chapter 3: Building a Collection That Really Pops

Baker, Sharon L. and Karen L. Wallace. *The Responsive Public
Library: How to Develop and Market a Winning Collection*, 2nd
ed. Englewood, CO: Libraries Unlimited, 2002.

Barr, Catherine. *Best New Media, K–12: A Guide to Movies,
Subscription Websites, and Educational Software and Games.*
Westport, CT: Libraries Unlimited, 2008.

Bartel, Julie. *From A to Zine: Building a Winning Zine Collection
in Your Library*. Chicago: American Library Association, 2004.

Bartel, Julie. "The Good, the Bad, and the Edgy." *School Library
Journal*, 51:7 (July 2005): 34–36. schoollibraryjournal.com/
article/CA621754.html.

Bartel, Julie. "Annotated List of Magazines." *School Library Journal*, 51:7 (July 2005): 37–41. www.schoollibraryjournal. com/article/CA621754.html.

Blyberg, John. blyberg.net. www.blyberg.net.

Brenner, Robin E. *Understanding Manga and Anime*. Westport, CT: Libraries Unlimited, 2007.

Codell, Esme Raji. *The PlanetEsme Plan: The Best New Children's Books from Esme's Shelf*. planetesme.blogspot.com.

Emmons, Mark. *Film and Television: A Guide to the Reference Literature*. Westport, CT: Libraries Unlimited, 2006.

Etches-Johnson, Amanda. Blog Without a Library. blogwithout alibrary.net.

Gallaway, Beth. *Game On!: Gaming at the Library*. New York: Neal-Schuman, 2008.

Gibson, Catherine. "How We Spent $2.7 Million—with the Help of Centralized Selection." *Library Journal*, 120:14 (1995): 128–130.

Goldsmith, Francisca. *Graphic Novels Now: Building, Managing, and Marketing a Dynamic Collection*. Chicago: American Library Association, 2005.

Hutchison, David. *Playing to Learn: Video Games in the Library*. Westport, CT: Libraries Unlimited, 2007.

Miller, Steve. *Developing and Promoting Graphic Novel Collections*. New York: Neal-Schuman, 2005.

Nichols, C. Allen, ed. *Thinking Outside the Book: Alternatives for Today's Teen Library Collections*. Westport, CT: Libraries Unlimited, 2004.

Pawuk, Michael. *Graphic Novels: A Genre Guide to Comic Books, Manga, and More*. Westport, CT: Libraries Unlimited, 2007.

Serchay, David. *A Librarian's Guide to Graphic Novels for Children and 'Tweens*. New York: Neal-Schuman, 2008.

Chapter 4: Advocacy, Marketing, Public Relations, and Outreach

American Association of School Librarians. AASL Advocacy Toolkit. American Library Association. www.ala.org/ala/aasl/aaslproftools/toolkits/aasladvocacy.htm.

American Library Association. "Advocacy Resource Center." www.ala.org/pio/advocacy.

American Library Association. ALA Store. www.alastore.ala.org.

American Library Association. *Library Advocate's Handbook*, 2nd ed. Chicago: American Library Association, 2006. www.ala.org/ala/advocacybucket/libraryadvocateshandbook.pdf.

Arant, Wendi and Pixey Anne Mosley, ed. *Library Outreach, Partnership, and Distance Education: Reference Libraries at the Gateway*. Binghamton, NY: Haworth Information Press, 2000.

Baker, Sharon and Karen Wallace. *The Responsive Public Library*, 2nd ed. Englewood, CO: Libraries Unlimited, 2002.

Bartel, Julie. *From A to Zine: Building a Winning Zine Collection in Your Library*. Chicago: American Library Association, 2004.

Benun, Ilise, Peleg Top, and Colleen Wainwright. "The Marketing Mix: The Official Blog from Marketing Mentor." www.marketingmixblog.com/blog.

Blowers, Helene and Robin Bryan. *Weaving a Library Web: A Guide to Developing Children's Websites*. Chicago: American Library Association, 2004.

Brenner, Robin. "Graphic Novels 101 FAQ." *The Horn Book*, 82 (March/April 2006): 123–125.

Bruggeman, Lora. "Zap! Whoosh! Kerplow: Build High-Quality Graphic Novel Collections With Impact." *School Library Journal*, 43:1 (January 1997): 22–27.

Byrd, Susannah Mississippi. *¡Bienvenidos! ¡Welcome! A Handy Resource Guide for Marketing Your Library to Latinos*.

Chicago: American Library Association, in collaboration with Cinco Puentos Press, El Paso, TX, 2005.

Curzon, Susan Carol. *Managing Change: A How-to-Do-It Manual for Librarians,* rev. ed. New York: Neal-Schuman, 2005.

Dewey, Barbara I. and Loretta Parham, eds. *Achieving Diversity: A How-to-Do-It Manual for Librarians.* New York: Neal-Schuman, 2006.

Dowd, Nancy. "Library Videos—The Best Of ..." libraryvideos.blogspot.com.

Dowd, Nancy. "The 'M' Word—Marketing Libraries." themword blog.blogspot.com.

Fisher, Patricia H., and Marseille M. Pride. *Blueprint for Your Library Marketing Plan: A Guide to Help You Survive and Thrive.* Chicago: American Library Association, 2006.

Foster, Katy. "Graphic Novels in Libraries: An Expert's Opinion." *Library Media Connection*, 22:5 (February 2004): 30–32.

Gorman, Michele. "What Teens Want." *School Library Journal*, 48:8 (August 2002): 42–47. www.schoollibraryjournal.com/article/CA236064.html.

Highlands Regional Library Cooperative. "Valuing Libraries—Demonstrating the Contributions Libraries Make to Their Communities." www.hrlc.org/funding/valuinglibs.htm.

Horrocks, Norman, ed. *Perspectives, Insights & Priorities: 17 Leaders Speak Freely of Librarianship.* Lanham, MD: The Scarecrow Press, 2005.

Lyga, Allyson A. W. "Graphic Novels for (Really) Young Readers." *School Library Journal*, 52 (March 2006): 56–61. www.schoollibraryjournal.com/article/CA6312463.html.

MacDonald, Heidi. "Drawing A Crowd." *School Library Journal*, 50 (August 2004): 20–22. www.schoollibraryjournal.com/article/CA439995.html.

Mates, Barbara T. *5 Star Programming and Services for Your 55+ Library Customers.* Chicago: American Library Association, 2003.

Neace, Melissa. "Building a Graphic Novel Collection." *Library Media Connection*, 23:7 (April/May 2005): 52.

O'Dell, Katie. *Library Materials and Services for Teen Girls*. Greenwood Village, CO: Libraries Unlimited, 2002.

Office for Literacy and Outreach Services. "Outreach and Literacy Services Tip Sheets." American Library Association. www.ala.org/ala/olos/outreachresource/outreachtipsheets.htm.

Office of Commonwealth Libraries (PA). "Training Resource Kit for Pennsylvania Public Library Trustees." WebJunction. www.webjunction.org/do/DisplayContent?id=14344.

Pfeil, Angela B. *Going Places with Youth Outreach: Smart Marketing Strategies for Your Library*. Chicago: American Library Association, 2005.

South Jersey Regional Library Cooperative. "Advocacy Resources." www.sjrlc.org/advocacy.

South Jersey Regional Library Cooperative. "Marketing Resources." www.sjrlc.org/marketing.shtml.

South Jersey Regional Library Cooperative. "Trading Spaces Resources." www.sjrlc.org/tradingspaces/index.shtml.

Stover, Jill. "Library Marketing—Thinking Outside the Book." librarymarketing.blogspot.com.

WebJunction Staff. "Demonstrating Impact: Making Your Case." WebJunction. January 4, 2004. www.webjunction.org/do/PrinterFriendlyContent?id=1204.

Young, Robyn. "Graphically Speaking: The Importance of Graphic Novels in a School Library Collection." *Library Media Connection*, 25:4 (January 2007): 26–28.

Chapter 5: Trendspotting

Anderson, Chris. *The Long Tail: Why the Future of Business Is Selling Less of More*. New York: Hyperion, 2006.

Gladwell, Malcolm. *The Tipping Point: How Little Things Can Make a Big Difference*. New York: Little, Brown and Company, 2000.

Huntley, Katharine E. Monahan. "'Working Girl' Review." Dramatica.com. www.dramatica.com/story/film_reviews/reviews/WorkingGirl.html.

Chapter 6: Information Technology Is Everyone's Job

American Library Association. ALA TechSource Blog. www.techsource.ala.org/blog.

Artman, Julie. "NextGen: Motivate Your Millennials!" *Library Journal* (February 15, 2008). www.libraryjournal.com/article/CA6529396.html.

Bolan, Kimberly and Robert Cullin. *Technology Made Simple: An Improvement Guide for Small and Medium Libraries*. Chicago: American Library Association, 2007.

Braun, Linda W. *Listen Up! Podcasting for Schools and Libraries*. Meford, NJ: Information Today, 2007.

Breeding, Marshall. "Next Generation Library Catalogs." *Library Technology Reports*, 43:4 (July/August 2007).

Brookover, Sophie. "Why We Blog." *Library Journal*, 132:19 (November 15, 2007). www.libraryjournal.com/article/CA6497263.html.

Farkas, Meredith, et al. Five Weeks to a Social Library. www.sociallibraries.com/course.

Farkas, Meredith. *Social Software in Libraries: Building Collaboration, Connection, and Community Online*. Medford, NJ: Information Today, 2007.

Gallaway, Beth, Jami Schwarzwalder, and Kelly Czarnecki. Game On: Games in Libraries. libgaming.blogspot.com.

Goodstein, Anastasia. "What Would Madison Avenue Do? Marketing to Teens." *School Library Journal* (May 1, 2008). www.schoollibraryjournal.com/article/CA6555544.html.

Howerton, Erin Downey. "Join My Network: A Cyber Six-Pack for Educators." *VOYA* (February 2008). pdfs.voya.com/VO/ YA2/VOYA200802join_my_network.pdf.

Levine, Jenny. "Gaming and Libraries: Intersection of Services." *Library Technology Reports*, 42:5 (September/October 2006).

Levine, Jenny. "Gaming and Libraries Update: Broadening the Intersections." *Library Technology Reports*, 44:3 (April 2008).

Neiburger, Eli. *Gamers ... in the Library?! The Why, What and How of Videogame Tournaments for All Ages.* Chicago: American Library Association, 2007.

Oder, Norman. "A New Jersey Library Starts Lending Kindles." *Library Journal* (December 13, 2007). www.libraryjournal.com/ article/CA6512445.html.

Ramsay, Karen M. and Jim Kinnie. "The Embedded Librarian: Getting Out There Via Technology to Help Students Where They Learn." *Library Journal* (April 1, 2006). www.library journal.com/article/CA6317224.html.

Risdahl, Aliza Sherman. *The Everything Blogging Book: Publish Your Ideas, Get Feedback, And Create Your Own Worldwide Network.* Cincinnati, OH: Adams Media, 2006.

Sauers, Michael P. *Blogging and RSS: A Librarian's Guide.* Medford, NJ: Information Today, 2006.

Stephens, Michael. "Handouts and Resources from ... Community Building Through Your Web Site: Blogs and RSS." South Jersey Regional Library Cooperative. www.sjrlc.org/web20/handouts.

Stephens, Michael. Tame the Web. www.tametheweb.com.

Stephens, Michael. "Web 2.0 and Libraries: Best Practices for Social Software." *Library Technology Reports*, 42:4 (July/August 2006).

Stephens, Michael. "Web 2.0 and Libraries, Part 2: Trends and Technologies." *Library Technology Reports*, 43:5 (September/October 2007).

Tennant, Roy, et al. TechEssence.info: The Essence of Techology for Library Decision-Makers. www.techessence.info.

Weil, Debbie. *The Corporate Blogging Book*. New York: Penguin Portfolio, 2006.

Chapter 7: Programming That Pops

Aguilar, Leslie and Linda Stokes. *Multicultural Customer Service: Providing Outside Service Against Cultures*. New York: McGraw Hill, 1996

Behen, Linda D. *Using Pop Culture to Teach Information Literacy*. Westport, CT: Libraries Unlimited, 2006.

Conlon, Susan. "Putting Your Teens in Focus with Films: How to Organize a Student Film Festival." *Voice of Youth Advocates* (August 2007): 212–215. pdfs.voya.com/VO/YA2/VOYA2007teens_in_focus.pdf.

Eberhart, George M., ed. *The Whole Library Handbook 4*. Chicago: American Library Association, 2006.

Kan, Kat, and Kristin Fletcher-Spear. "The Anime-ted Library." *Voice of Youth Advocates* (April 2005). pdfs.voya.com/VO/YA2/VOYA200504AntimetedLibrary.pdf.

Kan, Katharine L. *Sizzling Summer Reading Programs for Young Adults*, 2nd ed. Chicago: American Library Association, 2006.

Price, Nikol. "Dungeons & Dragons Adventures in the Library." *Voice of Youth Advocates* (February 2005): 454–456. pdfs.voya.com/VO/YA2/VOYA 200502DungeonsDragons.pdf.

Ranier, Raymond. *Programming for Adults: A Guide for Small and Medium Sized Libraries*. Lanham, MD: The Scarecrow Press, Inc., 2005

Robertson, Deborah A. with the Public Programming Office of the American Library Association. *Cultural Programming for Libraries: Linking Libraries, Communities and Culture.* Chicago: American Library Association, 2005.

Soltan, Rita. *Reading Raps: A Book Club Guide for Librarians, Kids, and Families.* Westport, CT: Libraries Unlimited, 2006.

Chapter 8: Pop Programming Year-Round: Pop Goes the Year

Bagdasarian, Adam. *The Forgotten Fire.* New York: Laurel-Leaf Books, 2002.

Balakian, Peter. *The Burning Tigris: The Armenian Genocide and America's Response.* New York: HarperCollins, 2003.

Colón, Connie. "Make A Rakhi for Your Brother Or Friend." *Highlights for Children*, 60:8 (August 2005): 11.

Deng, Alephonsion, Benson Deng, Benjamin Ajak, and Judy Bernstein. *They Poured Fire on Us from the Sky: The True Story of Three Lost Boys From Sudan.* New York: Public Affairs, 2005.

Filipoviç, Zlata. *Zlata's Diary: A Child's Life in Sarajevo.* New York: Viking, 1994.

Frank, Anne. *Anne Frank: Diary of a Young Girl.* New York: Pocket Books, 1958.

Glatshteyn, Yankev. *Emil and Karl.* New Milford, CT: Roaring Brook Press, 2006.

Ilibagiza, Immaculée and Steve Erwin. *Left to Tell: Discovering God Amidst the Rwandan Holocaust.* Carlsbad, CA: Hay House, 2006.

Isay, Dave. *Listening Is an Act of Love: A Celebration of American Life from the StoryCorps Project.* New York: Penguin Press, 2007.

Jansen, Hanna. *Over a Thousand Hills I Walk with You.* Minneapolis, MN: Carolrhoda Books, 2006.

Jungersen, Christian. *The Exception.* London: Wiedenfeld and Nicolson, 2006.

Kubert, Joe. *Fax From Sarajevo: A Story of Survival.* Milwaukie, OR: Dark Horse Comics, 1996.

Lowry, Lois. *Number the Stars.* Boston: Houghton Mifflin, 1989.

Menchú, Rigoberta and Elisabeth Burgos-Debray. *I, Rigoberta Menchú: An Indian Woman in Guatemala.* London: Verso, 1984.

Mikaelsen, Ben. *Red Midnight.* New York: HarperCollins, 2002.

Opdyk, Irene Gut and Jennifer Armstrong. *In My Hands: Memories of a Holocaust Rescuer.* New York: Knopf: Distributed by Random House, 1999.

Pausewang, Gudrun. *The Final Journey.* New York: Viking, 1996.

Rusesabagina, Paul and Tom Zoellner. *An Ordinary Man: An Autobiography.* New York: Viking, 2006.

Sacco, Joe. *Safe Area Gorazde.* Seattle: Fantagraphics, 2000.

Spiegelman, Art. *Maus: A Survivor's Tale.* New York: Pantheon, 1986.

Spiegelman, Art. *Maus II: A Survivor's Tale: And Here My Troubles Began.* New York: Pantheon, 1991.

Spinelli, Jerry. *Milkweed: A Novel.* New York: Alfred A. Knopf, 2003.

Stassen, Jean-Philippe. *Deogratias: A Tale of Rwanda.* New York: First Second, 2006.

Ung, Loung. *First They Killed My Father: A Daughter of Cambodia Remembers.* New York: HarperCollins, 2000.

Ung, Loung. *Lucky Child: A Daughter of Cambodia Reunites with the Sister She Left Behind.* New York: HarperCollins, 2005.

Zusak, Markus. *The Book Thief.* New York: Alfred A. Knopf, 2006.

ABOUT THE AUTHORS

Sophie Brookover is the Library Media Specialist at Eastern Regional Senior High School in Voorhees, NJ. She was previously a Senior Teen Librarian at the Vogelson Regional Branch of the Camden County Library System, also in Voorhees. In 2004 Sophie founded Pop Goes the Library (www.popgoesthelibrary.com), a blog about popular culture's place in librarianship, which has grown from a one-woman shop to an eight-blogger endeavor. Sophie has contributed to *Library Journal* and is a reviewer for *Voice of Youth Advocates*. Active in the YA Services Section of the New Jersey Library Association and in YALSA, Sophie is a frequent conference presenter on topics including pop culture, emerging technologies for public and school libraries, and services to young adults. She holds an MISt from the Faculty of Information Studies at the University of Toronto. In the battle between the Beatles and the Stones, Sophie chooses the Kinks (although her favorite band of all time is the Smiths).

Elizabeth Burns is the Head of Youth Services for the New Jersey Library for the Blind and Handicapped in Trenton, NJ. In 2005, she began contributing to Sophie's blog, Pop Goes the Library. Inspired by this work, she began blogging about books, movies, and TV at A Chair, a Fireplace and a Tea Cozy (yzocaet.blogspot.com). Liz is active in the YA Services Section of the New Jersey Library Association and in YALSA; she is a member of the 2009 Michael L. Printz Award Committee. Liz presents at conferences and workshops on Web 2.0 technologies and on blogging about children's literature. Prior to becoming a librarian, Liz worked for many years as a corporate attorney. She holds an MLIS from Rutgers University, SCILS, and a JD from Villanova Law School, Villanova University. *Buffy the Vampire Slayer* is her favorite television show. Ever.

INDEX

A

AADL catalog, 136
AARP, tax assistance, 193
Academy Awards, 186–188
adult services librarians, site visits, 25
Advergirl.com, 109
advertising, pop culture and, 16
advocacy
    ALA resources, 65
    for collections, 62
    demonstrating impact, 65–66
    internal, 70–71
    storytelling's role in, 62
    "Voices from the Field," 88–95
Advocacy Resource Center (ALA), 65
Advocacy Toolkit (AASL), 65
African American programming, 184–185
African drumming, 184

age groups, print materials for, 42
air force bases, 169
ALSC, trendspotting and, 107
Amazon Kindle, 115–116
Amazon.com, 35
American Association of School Librarians, 65
American Dairy Association, 158
American Girl, 42, 168
American Idol, 169
American Library Association (ALA)
    advocacy resources, 65
    Graphics Store, 75
    Office for Literacy and Outreach Services, 84
    Youth Book Awards, 176–178
anime clubs, 57, 84
anime collections, 5
Anime Festival, 172
Anime Insider, 99

AnimeFest, 107
Ann Arbor District Library, 79–80
Antiques Appraisal, 170
AOL Instant Messenger, 139, 147
Apple, 114–115, 116
April events, 192–196
archives, digital materials, 43
Armchair Travel, 170
art schools, outreach to, 85
artists, 85, 170. *see also* illustrators
Ask-a-Librarian campaign, 93
Ask-a-Librarian online, 58
"Ask Me!" buttons, 74
Association for Library Service to
      Children (ALSC), 176
attendance statistics, 155
Audacity, 137
audiences
    attendance statistics, 155
    children, 25
    relevance to, 17
    teens, 25
audiobooks, on circulating iPods,
    102
August events, 210–213
authors
    outreach to, 85
    as speakers, 184
Auto-Sync, 114
availability, pop culture and, 16
Avenick, Karen, 65

B

Baby Boomers, 7, 87
Baker, Sharon, 41, 72
Baker & Taylor, 49, 50
Bartel, Julie, 87
basketball, 176
Bastille Day, 207–208
battered materials, usage and, 28
beauty tips, 167
Benum, Ilise, 67–69
Binder Wiki, 125

Bitch magazine, 109
Black History Month, 183–186
Blogger, 44, 118
Blogging and RSS (Sauer), 124
Bloglines, 123
blogs, 124–125
    in the Children's Department,
        141–142
    continuous training and, 74
    focus group interviews using,
        28
    Google Blog Search, 43
    input from, 55
    internal, 74
    keeping up to date through, 34
    permission for, 92
    posts by patrons, 77
    as resource, 43
    in schools, 142
    trendsetting and, 110
    trendspotting and, 106–108
    use of, 99
    wikis and, 125–126
    wish lists on, 44
Blowers, Helene, 87
*Blueprint for Your Library
      Marketing Plan,* 62
Boards of Directors
    marketing to, 69–70
    reports to, 108
    support from, 92
Boing Boing, 32
Bon Appetit, 214
book clubs, 15, 179
book discussions, 75, 117
Book Expo, 107
book fairs, 166
Book Hooks, 179
Book Industry Study Group
    subject headings, 54
book reviews, 140
book stores, 44
book talks, 92

Booklist, 48
booklists, 30, 89
bookmarking
    online, 75
    social, 133–134
bookmarks, 75
bookmobiles, 83
booksellers, 72, 85
Bookslut, 43
Boys' Life, 42
Brad Bird comics, 155
brainstorming
    inspiration and, 155
    on library service development,
        25–26
    outreach programs, 84–85
    pop culture initiatives, 84
    with teachers, 75
    trendspotting and, 101
Braun, Linda W., 137
Bryan, Robin, 87
budgets
    collection development and, 24
    discretionary spending and, 48
    fundraising and, 161
    programming ideas and,
        160–161
    status of pop culture materials,
        57
    technology and, 141, 145
Buffy the Vampire Slayer, 203
bulletin boards
    3-D cases, 92
    marketing through, 92
    topics, 9
Bust, 108
butterfly gardening, 200
buzzwords, 31

C

cable TV ads, 94
cake decorating, 217

calendars, 92. *see also specific
        months*
call sheets, 86
calligraphy, 169
CamelCase, 127
Canada
    Canada Day, 205
    Victoria Day, 200–201
candy, 169
"Carrie on Copyright" (Minow),
        156
catalogs
    importance of, 53–54
    marketing and, 74
"Caught Reading" campaign, 157
celebrities
    chefs, 12
    news about, 153
    pop culture and, 17
    "spin" created by, 62
centralized selection, 50–51
A Chair, a Fireplace and a Tea
        Cozy, 119–121, 128
change
    expectations of, 67
    pop culture and, 16
    resistance to, 76–77, 94
Chanukah, 224–225
Charlotte's Web Country Fair, 169
children
    graphic novels for, 69–70
    print materials for, 42
    trendspotting and, 107
    varied reading "diets," 72
Children's Binder Wiki, 125
Chinese New Year, 179–181
Chirp, 42
Chocoholics Unanimous, 216
Christiansen, Betty, 168
Christmas, 224–225
churches
    outreach to, 90
    visits to, 25

Cinco de Mayo, 197
circulation statistics
    collection development and, 51,
        57
    "coolness" decisions and, 11
    determining interests from, 34
    information from, 28–30, 38
    magazine use, 22–23
    for pop culture collections, 82
City Hall, outreach to, 90
City of San Mateo (CA) Public
        Library, 134
classics
    impact of time on pop culture,
        18
    public opinion of, 72
CLEP/DANTES materials, 169
clubs, in schools, 45
clutter, be gone, 185–186
coffee shop posters, 94–95
Colbert Report, 55
collection development
    beyond books, 45, 48
    budgets and, 24
    buzzwords, 31
    cataloging, 54
    catalogs, 53–54
    centralized selection methods,
        50–51
    circulation statistics and, 34
    flexibility and, 99
    food-related materials, 214
    graphic novels in, 69–70
    the human factor, 43–45
    methodology, 48–53
    mistakes in, 54–55
    online tools, 42–43
    patron requests and, 34
    print tools, 41–42
    process of, 54–55
    starting small, 64–69
    strategies for, 40–41
    trendspotting and, 97–110
    "Voices from the Field," 55–59
    waiting lists and, 35

collection maintenance, 82–83
college students, 36
comic book stores
    in the Children's Room, 89
    interviewing owners of, 27
    outreach to, 85
    as resources, 44
    visits to, 82
comic books
    in collection development, 45
    literacy scores and, 85
    programming around, 154
Comic-Con, 107, 108, 208–209
Commonweal, 3
communication
    with the administration, 31
    essential sound bites, 68
    just talking, 31–38
    RSS feeds, 78
    trend tracking and, 104–105
communities
    collaboration with, 30
    collection development and, 40
    impact on collections, 21
    library card holders in, 28
    pop outreach programs, 83–84
    regional differences, 152
    support from, 61–62
community center visits, 25
community groups
    leaders of, 44
    outreach programs, 86
    outreach to, 90
complaints, 91, 95
conferences, 34, 106. see also
        Comic-Con; conventions;
        workshops
connectivity, pop culture and,
        17–18
Consumer Awareness Programs,
        161
contests, 85–86
controlled vocabulary, 126–129

conventions, outreach to, 85
cookbook collections, 12
cookbooks, library composed, 215
cooking, 11–12, 214–217
Cooking Light, 214
Cook's Illustrated, 214
"coolness," libraries and, 7, 10–11
Coretta Scott King Award, 177
CosmoGirl!, 42
costume character programs, 170,
    219
craft programs, 166
Creative Commons, 146
Creative Think, 109
Crocs shoes, 13
cross-training, 71–73
Crowther, Sue, 163
culture. *see also* demographics
    definition of, 2
    trends within, 4
customers. *see* patrons
Cute Overload, 109

D

daily lives, pop culture and, 17–18
The Daily Show, 55
Dairy Council Mid East, 158
Dangerous Surrender (K. Warren),
    3
Dark Horse comics, 155
DarkThrone, 141
Day of the Dead, 221–222
December events, 224–225
Declaration of Independence, 206
Defamer, 153
del.icio.us, 122, 133, 134, 145
demographics. *see also specific*
        events
    Chinese populations, 179–181
    enthusiasms and, 6–7
    Hispanic populations, 168
    programming built around, 168,
        169

demonstrating impact, 65–66
Department of Jobs and Family
        Services, 93
Dewey Decimal system, 28, 54,
    134
Diamond Comic Distributors, 155
Dictionary of Sociology, 2
Digg, 133
Discover Kids, 42
Disney, TV shows, 56
displays
    for the 4th of July, 206
    of cookbook collections, 12
    Flickr photos, 131
    high school sports, 176
    on hot topics, 9
    imaginative, 75
    themes for, 83
DIY programming, 160–161
domesticity, trends in, 11–12
donations, 69–70, 186
Dowd, Nancy, 62, 73
dragon dancers, 168, 169
Duff, Hilary, 98
Dunbar, Paul Laurence, 185
DVDs
    in collection development, 45
    cooking shows, 214
    movie collections, 40
    TV shows, 202–203

E

eBay for beginners, 192
ebranch librarians, 144
EBSCO, as resource, 43
Eclipse Prom, 220
Edge of the Forest, 43
Edible Book Festival, 216
Eid al-Fitr, 221
El Día de los Muertos, 221–222

email
  discussion lists, 43
  marketing through, 92
  mass mailings, 90–91
  trendspotting and, 105
entertainment information, 17–18
Entertainment Weekly, 34, 42
E!Online, 153
ephemora, pop culture and, 15
ESP Evening event, 220
Eurocup events, 176
Everyday Food, 214
Everyday with Rachael Ray, 214
The Everything Blogging Book (Sherman), 124
experts, as resources, 43–45

F

Facebook, 5, 129, 140, 147
faculty, wish list blogs, 44
Fagan Finder, 117–118
Faherty, Jill, 49, 51
Fair Use, 146
Family Jam, 171
fandom, 163–165
fantasy sports, 176
fashion, pop culture and, 17
Fashion Fabuloso, 172
Fear Food Factor programs, 215, 216
February events, 183–186
feed aggregators, 123–124
feedback. *see also* listening; surveys
  from focus groups, 26–28
  surveys used in, 23–26
  from teens, 22–23
Feng Shui, 167
Fight Club, 165
Filamentality, 145
film festivals, 181–183, 206

filters, 142, 145, 204
FindLaw, 153
5 Star Programming and Services for Your 55+ Library Customers (Mates), 87
flash drives, 113–114
flexibility, collections and, 99
Flickr, 75, 87, 112, 122, 130–133, 140, 144, 146
fliers, 93
focus groups, 26–28
folksonomy, 123, 126–129
food, trends and, 11–12
Food Network, 12
food-related events, 214–217
Forbes, 100
Ford, Harrison, 100–101
formats, pop culture and, 45–48
Fourth of July/Independence Day, 206–207
$40 a Day with Rachael Ray, 214
40 Developmental Assets, 89
Friends of the Library, 161, 166
From A to Zine (Bartel), 87
fun, pop culture and, 24
funders, demonstrating impact to, 66
fundraising, 161, 215

G

Gallaway, Beth, 134
GameBoy night, 167
GameCub, 167
Gamers...In the Library? (Neiburger and Gallaway), 134
games, 134–135
  cognitive benefits of, 89–90
  in collection development, 45
  electronic, 45
  in the library, 141

popularity of, 29, 57
programs build around, 167
PS2, 89, 91
table top, 45
gardening
    programming built around,
        198–200
    publications, 199–200
    TV programs, 200
    websites, 200
gay, lesbian, bisexual, transgen-
        dered, and intersex
        (GLBTI) community, 204
Gay Pride Month, 203–205
genealogy programs, 171
generation X, enthusiasms of, 6–7
generation Y, enthusiasms of, 6–7
genocides, 194–196
Go Fug Yourself, 32
Godin, Seth, 109
Good Deal with Dave Lieberman,
    214
Google, 133
    Blog Search, 43
    Groups, 92
    Reader, 124
    wikis, 125
    YouTube and, 137–138
"Got Milk" campaign, 156–157
Gourmet, 214
grade schoolers, 6. see also
        children
graphic novels
    for children, 72
    classroom use of, 75
    in collection development, 45
    for older readers, 72
    rationale for, 69–70
Graphics Store (ALA), 75
grass-roots movements, 15
The Greatest Generation, 7
Griffith, Melanie, 100–101
Guitar Hero III, 135
Gutman, Dan, 179

H

hair styling, 167
Halloween, 219–220
hand selection plans, 48–53
Hanna Montana, 56
Harry Potter, 220
    fandom, 163–164
    pop culture status of, 15
    programming events around, 31,
        159, 168
Hasbro site, 153
health class collaboration, 166
Heeb, 3
Helmrich, Erin, 134
Hennepin County Library, 79, 136
Herz, Christine, 198
HGTV, 12
High School Musical 2, 56
Highland Regional Library
        Cooperative, 66
hip-hop, 184, 185
historical societies, 84
hobbyists, as resources, 44
Hokey Pokey, 171
Holiday dilemma, 224–225
home schoolers, 85, 210

I

"Idea Boxes," 35. see also
        suggestion boxes
illustrators, 75, 85. see also artists
IMC (Instructional Media Centers),
        58
IMDb, 109
iMixes, 116, 117
immigrant populations, 41. see
        also demographics;
        specific events
improv groups, 170
In Flander's Fields (McCrae), 223

in-services, trendspotting and, 105
incentives. *see also* motivation
  contests, 179
  for library use, 72
  paperback coupons, 37
  prizes, 166
  raffles, 75, 76
information literacy, 8–10, 91
Information Literacy Standards, 89
information technology (IT),
  111–149
inhibitors, to library use, 72
inspiration, 9, 152–160. *see also*
  incentives; motivation
instant messaging (IM), 27–28,
  139, 147–148
InStyle, 62
Intelliwriters, 141
inter-library loans, 15
Internet
  access to, 91
  fear of, 125
  online surveys, 26, 31
  research using, 32
  trendspotting and, 105, 106, 109
Internet@Schools conferences, 108
interviews
  by celebrities, 62
  focus groups, 26–27
  in-person surveys, 25
  local history, 223
iPods, 102, 114–115
Iron Chef, 216
iTunes, 114, 115

J

J-14, 42
January programming, 174–183
jazz, 184
Jeopardy-style programming, 168
Jolie, Angelina, 62–63

July events, 205–209
June events, 202–205

K

karaoke, 184
knitting programs, 166, 168, 170
Krumholtz, David, 164

L

Lawson, Nigella, 12
Lebanese dancing, 167
Librarian Avengers blog, 109
librarians
  collection development and, 21
  personalities, 67–69
libraries
  advocacy for, 62
  demonstrating impact, 65–66
  donations to, 70
  external constituents, 69–70
  missions of, 73, 79–80
  product successes, 72
  relevancy of, 47
  RSS feeds, 78
  strategic planning, 73
  views of, 7, 10
Library Arts Café, 168
Library Journal, 42
Library Marketing blog, 109
Library of Congress system, 28, 54
"Library Oscars," 24
Library Success, 134
library wholesalers, 50–51
LibraryElf, 140
LibraryLaw blog, 156
LibrarySuccess, 125
LibraryThing, 135, 145
Lieberman, Dave, 12, 214
Lifehacker, 109

Listen Up! (Braun), 137
listening, 24, 77, 106, 109
listserves, trendspotting and, 105
LISWiki, 139
literacy, graphic novels and, 69–70, 85
Literary Luncheons, 172
literary value, 18
Live Homework Help, 146
LiveJournal, 125, 144
Logan, Debra Kay, 8–10, 156–158

M

Mac, 114
Macaluso, Judy, 4–5
Madison-Jefferson County Public Library, 79
magazines
    circulation statistics, 22
    in collection development, 45
    digital formats, 43
    food-related, 214
    programming ideas, 154
    on school visits, 23
    trendspotting and, 105
Magazines for Libraries, 42
mainstream consciousness, 16
makeup lessons, 167
manga collection, 5
maps, 81
March events, 186–192
Mario Baseball tournament, 176
marketing
    campaigns, 62
    collection placement and, 80–82
    of collections, 62
    contests, 85–86
    displays for, 74
    Flickr photos, 132
    getting over shyness, 67–69
    internal, 70–71
    keeping fresh, 78
    of library service, 72
    options, 92
    outreach programs, 86
    pop culture and, 16
    print materials, 90
    sound bites, 68
    to staff, 76
    strategies for, 64–65
    "Voices from the Field," 88–95
Marketing Mentor, 67
marquees, 90
Mates, Barbara T., 87
Matteo, Christine, 101–104
Matthews, Brian, 138
May events, 197–201
Mays group, 107
McCrae, John, 223
media
    leads through, 56
    outreach programs, 86
    pop culture and, 62
Mediawiki, 125
Meebo, 139
meetings
    bringing books to, 92
    electronic, 74
    in-person, 73–74
    trendspotting and, 109
merchandising training, 91
Michael L. Printz Award, 177
micromanagement, 112
microphones, 137
Microsoft Publisher, 10, 167
Minow, Mary, 156
mission statements
    collections and, 95
    for libraries, 79–80
    programming and, 162
mistakes
    fear of failure, 98–99
    learning from, 54–55, 78–82

MMPORGs (massively multi-player online role-playing games), 135
mock awards, 177–178, 179
mock trials, 207
Monopoly, 152–153
Montessori, 142–143
mosques, visits to, 25
motivation, 9–10. *see also* incentives; inspiration
MP3 players, 115
murder mystery dinner, 171–172
music
    African drumming, 184
    awards, 187–188
    in collection development, 45
    definition of pop culture and, 15
    Family Jam, 171
    hip-hop, 184, 185
    iMixes, 116–117
    jazz, 184
    sixties programming, 167
    Teen Tech Week and, 191–192
music shops, as resources, 44
MySpace, 5, 129, 141, 142, 143, 146
Mystery Game Night, 172

N

name recognition, 14
National Candy Month, 169
National Public Radio, 36
National Women's History Project, 189
needlework collection, 33
Neiburger, Eli, 134
Netflix lists, 57
New Blogger Tag Cloud, 127
New York Times online, 122
Newberry Award, 177

newsletters, 77
    marketing through, 89, 92
    teen magazines, 167
newspapers
    features in, 93
    library information through, 87
    trendspotting and, 105, 109
Newsweek, 34
niche markets
    pop culture *versus,* 15
    "Voices from the Field," 30–38
Nichols, C. Allen, 45–47
Nigella Express, 214
9/11, 12–13, 217
Ning, 142
Nintendo Night, 167
non-print materials, 94. *see also specific* materials
nostalgia, seniors and, 40
notification lists, 50
November events, 221–224
NPR Podcast Directory, 137
Numb3rs fandom, 163–164

O

Ocean County Library, 101–104
October events, 217–221
Odeo Studio, 137
Office for Literacy and Outreach Services (ALA), 84
Officer Buckle and Gloria (Rathman), 157
Oktoberfest, 217–218
Oliver, Jamie, 12
online gardening publications, 199–200
online surveys, 31
online tools, 42–43
OPACs, 54, 79, 135, 212
Oprah book club, 15
orientation packs, 94, 212
Oscar parties, 186–188

Otaku USA, 99
outdoor activities, 24
outreach programs
    collections and, 82
    community events and, 90
    Department of Jobs and Family
        Services, 93
    pop culture themed, 83–84
    possibilities, 85–88
    toolkits, 86
    "Voices from the Field," 88–95

P

Paone, Kimberly, 202
paranormal investigators, 220
parent-teacher organizations, 85
parents
    orientation packs for, 94
    outreach to, 85
    print materials for, 42
Parents, Families and Friends of
        Lesbians and Gays
        (PFLAG), 204
Patriot Day (9/11), 217
patrons
    contributions by, 77
    Flickr photos, 132
    participation in marketing, 76
    relationships with, 88
    requests, 34, 37, 59
    as resources, 21–22
    trendspotting and, 106
PBwiki, 125
PDAs, 140
PennTags, 136
People, 34, 42, 62
pervasiveness, of pop culture, 16
PFLAG, visits to, 25
photo albums, digital, 114
photo sharing, 130–133, 143
Pirate Ball, 172

placement, of materials, 80–81
plant databases, 199
Playaway, 116
Playstation Portable (PSP), 114
PLCMC program, 144
podcasting, 95, 136–137, 146
Podcast.net, 137
PodOmatic, 137
Pokemon tournament, 168
policies
    social networking sites and,
        141, 142
    on technology, 145
pop culture
    creating niches within libraries,
        21–38
    definitions, 1–4, 14–18
    impact of time on, 18
    justification for collections, 94
    library's mission and, 80
    literary value *vs.,* 18
    "Voices from the Field," 14–18
Pop Goes the Library
    blog, 109, 110, 118, 119
    Blogger tags, 127
    RSS feed, 118–121, 119
    website, 118
popular press, leads through, 56
portable media players (PMPs),
        114–117
posters, 75, 94
PostSecret, 109
potluck, 175
PR departments, 93
PR for Dummies (Benun), 67
preparation, for programs,
        152–160
press releases
    marketing through, 92
    outreach programs, 86
    use of, 74, 76
print materials, 90
print tools, 41–42

prizes, contests and, 179
programming
    attendance statistics, 82, 155
    book-related, 178–179
    fan fiction and, 163–165
    food-related, 214–217
    inspiration for, 152–160
    marketing and, 74
    marketing collections using, 75
    mission statements and, 162
    preparation for, 152–160
    press releases, 76
    promotions for, 155
    refreshments and, 168
    seasonal guides to, 90
    successful, 151–172
    "Voices from the Field," 166–172
    year-round, 173–225
programs, Flickr photos of, 131
promotional materials, 132, 155.
    see also marketing
PS2 games, 89
public opinion
    about libraries, 7
    about pop culture, 14–15, 46–47
punk shows, 108
The Purpose-Driven Life (R. Warren), 3

R

radio stations, 36, 87
raffles, 75, 76
Rakhi, 212–213
Ralph Caldecott Medal, 177
Ramadan, 220–221
Rathman, Peggy, 157
Ray, Rachel, 12, 214
Read Across America campaign, 158
Reader's Advisory librarians, 50
reading, trendspotting and, 108, 109

recommendations. see also book clubs
    booklists, 30, 89
    cross-media lists, 30
    recommendation chains, 36
reference librarians
    input from, 56
    roving reference, 139, 142
    sites to visit, 25
reference meetings, 107
reference questions, analysis of, 31, 34, 55
refreshments, 175, 185
Refworks, 143
relevancy, of libraries, 47
Remembrance Day, 222–224
resources. see also Appendix A; specific resources
    identification of, 100–101
    reference, 133
The Responsive Public Library (Baker and Wallace), 41, 72–73
restaurants, posters in, 94–95
Right On!, 42
Ripley's Believe It or Not program, 216
Risdahl, Aliza Sherman, 124
The Rocky Horror Picture Show, 164
Rolling Stone, 34
roving reference, 139, 142
RSS feeds, 117–122, 146
    aggregators, 123–124
    New York Times, 122
    trendspotting and, 110
    use of, 78
RSS2Java, 122
RuneScape, 135, 141

S

Saint Joseph Public Library, IN, 126
sales promotions, 16
Sauers, Michael, 124
scavenger hunts, 166, 171
Schachner, Judy, 179
Scholastic orders, 57
School Library Journal, 42–43, 48, 70, 156
schools
  curricula, 37
  end of, 202
  libraries, 8–10, 31
  media specialists, 25, 45
  missions of, 75
  newspapers, 91
  notebook decorating, 212
  outreach to, 85
  start of, 210–211
  visits to, 23, 25
Second Life, 143
security issues, technology-related, 146
senior residences, 25
seniors
  5 Star Programming and Services for Your 55+ Library Customers (Mates), 87
  books to, 172
  collections development and, 40
  feedback from, 26
  September events, 213–217
Serenity, 164
Series Binder Wiki, 89
Seventeen magazine, 109
shyness, working through, 67–68
signage, 74, 81
silo effect, 71
sixties programming, 167
Skype, 137

SLAM, 42
slang, pop culture and, 17
Smart Mobs, 109
Smartboards, 141
SnapShirts, 127
soccer, 176
social bookmarking, 133–134
social catalogs, 135–136
social marketing, 90
social networking, 129, 141, 142, 144
social OPACs, 135
Sony Reader, 115–116
sound bites, 68
Spa programs, 169
Spanish speakers, 168
speakers
  authors, 85, 184
  illustrators, 75, 85
  marketing collections using, 75
paranormal investigators, 220
Spears, Britney, 3, 4
SPIN, 42
Spongebob Squarepants, 35
sports, high school displays, 176
Sports Illustrated for Kids, 42
sports-related programming, 174–176
Spring cleaning, 185–186
Spring Festival (Chinese New Year), 179–181
staff
  complaints by, 91
  continuous training, 73–74
  cross-training of, 71–73
  education about collections, 30
  empowerment of, 98
  marketing to, 76
  presenting trends to, 103
  support from, 70–71
  technology used by, 111–112
  wish list blogs, 44

stakeholders. *see also* audiences; patrons
  demonstrating impact to, 66
  external constituents, 69–70
  questions from, 28
  support from, 61–62
standing order plans, 48–53
Star Trek, 165
Star Wars, 170
statistics
  information from, 28–30
  tracking reference questions, 31
Stephen's, Michael, 124
Stomp the Yard, 169
Stop Pushing Me Around (Benun), 67
StoryCorps project, 189
storytelling, advocacy and, 62, 65
Stover, Jill S., 76–78
strategic planning, 103
student projects, 132
sub-cultures, pop culture and, 16
success, definitions of, 98
suggestion boxes, 58. *see also* "Idea Boxes"
summer reading programs, 167
Sundance Film Festival, 181–183
Super Bowl, 174–176
SurveyMonkey.com, 14
surveys, 36
  for feedback, 23–26
  in-person, 25
  objectives of, 23
  online, 26, 31
  phrasing questions for, 23
synagogues, visits to, 25

T

table tents, 94
tag clouds, 127
tagging, 126–129
talk shows, 36

ataxes, programming around, 192–194
taxonomies, folksonomy, 126–129
Tea Cozy, tagging in, 128
Tea Cozy blog, 118
teacher book clubs, 179
tech literacy, 190
technology
  budgets, 141, 145
  learning curves, 112–113
  programming built around, 171
  resistance to, 148
  security issues, 146
  use of, 95
  "Voices from the Field," 140–148
Technorati, 43
Teen Advisory Boards (TABs)
  collection decisions and, 33
  input from, 22, 32, 33, 57
  online catalog orders and, 57
  Teen Tech Week and, 191–192
  working with, 5
teen magazines, 167
Teen Read Week, 166, 170
Teen Reading Program, 172
Teen Tech Week, 190–192
Teen Vogue, 42
teens
  enthusiasms of, 6
  input from, 55
  print materials for, 42
  technology and, 140
temples, visits to, 25
testimonials, showcasing of, 77
text messaging, 140, 143
That's So Raven, 56
Thrasher, 42
tie-ins, 101–105
Time, 34
time constraints, 162
time management, 53
tiny tots, enthusiasms of, 6
tip sheets (ALA), 84
Toledano, Yann, 23

Totally Wired, 109
tours, 131
travelogues, 166, 170
trends
    ephemeral nature of, 13
    leveraging, 13
Trends & Tudes, 5
Trendspotter Committees, 102–104
trendspotting, 97–110
Trillian, 139, 144
trust
    establishment of, 101–105
    in libraries, 7
TV
    ads, 94
    Disney shows, 56
    DVDs, 202–203
    fandom, 163–164
    gardening shows, 200
    internal projectors, 141
    licensing issues, 203
    season premieres, 213
    series finales, 202–203
    show popularity, 36
    trendspotting and, 107
tweens, enthusiasms of, 6

U

The Ubiquitous Librarian, 138
Us Weekly, 62
USA Today, 36
USB drives, 113–114

V

Valueing Libraries (HRLC), 66
Vanity Fair, 42
Veteran's Day, 222–224
Veterans of Foreign Wars (VFW),
    223
VIBE, 42

Victoria Day, 200–201
video conferences, 179
video sharing, 137–138
virtual learning, 146
virtual reference, 142
visibility, pop culture and, 16
Vogue, 42
Voice of Youth Advocates, 70
Voice over Internet Protocol
    (VoIP), 137
"Voices from the Field"
    on back-to-school events, 212
    on Black History Month,
        184–185
    on book-related programming,
        178–179
    on collection development,
        55–59
    creating a pop niche, 30–38
    film-related comments, 183
    on food-related programming,
        215–217
    on Halloween programs, 220
    on marketing, 88–95
    on music awards, 187–188
    pop culture definitions, 14–18
    on programming, 166–172
    on sports-related programming,
        175
    on Spring cleaning, 186
    on technology, 140–148
    on Teen Tech Week, 191–192
    on trendspotting, 105–110
volunteers, 25, 37, 86
VOYA magazine, 109

W

waiting lists, collection develop-
    ment and, 35
Walden Media, 109
Wallace, Karen, 41, 72
Warren, Rick, 3

Weaving a Library Web (Blowers and Bryan), 87
Web 2.0, 144
Web librarians, 35
Web polls, 36
Webber, Carlie, 163–165
WebJunction, 65–66
websites
  communication via, 90
  interactive, 83, 95
  lack of traffic to, 145–146
  marketing via, 90, 92
  micromanagement of, 112
  online surveys, 26
  outreach initiatives, 87–88
  trendspotting and, 108
weeding guidelines, 80
Wegmans supermarket, 81
Weird Science, 171
Westerfeld, Scott, 98
White, Katy, 49, 51
Whose Line Is It Anyway, 169, 170
Wii bowling, 135
Wii culture, 17
Wii sports tournaments, 176
Wikipedia, 125
wikis, 125–126
Windows Live Messenger, 139
wish lists, blogs, 44
With Amusement for All (LeRoy), 2–3
Withrow, Mary Ellen, 157
Women's History Month, 117, 188–190
word of mouth marketing, 89, 92, 93, 106

WordPress, 44
Working Girl, 100–101
workshops
  for cross-training, 71
  on illustration, 154
  marketing collections using, 75
  on pop culture, 4
  trendspotting and, 105
World Future Society conferences, 103
WWE, 42
WYSIWYG editors, 124

Y

YA-YAAC listserv, 22
Yahoo!, 133
Yahoo! Messenger, 139
YALSA (Young Adult Library Services Association), 22, 107, 125, 176–177, 190
Yom HaShoah/Holocaust Remembrance Day, 194–196
Youth Book Awards (ALA), 176–178
YouTube, 89, 112, 137–138
YPulse, 5, 109

Z

zines, 42. *see also* magazines
ZoomClouds, 127

More Great Books from Information Today, Inc.

The Thriving Library
Successful Strategies for Challenging Times

By Marylaine Block

Here is a highly readable guide to strategies and projects that have helped more than 100 public libraries gain community support and funding during challenging times. The author integrates survey responses from innovative library directors with her research, analysis, and extended interviews to showcase hundreds of winning programs and services. The strategies explored include youth services, partnerships, marketing, Library 2.0, and outreach.

352 pp/softbound/ISBN 978-1-57387-277-5 $39.50

The NextGen Librarian's Survival Guide

By Rachel Singer Gordon

Here is a unique resource for next generation librarians, addressing the specific needs of GenXers and Millenials as they work to define themselves as information professionals. The book focuses on how NextGens can move their careers forward and positively impact the profession. Library career guru Rachel Singer Gordon—herself a NextGen librarian—provides timely advice along with tips and insights from dozens of librarians on issues ranging from image to stereotypes, to surviving library school and entry-level positions, to working with older colleagues.

224 pp/softbound/ISBN 1-57387-256-3 $29.50

Social Software in Libraries
Building Collaboration, Communication, and
Community Online

By Meredith G. Farkas

This guide provides librarians with the
information and skills necessary to
implement the most popular and effective
social software technologies: blogs, RSS,
wikis, social networking software,
instant messaging, and more. Novice
readers will find ample descriptions and
advice on using each technology, while
veteran users of social software will discover new applications and approaches.

344 pp/softbound/ISBN 978-1-57387-275-1 $39.50

Listen Up!
Podcasting for Schools and Libraries

By Linda W. Braun

Here is a timely guide for teachers,
librarians, and school media specialists who
need to get quickly up-to-speed on
podcasting. Linda Braun explains what
podcasting is and why it is such a useful
tool for schools and libraries. She covers
both content and technical issues, sharing
tips for finding and using podcasts, and
guidance on getting the word out to
students, staff, patrons, and other users.

120 pp/softbound/ISBN 978-1-57387-304-8 $29.50